More Quizzes for
Great Children's Books

More Quizzes for
Great Children's Books

The Quest Motivational Reading Program

POLLY JEANNE WICKSTROM
and
JAMES MARK WICKSTROM

1996
TEACHER IDEAS PRESS
A Division of
Libraries Unlimited, Inc.
Englewood, Colorado

TO OUR PARENTS:
Suzan Buelow
Nancy and Gordon Wickstrom
Arthur J. King

TEACHER IDEAS PRESS
A Division of Libraries Unlimited, Inc.
P.O. Box 6633
Englewood, CO 80155-6633
1-800-237-6124

Production Editor: Kevin W. Perizzolo
Copy Editor: Tama Serfoss
Layout and Interior Design: Kay Minnis

Library of Congress Cataloging-in-Publication Data

Wickstrom, Polly Jeanne, 1959-
    More quizzes for great children's books : the quest motivational
reading program / Polly Jeanne Wickstrom and James Mark Wickstrom.
    ix, 196 p. 22x28 cm.
    ISBN 1-56308-250-0
    1. Literature--Study and teaching (Elementary) 2. Children's
stories, English--Examinations, questions, etc. 3. Reading
comprehension--Examinations, questions, etc. 4. Children--Books and
reading. I. Wickstrom, James Mark. II. Title.
LB1575.W53   1996
372.4'147'076--dc20   95-45696
                                                                CIP

Contents

PREFACE vii

INTRODUCTION ix

PART I—TEACHER'S MANUAL 1

Introduction—About the Book Format 3
    The Teacher's Manual 3
    The Album of Tests 3
    The Answers 3
    The Children's Catalog 3
The Program Mechanics 3
    Categories of Books 3
    Point Value Assignments 4
Exploring the Options for Program Use 4
    Using the Program as a Basis for Determining Grades 4
    An Individualized Grades Approach 6
    Using the Program as a Basis for a Reading Contest 6
Preparing to Implement the Program in a Classroom Setting 8
    Preparing the Classroom 8
    Preparing a Time Schedule 9
    Preparing the Students 9
Scheduling 9
    Test Taking 9
    The Sustained Silent Reading Period 10
    Record Keeping 10
    Questions and Answers 10
Using the Program for Homeschoolers 10
Record Keeping 11
    Criteria for Passing the Tests 11
    Record Keeping Plan One 11
    Instructions for Record Keeping Plan One 12
    Record Keeping Plan Two 12
    Instructions for Record Keeping Plan Two 12
    The Data Sheets 13
    A Sample Data Sheet 13
    The Cumulative Record Sheets 14
    A Sample Cumulative Record Sheet 14
Expanding the Program 16
    Writing the Tests 16
    Numbering the Books 16
    Categorizing 17
    Assigning Point Values 17
    The Cumulative Record Sheets 17
    Advertising New Books 17

PART I—TEACHER'S MANUAL (*continued*)

About the Black-Line Masters 18
    The Answer Sheet 18
    The Student/Teacher Contract 18
    The Data Sheet 18
    The Cumulative Record Sheet 18
    The Cumulative Record Sheet 2 18
    The More Quizzes List of Great Children's Books 18
    Cumulative Listing 18

PART II—ALBUM OF TESTS 33

PART III—ANSWERS 155

Answer Key 157

PART IV—CHILDREN'S CATALOG 169

Introduction 171
List of Subjects 172
Subject Index 173
Annotations—Category A 186
Annotations—Category B 188
Annotations—Category C 190
Annotations—Category D 193
Annotations—Category E 195

Preface

One Teacher's Story

I've always had an insatiable hunger for books, and when I taught sixth-grade language arts, I wanted to pass the rich tradition of reading on to my students. So I began with the age-old method of asking my students to read books and to provide written and sometimes oral reports on what they had read.

Using this traditional method, however, I ran into some problems. For example, some children seemed capable of producing beautifully written book reports, but incapable of answering a few simple, informal questions about the plot of the book. Other students seemed to dread giving the oral book report or to dread writing the book report—or both—and thus I had the problem of associating something negative with something I wanted to be a very positive experience for my students: that of reading a good book.

After considering these problems, I decided one year that I would try something altogether different. Having selected 20 children's books, I read the books and then wrote short tests for each book. When the tests were prepared, I presented the list of books to my students and asked them to read not one, but several of the books on the list. I explained that no book report and no oral report would be required. Instead, all the students would have to do to receive credit for reading a book would be to take a short and simple objective test about the book. I assured the students that the tests would be easy for anyone who read the books. No trick questions and certainly no studying would be required. Just reading and enjoying the books was the main objective.

The response to this simple system was overwhelming. My students loved not having to write book reports and not having to give oral reports every time they read a book, requirements which I suspected inhibited their reading rather than promoted it, and they loved the simplicity of taking the short test to receive credit for books they read. I noticed that the children seemed to enjoy a feeling of accomplishment that came as a result of having read an entire book on their own, and as success has a way of breeding more success, I observed my students beginning to read more and more books.

In response to my students' enthusiasm, I began to add more quizzes to the program and to develop the program further by assigning point values to books based on their length and complexity. For the following school year, I prepared and launched a full-blown book reading contest with an offering of 50 titles for my students to choose from. The results were staggering. Reading became the "in" thing among sixth graders at the junior high school where I taught, and I had students who read all 50 books in one semester and came to me asking for more. One afternoon I remember in particular, I was in charge of a study hall with over 60 sixth-grade students in a large double room. Supervising study halls was not a favorite task among teachers as the environment too often seemed to lend itself to chaos and disorder. On this particular day, however, the entire room of 60 students was silent and in each set of hands was a book. Behind each book was the face of a child obviously engrossed in a book. It was so quiet in the room, with no sound except the soft rustling of turning pages, you could have heard a pin drop. When another teacher walked in the room to deliver a memo, she stopped in her tracks and stared out over the room with me, sharing my pleasure at this strange and beautiful sight.

As the year went on, the students were reading so fast and asking for more and more titles, that keeping up with the task of writing the quizzes became overwhelming. Thus, the next year, when I left teaching to give birth to my first child, I decided to devote myself to the task of adding many more titles to the program and to seek publication. This is how the *Quizzes* program was born.

In this second volume of *Quizzes*, I am pleased to introduce my husband, James Wickstrom, as co-author. Jim and I pass this book on to teachers, library school media specialists, parents, and college professors with the hope that it will be a useful tool in accomplishing the worthy goal of launching children into the wonderful world of books.

—Polly Wickstrom

Introduction

A comprehensive reading program not only teaches young people the skill of reading, but also encourages them to develop a lifelong enjoyment of literature. Research tells us that students build reading skills by reading: the more, the better.

For a number of years, teachers have used the book report as the major evaluative component of an individualized reading program. *Quizzes for 220 Great Children's Books* and *More Quizzes for Great Children's Books* provide an alternative to book reports as a method of determining what, how much, and how well young people read.

In the *Quizzes* program, the student chooses a book from the *Children's Catalog*, reads the book, and then takes a 14-question test about the book. The test is designed both as a comprehension check and to see that the book was finished. After students complete the test successfully, they receive credit or points for their accomplishment. The program is designed to provide teachers with a method of distributing credit fairly to students based on the length and difficulty of the books they read.

The primary audience of *Quizzes* is students in grades three through eight. However, the program is flexible and can be adapted to almost any grade level. It could be used as part of a program for gifted students in the first or second grades. It could be used by high school teachers, librarians sponsoring summer reading programs, and even by college professors teaching courses in children's literature.

School library media specialists and classroom teachers can use the system to integrate library motivational reading programs with reading skills instruction. *Quizzes* can also provide a means for parents who teach their children at home and encourage children to read widely and carefully.

Not only is the program flexible, it is also expandable. As it stands, the program tests 340 children's books. (*Quizzes for 220 Great Children's Books* provides tests for 220 books; *More Quizzes for Great Children's Books* provides tests for 120 books.) That in itself will provide a wide variety of reading materials from which students can choose. The user, however, can easily add an unlimited number of additional books. This option keeps the program from growing stale.

Quizzes takes into consideration the heavy responsibilities of today's teachers and library media specialists by providing several simple methods of tracking what young people read. Perhaps even more importantly, it provides a means for adults to *motivate* children to read and to lay the foundation for a lifelong love of books.

PART
I

Teacher's Manual

Introduction—About the Book Format

The Teacher's Manual

The *Teacher's Manual* describes the program and outlines various methods by which the teacher, library media specialist, or parent can implement the program. The manual also includes a set of black-line masters to be used in record keeping.

The Album of Tests

This volume of *Quizzes* contains a total of 120 tests covering books that have been carefully selected to provide a wide sampling of high-quality children's literature. (*Note:* The first volume of *Quizzes*, *Quizzes for 220 Great Children's Books* contains an additional 220 tests.)

Each test contains 14 objective questions that test the extent to which students have read and comprehended given books. Most of the questions included on the tests are comprehensive in nature, covering major events that occurred in the book. Some of the questions are literal questions asking the student to recall facts about the characters portrayed in the books. However, the literal questions are *always* questions that should be obvious to any student who actually read that book. For example, a question such as "Did Mrs. Smith have red hair?" would never be asked unless the fact that Mrs. Smith had red hair was part of the story line and was continually repeated throughout the book.

The Answers

A complete set of answers for the 120 tests are in part III. The user may use binder clips to fasten these pages together while students are using the book to take tests.

The Children's Catalog

The first half of the *Children's Catalog* provides a Subject Index of all the books listed in the program. The second half of the catalog provides brief motivational blurbs about each book. The catalog is designed to help students select books that they will find interesting and books that will be suited to their reading abilities.

The Program Mechanics

Categories of Books

The books have been divided into five categories based on the subject matter, vocabulary, and complexity of plot in each book. Following are the various categories and the appropriate reading levels for participants in the *Quizzes* reading program.

Category	Reading Level
A	Grades 3 and 4
B	Grades 4 and 5
C	Grades 5 and 6
D	Grades 6 and 7
E	Grades 7 and 8

These categories enable the teacher, the library media specialist, or parent to guide students to the category of books best suited to their interests and reading abilities. The categories are meant to serve as general guidelines only. Because of the wide range of preferences and reading abilities within even the same grade level, the user must make the final decision regarding categorical assignments for individual students.

Point Value Assignments

Each book in the program has been assigned a point value based on the length of the book. The point value assignments are as follows:

125 pages or less	5 pts.
126–200 pages	10 pts.
201–275 pages	15 pts.
276–350 pages	20 pts.
351–425 pages	25 pts.
426 pages or more	30 pts.

These point value assignments enable the user to distribute credit fairly to students based on the length of the books they have read.

Note: Because of the large print and very simple vocabulary of some books, these titles have been assigned a low point value regardless of their length in pages.

 # Exploring the Options for Program Use

There are many different contexts in which the *Quizzes* program could be used and many different methods through which it could be implemented. The teacher, library media specialist, or parent may want to use one of the suggestions discussed in this section, or may very well devise a personal system of putting the program to work, so that it will effectively meet local needs.

Using the Program as a Basis for Determining Grades

In a classroom setting, the teacher may want to use the program as a basis for determining part of the students' grades in reading. This could be done by setting up a scale using points. The method for keeping track of the number of points each student has earned over a given period of time will be discussed in the section "Record Keeping."

The first step in setting up a grading scale would be to decide how many average-length books (201–275 pages) the students would need to read over a given period of time to earn an A. Because average-length books are worth 15 points, the teacher would multiply 15 times the number of books to be read. Thus, if the teacher wanted the students to read five average-length books over a period of nine weeks to earn an A, the students would need to earn approximately 75 points.

(*Note:* Average-length books are chosen only for the purpose of setting up a grading scale. Once the grading scale has been established, the student may be invited to read any combination of books to earn points. For example, instead of reading five 15-point books to earn an A, the student could read six 10-point books and three 5-point books. Alternatively, the student could read three 20-point books, one 10-point book, and one 5-point book, etc.)

Teachers can set up their own grading scale by using the following mathematical formula:

X = The number of average-length books students would have to read over a given period of time to earn an A.

$Y = X \times 15$

.90 x Y = Minimum number of points a student would need to earn an A.
.80 x Y = Minimum number of points a student would need to earn a B.
.70 x Y = Minimum number of points a student would need to earn a C.
.60 x Y = Minimum number of points a student would need to earn a D.

Returning to the example of setting a criterion of reading five average-length books to earn an A, the formula used to set up a grading scale would be as follows:

X = 5
Y = (5x15) or 75

By multiplying .90 x 75, the teacher would come up with the minimum number of points a student needs to earn an A. By multiplying .80 x 75, the teacher would come up with the minimum number of points a student needs to earn a B, and so on. Thus, the grading scale for a requirement of five average-length books to earn an A would look like this:

67–75 pts.	A
60–66 pts.	B
52–59 pts.	C
45–51 pts.	D
44 and below	F

A set of model grading scales appears below. Each scale is based on a different number of average-length books that would have to be read by students over a given period of time to earn an A.

Model Grading Scales

2 average-length books per grading period:

27–30	A
24–26	B
21–23	C
18–20	D
17 and below	F

3 average-length books per grading period:

40–45	A
36–39	B
31–35	C
27–30	D
26 and below	F

4 average-length books per grading period:

54–60	A
48–53	B
42–47	C
36–41	D
35 and below	F

5 average-length books per grading period:

67–75	A
60–66	B
52–59	C
45–51	D
44 and below	F

6 average-length books per grading period:

81–90	A
72–80	B
63–71	C
54–62	D
53 and below	F

7 average-length books per grading period:

94–105	A
84–93	B
73–83	C
63–72	D
62 and below	F

8 average-length books per grading period:

108–120	A
96–107	B
84–95	C
72–83	D
71 and below	F

9 average-length books per grading period:

121–135	A
108–120	B
94–107	C
81–93	D
80 and below	F

10 average-length books per grading period:

135–150	A
120–134	B
105–119	C
90–104	D
89 and below	F

An Individualized Grades Approach

If the teacher decides to use the program as a basis for determining grades, those grades should be based on the individual abilities of the students. For example, an advanced reader may be required to accumulate 75 points to earn an A, while a less proficient reader would only be required to earn 50 points. An excellent way to accomplish this individualization would be to use the Student-Teacher Contract. (See the Black-Line Masters section of this manual.)

In setting up Student-Teacher Contracts, the teacher may want to follow some or all of the six steps outlined below:

STEP ONE: Set aside a time during the day to meet with each student for approximately five minutes. Make enough copies of the Student/Teacher Contract so that there is at least one blank contract available for each student.

STEP TWO: During the conferences with the students, be as positive and encouraging as possible. Stress to the students that the information printed on each contract is to remain confidential between the teacher and the student. Try to discourage students from comparing their contracts with those of their classmates.

STEP THREE: Negotiate with the student concerning the number of books that should be read over an agreed upon period of time to earn an A. Once an agreement has been reached, fill in the information on the student's contract.

STEP FOUR: Use the model grading scales or follow the directions given in the previous section to come up with the point scale that will be used to determine that student's grade.

STEP FIVE: Write the scale at the bottom of the student's contract. The contract can then be used at the end of the grading period to determine the student's grade.

STEP SIX: Optionally, the teacher might create a chart similar to the one in figure 1, which shows student progress as a percentage of the goal. The emphasis for all the students is to complete the goal, rather than to compare the number of contracted points.

Using the Program as a Basis for a Reading Contest

The *Quizzes* program lends itself nicely to organizing a book-reading contest within a classroom, a school, a home, or in the case of a very ambitious person, a whole town! The contest could be based on the number of points earned by participants over a period of time. The student earning the most points could be declared the winner, or better yet, the contest could be designed so that every reader is a winner.

One way to track points earned in a reading contest would be to use a large chart. As students earn points by passing tests on books they have read, the teacher or library media specialist fills in the number of points earned by the student on the chart. The chart would look something like figure 2.

Percent of Goal										
	10%	20%	30%	40%	50%	60%	70%	80%	90%	100%
Amy	███	███	███	███	███	███				
Tommy	███	███								
Jared	███	███	███	███	███	███	███	███		
Allison	███	███	███	███	███					
Heather	███	███	███	███	███	███	███	███		
Nathan	███	███	███	███	███					
David	███	███	███	███	███	███	███	███	███	███
Kirsten	███	███	███							

Fig. 1. Chart showing student progress as a percentage of an individual goal.

Number of Points									
	10	20	30	40	50	60	70	80	90
Amy	███	███	███						
Tommy	███								
Jared	███	███							
Allison	███	███	███	███	███				
Heather	███	███	███	███	███	███	███	███	
Nathan	███	███	███						
David	███	███	███	███	███	███			
Kirsten	███								

Fig. 2. Chart showing student progress based on earned points.

Regardless of the method (charts or individual record sheets) selected to track progress, the *Quizzes* program can be used in countless ways to implement motivational reading programs for children. For example, at a local library, a program was held in which children ages 9–12 received a ticket every time they read 250 pages. Each ticket earned was signed by the student and then placed in a large box. At the end of the contest, a raffle was held with prizes donated by local businesses. Each child who participated in the contest received a token prize, but additionally, each child had a chance to have his or her ticket drawn in the raffle. The more tickets earned, the more chances the child had of winning extra prizes. The *Quizzes* program could easily be used with ideas similar to this one. Rather than receiving tickets for the number of pages read, children could receive tickets based on the number of points earned.

It should again be emphasized that the ideas suggested in this manual are only a few of the ways in which the *Quizzes* program can be implemented. Other ways in which the program can be used are limited only by the imagination, purposes, or ambitiousness of the user.

Preparing to Implement the Program in a Classroom Setting

As the teacher prepares to incorporate the program into the daily curriculum, there are several things that might enhance the program's effectiveness. While many of the suggestions outlined in this section would be advantageous, they are not crucial to the program's success. The teacher will want to follow some of the suggestions, disregard some of them, and modify others to make them coincide with specific resources, capabilities, and conditions.

Preparing the Classroom

In preparing the classroom, the teacher might do any of the following:

1. Set up an area of the room where students could go to read. One or two beanbag chairs and a small bookcase containing books from the *Quizzes List* (see Black-Line Masters) would make an excellent start for such an area. Later, if resources allow, a few large pillows, posters, a colorful rug, and even a rocking chair could be added to create an inviting place for students to read.

2. Set up a "testing center" where students could sit when taking tests. The testing center could simply be a desk close to the teacher, or it could be a table set up in a corner of the room. Materials that should be kept near the testing center include pencils, blank answer sheets (see Black-Line Masters), and a tray or basket where students could place completed answer sheets.

3. Have as many books as possible from the *Quizzes List* available in the classroom for the students to check out and browse through. Students could be encouraged to bring in old books from the *Quizzes List* that they may have at home, or the books could be purchased inexpensively at used bookstores.

4. Pull books from the school library media center or the public library for use as a temporary room collection.

5. Put up a motivational bulletin board about reading.

6. Display a classroom chart or purchase a set of individual charts (available at most teacher supply stores) to plot students' progress.

Preparing a Time Schedule

One of the nice things about the program is that it provides purposeful activity for the students to engage in when they have completed their other assignments or when the teacher is working with a small group. Students can read silently at any time during the school day, but it would be a good idea for the teacher to set aside a 20-minute period each day entirely devoted to the program.

During this 20-minute period, called the Sustained Silent Reading period, all of the students would read silently. The teacher might also participate in the program and chart personal progress along with the students.

If time permits, the teacher might schedule five minutes before and after the Sustained Silent Reading period to allow students to take tests and to complete the record keeping part of the program. The Sustained Silent Reading period and aspects of scheduling will be discussed in greater detail in the next section.

Preparing the Students

The teacher may want to spend a day or two familiarizing students with the program, outlining expectations for them, getting them excited about reading, answering any questions they might have, and helping them to make book selections. This initial investment of the teacher's time will pay off in the long run by avoiding a barrage of questions and misunderstandings later on.

One way of familiarizing the students with the program and getting them motivated to read books would be to read aloud the introduction to the *Children's Catalog*. The next step would be to allow the students to take turns browsing through the catalog and writing down titles that interest them. Also, if the teacher is planning to assign readings from specific categories of books, this would be a good time to make those assignments.

On the second day, the teacher might take the students to the school library media center so they could check out books. The teacher might also make copies of the *Quizzes List* for students to take home. Having a copy of the *Quizzes List* at home will allow parents to aid their children in the selection of books.

Once every student had a book from the *Quizzes List*, the teacher would be ready to begin.

 # Scheduling

To keep the *Quizzes* program running smoothly in a classroom setting, three types of activities—test taking, silent reading, and record keeping—will need to be planned each day. This section suggests scheduling brief periods of time throughout the school day or period to attend to each of these activities separately. However, the program could just as easily be implemented by combining these activities so that they are all accomplished in one 20-minute period.

Test Taking

Each day before the Sustained Silent Reading (SSR) period begins, teachers might wish to set aside a 5–10 minute period for students to take tests. Test taking could be done at the beginning of the SSR period, and if it is taken care of beforehand, the SSR period can be enjoyed without interruptions.

At the beginning of the testing period, students needing to take tests should raise their hands so that the teacher can write their names on the chalkboard. After writing names on the board, the teacher should place this book at the testing center. (*Note:* If desired, the teacher may clip the pages of the *Answers* section together at this time.) Next, the teacher should make a quick check to see that the testing center supplies (pencils and blanks answer sheets) are fresh and that a tray for completed answer sheets is in place.

When the testing center is ready, the child whose name appears first on the list should go to the testing center, find the appropriate test in the book, and complete the test using a blank answer sheet to record his or her answers. When a student is finished taking a test, he should place his answer sheet in the tray and cross his name off the list on the chalkboard, signifying the next person's turn to use the testing center.

Students who finish taking a test could then spend some time browsing through the *Children's Catalog* and writing down the titles of books that interest them. Some students might be given permission to go to the library media center at this time to review and check out books.

The Sustained Silent Reading Period

The Sustained Silent Reading period is the 20-minute reading period discussed in the last section. During the SSR period, it would be a good idea to have students clear everything off their desks except for the books that they are reading. If a classroom reading area is available, some students might be allowed to take their books to that area. The students should then be asked to read quietly during this time.

Since teachers as well as students need to explore the rich heritage of children's literature, the author recommends that the teacher also use the SSR period to read. The teacher could read books that are not a part of *Quizzes*, adding new books and tests to the program. Over time, the program would grow and become relevant to the particular collection of children's books held in a school or library.

Record Keeping

The teacher will have to complete the record keeping part of the program. Tests need to be graded and the results recorded on the students' individual Data Sheets or the classroom chart. However, this process should take only a minimum amount of time and could be completed during the last five minutes of the SSR period or at some other time during the school day. In fact, students may monitor their own tests and charting depending on each student's ability and responsibility.

Questions and Answers

What should the teacher do if students forget to bring the books that they are reading during SSR time?
These students could be allowed to read one of the books from the *Quizzes List* available in the classroom. By all means, though, the teacher should insist that the students read *something* during SSR time, even if a book from the *Quizzes List* is not available.

What should the teacher do if more than one student at a time wants to browse through the Children's Catalog after having taken a test?
It is probably advisable to allow only one student at a time to look through the student catalog, but the other students could be allowed to browse through the books available in the classroom. Also, if such an arrangement is acceptable to the school library media specialist, students could be given a copy of the *Quizzes List* to use in reviewing books at the school library media center.

 # Using the Program for Homeschoolers

The *Quizzes* program is an excellent choice for parents and children involved in homeschooling. Each child may be given a goal for attaining a certain number of points, and progress may be charted. The author recommends that parents adopt any of the ideas and forms listed in this guide for use with individual students.

Books not already a part of the program can be added easily. For example, instead of creating new tests for new titles, the child might read a book, then create a list of four things to discuss with the parent about the book. This list would be used by the parent to ascertain whether the child has read the book and would substitute for the test. The new title and discussion points could be added to the program for use by another child.

Cumulative records like those described in the next section provide a "reading diary" for the student over a period of years. Such a diary can build a source of pride as progress is made in reading more complex and longer books and a wide variety of literature. Parents should remember that the purpose of *Quizzes* is to build reading enjoyment. Reading skill will improve as the number of books read increases. Parents should be careful not to make the *Quizzes* program seem like a negative, work-filled task. Its purpose is positive, fun, and exciting as the personal reading diary grows.

 # Record Keeping

In this section, two different methods that teachers can employ to keep track of students' progress in the *Quizzes* program will be described. The methods differ in the amount of paperwork they require teachers to handle and in the purposes each accomplishes. By reading the brief description of each method, teachers can decide which method will be best suited to their individual needs and preferences.

In addition to these methods, the criteria that students must meet to pass the tests will be discussed. The Data Sheets and the Cumulative Record Sheets will also be mentioned and the purposes for using them will be explored.

Criteria for Passing the Tests

For students to receive credit for a book, they must pass the test on that book. The criteria for passing the tests are set by the teacher, but the author recommends that students be required to answer at least 10 out of 14 questions correctly. These criteria should be easily met by any student who has read a book.

If the student is not able to answer at least 10 out of 14 questions correctly, the teacher should try to discern why the student failed the test. The teacher might set aside a time when the student and teacher can sit down together with the book to discuss it. If the teacher determines that the student actually read the book but the test itself was a problem, then partial or full credit should be given. The emphasis should be placed on reading, not test taking. Teachers should make the entire experience positive—never negative!

It is probably not a good idea to allow students to "study" books repeatedly to pass the tests. Such a practice misses the point of the program.

Record Keeping Plan One

Using Plan One, the teacher uses individual Data Sheets (see Black-Line Masters) to record each student's accumulation of points. In addition to recording point accumulation, the teacher records other information, including the dates on which tests were taken, the number of questions that were answered correctly on each test, and the titles of books read.

One advantage of this method is that it enables the teacher to analyze patterns that may develop in students' progress for the purposes of diagnosis and remediation. For example, a teacher might notice that a student has been taking a test every other day and has been consistently failing the tests. In this case, the teacher might conclude that the student is not reading but probably only skimming the books. The teacher can then encourage that student to devote more time to each book—reading perhaps only a few chapters each day.

On the other hand, a teacher might notice that another student has never attempted to take a test about a book. In this case, the teacher might decide to confer privately with that student to find out what the problem is.

Another advantage of this method is that the Data Sheets provide excellent feedback for parents. By looking at the Data Sheets, parents are able to get a clear picture of the progress their child is making in the program.

Instructions for Record Keeping Plan One

STEP ONE: Make several copies of the Data Sheet and of the Cumulative Record Sheet (see Black-Line Masters). Next, print each student's name on a Data Sheet and on a Cumulative Record Sheet.
Note: If the students participated in the program the preceding year, the teacher would not need to make copies of the Cumulative Record Sheets. Instead, obtain the records from the students' previous teacher.

STEP TWO: Grade any tests that were taken before or during the Sustained Silent Reading period. Write the number of questions the student answered correctly, the point value assignment of the book, and the credit received in the space provided at the bottom of each answer sheet. If the student answered fewer than 10 out of 14 questions correctly on the test, write a question mark in the blank next to credit received. This will indicate to the student that you wish to meet with him or her to discuss the book before determining the amount of credit that will be given.

STEP THREE: Fill out the Data Sheet for each student who took a test.

STEP FOUR: Fill out the Cumulative Record Sheet for each student who took a test.

STEP FIVE: If the program is being used as a basis for a reading contest, plot each student's additional points on a classroom chart.

STEP SIX: Return the graded answer sheets to the students. If there was a student who failed a test, make arrangements to have a conference with that student and reassure the student that the two of you will discuss the book and the test together and that a joint decision will be made regarding the amount of credit to be received.

Record Keeping Plan Two

Using Record Keeping Plan Two, the teacher will not use the Data Sheets but will only use a classroom chart to record accumulation of points by students. This method has the advantage of requiring very little paperwork on the part of the teacher while still allowing the teacher to use the program to meet the objectives stated in the introduction.

Instructions for Record Keeping Plan Two

STEP ONE: Prepare a classroom chart that will be used to plot each student's point accumulation. The chart should look something like figure 2 (see page 7).

STEP TWO: Make copies of the Cumulative Record Sheet (see Black-Line Masters). Print each student's name on a Cumulative Record Sheet.
Note: If the students participated in the program the preceding year, the teacher would not need to follow this step. Instead, obtain the records from the students' previous teacher.

STEP THREE: Grade any tests that were taken before or during the Sustained Silent Reading period. Write the number of questions the student answered correctly, the point value assignment of the book, and the credit received in the space provided at the bottom of each answer sheet. If the student answered fewer than 10 out of 14 questions correctly on the test, write a question mark in the blank next to credit received. This will indicate to the student that you wish to meet with him or her to discuss the book before determining the amount of credit that will be given.

STEP FOUR: Shade in the appropriate boxes on the classroom chart for each student who passed a test.

STEP FIVE: Fill out the Cumulative Record Sheet for each student who took a test.

STEP SIX: Return the graded answer sheets to the students. If there was a student who failed a test, make arrangements to have a conference with that student and reassure the student that the two of you will discuss the book and the test together and that a joint decision will be made regarding the amount of credit to be received.

The Data Sheets

The Data Sheets provide detailed information regarding students' progress in the *Quizzes* program. The first three columns of the Data Sheet provide space for the teacher to record the dates on which tests were taken, the number of questions that were answered correctly on each test, and the titles of books read. The fourth column of the Data Sheet provides space to record the number of points the student earned for reading a book along with the point-value assignment of that book. In most cases, the points earned and the point-value assignment will be the same. In the case of a student who failed a test and received partial credit, however, the teacher would note the amount of credit which was given in relation to the amount of credit available for that book.

For example, the book, *The Grand Escape*, has a point-value assignment of 10 points. If a decision was made that a student would receive partial credit of eight points for that book, the teacher would write 8/10 in the fourth column of the Data Sheet.

The final column on the Data Sheet allows the teacher to keep track of the total amount of points earned.

A Sample Data Sheet

Figure 3 is a sample Data Sheet illustrating how a teacher would use the form to record information. (*Note:* A blank Data Sheet is provided in the Black-Line Masters.)

By studying the sample Data Sheet, the teacher can see that this student took six tests over a period of approximately six weeks. The student passed four of the tests and received full credit for each of those tests. On the test for *Behind the Attic Wall*, however, the student answered only 8 of 14 questions correctly. After a conference with the student, it was decided that partial credit of 15 points instead of the full 20 points would be given.

Data Sheet				
Name: *Jeff Thompson*				
Date	**Title of Book**	**Number Correct**	**Points Earned/ Point Value Assignment**	**Total Points**
9/15	The Indian in the Cupboard	14	10/10	10
9/23	Fudge	13	5/5	15
10/4	Monkey Island	12	10/10	25
10/15	Behind the Attic Wall	8	15/20	40
10/21	Hatchet	14	30/30	70
10/30	The Winter Room	7	?/10	

Fig. 3. Sample Data Sheet.

The final entry on the sample Data Sheet shows that the student took the test for *The Winter Room* and answered only 7 of 14 questions correctly. Thus, the teacher wrote a question mark in the fourth column indicating that a decision had not yet been made regarding the credit to be given for that book.

In the last column, the teacher kept a running total of all the points earned by the student. Each time a student took a book test, the credit received for that book was added to the previous total. Keeping a running total in the last column saves the teacher time at the end of the grading period.

Note: Start a new Data Sheet for each grading period. Old sheets can be discarded or saved for parent-teacher conferences.

The Cumulative Record Sheets

The Cumulative Record Sheets are forms the teacher uses to keep a record of books the students have read and been tested on. These sheets provide continuity in the program as students progress from one grade to the next. At the end of each school year, the Cumulative Record Sheets are passed on to the students' next teacher so that the progress each student has already made in the program forms the basis for greater challenges.

One simple method allows the teacher to record information about several different aspects of students' progress in the *Quizzes* program. For each test that is taken, the teacher would record the following:

1. The grade that the child is currently in.

2. In parentheses, the number of questions answered correctly on the test.

3. The number of points earned.

If partial credit was given for a book, the teacher might wish to indicate this by writing an asterisk next to the number representing points earned.

For example, Book #288, *The Night Journey*, is a Category C book worth 10 points. If a fifth-grade student answered 13 out of 14 questions correctly on this test, the teacher would write the following in the cell marked 288 in the Category C column of the record sheet:

> 5 (+13/14) 10

If a fifth-grade student answered 8 of 14 questions correctly on this same test and partial credit of eight points was earned, the teacher would write:

> 5 (+8/14) 8*

If a fifth-grade student answered 2 of 14 questions correctly on this same test and no credit was earned, the teacher would write:

> 5 (+2/14) 0

Teachers might wish to make progress in each grade even clearer by using a light-colored highlighting marker to highlight all the entries for a given school year. Teachers could agree on a universal color-code system such as third grade = pink, fourth grade = blue, fifth grade = orange, etc., which is appropriate for their school. Writing the color code at the bottom of the record sheet will make the entries easily interpretable.

A Sample Cumulative Record Sheet

Figure 4 is a sample Cumulative Record Sheet illustrating how a teacher might use the form to record information. By studying this form, the teacher can see exactly what type of progress a student made during two years of participation in the program. (*Note:* A blank Cumulative Record Sheet has been provided in the Black-Line Masters section of this manual.)

Cumulative Record Sheet

More Quizzes Great Children's Books

Student's Name: *Sarah Miller*

Category A—Grades 3 & 4	Category B—Grades 4 & 5	Category C—Grades 5 & 6	Category D—Grades 6 & 7	Category E—Grades 7 & 8
221—3 (+14/14) 5	230—4 (+14/14) 10	226—	227—	228—
222—3 (+14/14) 5	231—4 (+12/14) 10	229—	232—	270—
223—3 (+13/14) 5	233—4 (+13/14) 10	235—	237—	271—
224—3 (+12/14) 5	234—4 (+13/14) 10	236—	242—	272—
225—3 (+13/14) 5	244—4 (+14/14) 10	238—	243—	289—
241—	245—4 (+14/14) 10	239—	256—	302—
251—	246—	240—4 (+12/14) 10	267—	305—
252—	247—	249—4 (+7/14) 15*	276—	306—
253—	248—	250—	277—	307—
254—	261—	257—	279—	313—
255—	262—4 (+2/14) 0	258—	280—	314—
275—4 (+14/14) 5	263—4 (+11/14) 10	259—	281—	317—
290—3 (+13/14) 10	264—	260—	287—	323—
291—3 (+11/14) 10	265—	268—4 (+12/14) 5	295—	324—
292—3 (+12/14) 10	266—	269—	296—	333—
298—	282—	273—	304—	334—
299—	283—	274—	315—	
335—	284—3 (+13/14) 10	278—	316—	
336—	285—3 (+14/14) 10	288—	319—	
337—	286—	297—	320—	
	293—	300—4 (+14/14) 10	322—	
	294—	301—	325—	
	303—	308—	330—	
	310—	309—	331—	
	311—3 (+6/14) 6*	312—		
	328—	318—		
	329—	321—		
	332—	326—		
		327—		
		338—		
		339—		
		340—		

Fig. 4. Sample Cumulative Record Sheet.

Looking at figure 4, one would be able to determine that:

- In the third grade, this student read and was tested on a total of 11 books. The student received full credit for 10 of the books and partial credit for one book, Book #311.

- In the fourth grade, this student read and was tested on a total of 13 books. The student received full credit for 11 of the books and partial credit for one book, Book #249. The student answered only 2 of 14 questions correctly on the test for Book #262 and received no credit for that book.

At the end of the school year, the teacher might use the Cumulative Record Sheets to compile individual summaries of each student's progress in the *Quizzes* program to give to parents. The summaries could contain statements such as the ones provided above, or the summaries could be more detailed, providing the titles and other information about each book the child read that year.

 # Expanding the Program

This book includes tests on 120 books. The first volume of *Quizzes, Quizzes for 220 Great Children's Books*, includes tests for an additional 220 books, making tests for a total of 340 books currently available. In addition to tests provided in these volumes, teachers can expand the program even further by adding tests they write themselves. This section will suggest tips for teachers as they write tests and incorporate them into the program.

Writing the Tests

In writing new tests, teachers should attempt to ask questions that cover major events that occurred in the book rather than questions that focus on details. It is also recommended that teachers avoid asking questions that are unrelated to the story line such as, "Who is the author of this book?"

Teachers will find that some books lend themselves to true-false questions while it is easier to write multiple choice questions for other books. Teachers can write the type of questions that best coincide with the book they have read, and they do not need to worry about the ratio of true-false to multiple choice questions in the tests.

After writing the tests, the teacher will want to write corresponding answer keys. One way of storing answer keys for teacher-made tests would be to write them on index cards and then to store them in a card file.

Numbering the Books

When the teacher writes a test for a new book, a book number should be assigned. Any number would work starting from #341, but the author recommends a beginning number of A1, A2, etc. This will allow the author to add additional volumes of *Quizzes* without interfering with local additions.

Categorizing

The teacher should assign a category to each new book that will be tested—A, B, C, D, or E. The approximate reading level of each category of books is as follows:

Category	Reading Level
A	Grades 3 and 4
B	Grades 4 and 5
C	Grades 5 and 6
D	Grades 6 and 7
E	Grades 7 and 8

Assigning Point Values

The teacher will also want to assign each new book a point value. The scale for assigning point values is as follows:

125 pages or less	5 pts
126–200 pages	10 pts.
201–275 pages	15 pts.
276–350 pages	20 pts.
351–425 pages	25 pts.
426 pages or more	30 pts.

The Cumulative Record Sheets

The teacher can use the form called Cumulative Record Sheet #2 (see Black-Line Masters) to add the book numbers of the additional tests that have been written. However, because the Cumulative Record Sheets are intended to be passed from teacher to teacher at the end of each school year, all of the teachers using the program in the same school will probably want to devise a system that would enable them to know what numbers their colleagues have assigned to new books. Otherwise, a confusing situation could occur.

For example, if Miss Adams, a third-grade teacher, read *Winnie the Pooh* and assigned it a book number of A1, and Mrs. Roberts, a fourth-grade teacher, read *The Wind in the Willows* and also assigned it a book number of A1, the program would begin to lose some of its continuity as far as the Cumulative Records are concerned.

One way of avoiding this situation would be for teachers to meet occasionally and to pool any new tests that they have developed. This way, a universal system of numbering books could be developed, and the program would maintain its continuity. For example, Mrs. Smith could devise tests S1, S2 . . . Mrs. Roberts, R1, R2 . . .

Advertising New Books

As teachers create tests on new books, they will want to let their students know that these new books are available. To do this, teachers may wish to create supplements to add to the *Children's Catalog*.

About the Black-Line Masters

This section of the *Teacher's Manual* contains Black-Line Masters that can be copied and used in conjunction with the implementation of the *Quizzes* program.

The Answer Sheet

Students may use the answer sheet to record answers when taking tests.

The Student/Teacher Contract

A form that may be used during student-teacher conferences to set mutually agreed upon reading goals.

The Data Sheet

A form that may used to record detailed data regarding the reading progress of individual students.

The Cumulative Record Sheet

A form that can be used to record data regarding the reading progress of individual students over several years' time.

The Cumulative Record Sheet 2

A blank form that can be used to add book numbers when the program is expanded by the user.

The More Quizzes List of Great Children's Books

A comprehensive list of the 120 books included in the program arranged alphabetically according to author. The teacher might wish to make copies of this list to send home with students at the beginning of the program so that parents can assist their children in the selection of books.

Cumulative Listing

For those using both *Quizzes for 220 Great Children's Books* and *More Quizzes*, this is a comprehensive list of all 340 books arranged alphabetically according to author.

The Answer Sheet

Name: _____

Date: _____

Title of Book: _____

1.	True	False	A	B	C	D
2.	True	False	A	B	C	D
3.	True	False	A	B	C	D
4.	True	False	A	B	C	D
5.	True	False	A	B	C	D
6.	True	False	A	B	C	D
7.	True	False	A	B	C	D
8.	True	False	A	B	C	D
9.	True	False	A	B	C	D
10.	True	False	A	B	C	D
11.	True	False	A	B	C	D
12.	True	False	A	B	C	D
13.	True	False	A	B	C	D
14.	True	False	A	B	C	D

+ _____/14   Point Value Assignment: _____

Credit Received: _____

STUDENT/TEACHER CONTRACT

NAME OF STUDENT:_____

DATE:_____

CATEGORY	A	B	C	D	E
ASSIGNMENT:					

I agree to earn _____ points to receive an A. To earn the _____
points, I will read a combination of books similar to the following:

_____   5-POINT BOOKS

_____   10-POINT BOOKS

_____   15-POINT BOOKS

_____   20-POINT BOOKS

_____   25-POINT BOOKS

STUDENT'S SIGNATURE:_____

TEACHER'S SIGNATURE:_____

Data Sheet				
Name:				
Date	Title of Book	Number Correct	Points Earned/ Point Value Assignment	Total Points

Cumulative Record Sheet

More Quizzes for Great Children's Books

Student's Name:

Category A— Grades 3 & 4	Category B— Grades 4 & 5	Category C— Grades 5 & 6	Category D— Grades 6 & 7	Category E— Grades 7 & 8
221—	230—	226—	227—	228—
222—	231—	229—	232—	270—
223—	233—	235—	237—	271—
224—	234—	236—	242—	272—
225—	244—	238—	243—	289—
241—	245—	239—	256—	302—
251—	246—	240—	267—	305—
252—	247—	249—	276—	306—
253—	248—	250—	277—	307—
254—	261—	257—	279—	313—
255—	262—	258—	280—	314—
275—	263—	259—	281—	317—
290—	264—	260—	287—	323—
291—	265—	268—	295—	324—
292—	266—	269—	296—	333—
298—	282—	273—	304—	334—
299—	283—	274—	315—	
335—	284—	278—	316—	
336—	285—	288—	319—	
337—	286—	297—	320—	
	293—	300—	322—	
	294—	301—	325—	
	303—	308—	330—	
	310—	309—	331—	
	311—	312—		
	328—	318—		
	329—	321—		
	332—	326—		
		327—		
		338—		
		339—		
		340—		

Cumulative Record Sheet

Student's Name:

Category A— Grades 3 & 4	Category B— Grades 4 & 5	Category C— Grades 5 & 6	Category D— Grades 6 & 7	Category E— Grades 7 & 8

The More Quizzes List of Great Children's Books

Adler, Susan S. (American Girls Collection) *Meet Samantha.*
AVI. *Blue Heron.*
AVI. *Punch with Judy.*
AVI. *The True Confessions of Charlotte Doyle.*
AVI. *Who Was That Masked Man, Anyway?*
Banks, Lynne Reid. *The Indian in the Cupboard.*
Banks, Lynne Reid. *The Mystery of the Cupboard.*
Banks, Lynne Reid. *One More River.*
Banks, Lynne Reid. *The Return of the Indian.*
Banks, Lynne Reid. *The Secret of the Indian.*
Bauer, Marion Dane. *Face to Face.*
Bauer, Marion Dane. *On My Honor.*
Bellairs, John. *The House with a Clock in Its Walls.*
Bellairs, John. *The Letter, the Witch, and the Ring.*
Bellairs, John. *The Mansion in the Mist.*
Blume, Judy. *Are You There God? It's Me, Margaret.*
Blume, Judy. *Fudge-A-Mania.*
Blume, Judy. *Here's to You, Rachel Robinson.*
Blume, Judy. *Then Again, Maybe I Won't.*
Byars, Betsy. *A Blossom Promise.*
Byars, Betsy. *The Blossoms and the Green Phantom.*
Byars, Betsy. *The Blossoms Meet the Vulture Lady.*
Byars, Betsy. *The Not-Just-Anybody Family.*
Byars, Betsy. *Wanted . . . Mud Blossom.*
Cassedy, Sylvia. *Behind the Attic Wall.*
Cassedy, Sylvia. *Lucie Babbidge's House.*
Christopher, Matt. *Front Court Hex.*
Christopher, Matt. *Johnny Long Legs.*
Christopher, Matt. *No Arm in Left Field.*
Christopher, Matt. *Red-Hot Hightops.*
Cleary, Beverly. *Muggie Maggie.*
Cleary, Beverly. *Strider.*
Coville, Bruce. *The Ghost in the Big Brass Bed.*
Coville, Bruce. *The Ghost Wore Gray.*
Coville, Bruce. *My Teacher Flunked the Planet.*
Coville, Bruce. *My Teacher Is an Alien.*
Dahl, Roald. *Charlie and the Chocolate Factory.*
Dahl. Roald. *Charlie and the Great Glass Elevator.*
Dahl, Roald. *James and the Giant Peach.*
Dahl, Roald. *The Witches.*
Dorris, Michael. *Morning Girl.*
Fleischman, Sid. *Jim Ugly.*
Fleischman, Sid. *The Midnight Horse.*
Fleischman, Sid. *The Whipping Boy.*
Fox, Paula. *Monkey Island.*
Freedman, Russell. *Franklin Delano Roosevelt.*
Freedman, Russell. *Lincoln: A Photobiography.*
Freedman, Russell. *The Wright Brothers.*
George, Jean Craighead. *The Missing 'Gator of Gumbo Limbo.*
George, Jean Craighead. *Shark Beneath the Reef.*
Graeber, Charlotte Towner. *Fudge.*
Hahn, Mary Downing. *Wait Till Helen Comes: A Ghost Story.*
Hamilton, Virginia. *Cousins.*
Hamilton, Virginia. *Zeely.*
Hinton, S. E. *The Outsiders.*
Hinton, S. E. *Tex.*
Hinton, S. E. *That Was Then, This Is Now.*
Howe, Deborah, and James Howe. *Bunnicula: A Rabbit Tale of Mystery.*
Howe, James. *The Celery Stalks at Midnight.*
Howe, James. *Howliday Inn.*
Howe, James. *Return to Howliday Inn.*
King-Smith, Dick. *Harry's Mad.*

Konigsburg, E. L. *T-Backs, T-Shirts, COAT and Suit.*
Lasky, Kathryn. *The Night Journey.*
Lasky, Kathryn. *Shadows in the Water.*
Lindgren, Astrid. *Pippi Goes on Board.*
Lindgren, Astrid. *Pippi in the South Seas.*
Lindgren, Astrid. *Pippi Longstocking.*
Lowry, Lois. *All About Sam.*
Lowry, Lois. *Attaboy, Sam!*
Lowry, Lois. *The Giver.*
Lowry, Lois. *Number the Stars.*
MacBride, Roger Lea. *Little House on Rocky Ridge.*
MacDonald, Betty. *Mrs. Piggle-Wiggle.*
MacDonald, Betty. *Mrs. Piggle-Wiggle's Farm.*
MacLachlan, Patricia. *Baby.*
MacLachlan, Patricia. *Journey.*
Magorian, Michelle. *Good Night, Mr. Tom.*
Martin, Ann M. *Ten Kids, No Pets.*
McKissack, Patricia C. *The Dark-Thirty: Southern Tales of the Supernatural.*
McKissack, Patricia C., and Fredrick McKissack. *A Long Hard Journey: The Story of Pullman Porter.*
Montgomery, L. M. *Anne of Avonlea.*
Montgomery. L. M. *Anne of Green Gables.*
Naylor, Phyllis Reynolds. *The Agony of Alice.*
Naylor, Phyllis Reynolds. *Beetles, Lightly Toasted.*
Naylor, Phyllis Reynolds. *The Boys Start the War.*
Naylor, Phyllis Reynolds. *The Grand Escape.*
Naylor, Phyllis Reynolds. *Shiloh.*
Nixon, Joan Lowery. *The Kidnapping of Christina Lattimore.*
Nixon, Joan Lowery. *The Other Side of Dark.*
O'Dell, Scott. *My Name Is Not Angelica.*
Paterson, Katherine. *Lyddie.*
Paterson, Katherine. *Of Nightingales That Weep.*
Paterson, Katherine. *Park's Quest.*
Paulsen, Gary. *Hatchet.*
Paulsen, Gary. *Nightjohn.*
Paulsen, Gary. *The Voyage of the* Frog.
Paulsen, Gary. *The Winter Room.*
Peck, Richard. *Are You in the House Alone?*
Peck, Richard. *Don't Look and It Won't Hurt.*
Peck, Richard. *The Ghost Belonged to Me.*
Porter, Connie. (American Girls Collection) *Meet Addy.*
Reeder, Carolyn. *Shades of Gray.*
Rylant, Cynthia. *Missing May.*
Sachar, Louis. *There's a Boy in the Girls' Bathroom.*
Shaw, Janet. (American Girls Collection) *Meet Kirsten.*
Smith, Robert Kimmel. *The War with Grandpa.*
Spinelli, Jerry. *Maniac Magee.*
Spinelli, Jerry. *Space Station Seventh Grade.*
Stolz, Mary. *Stealing Home.*
Taylor, Mildred D. *Let the Circle Be Unbroken.*
Taylor, Mildred D. *The Road to Memphis.*
Tripp, Valerie. (American Girls Collection) *Meet Felicity.*
Tripp, Valerie. (American Girls Collection) *Meet Molly.*
Warner, Gertrude Chandler. *The Boxcar Children.* (Boxcar Mystery #1)
Warner, Gertrude Chandler. *Surprise Island.* (Boxcar Mystery #2)
Warner, Gertrude Chandler. *The Yellow House Mystery.* (Boxcar Mystery #3)
Wright, Betty Ren. *Christina's Ghost.*
Wright, Betty Ren. *The Dollhouse Murders.*
Wright, Betty Ren. *Ghosts Beneath Our Feet.*

Cumulative Listing

Author	Title	Vol. I	Vol. II
Alcott Louisa May	*Little Men*	•	
	Little Women	•	
Alexander, Lloyd	*The Black Cauldron*	•	
	The Book of Three	•	
	The Castle of Llyr	•	
	The Cat Who Wished to Be a Man	•	
	The High King	•	
	Taran Wanderer	•	
	The Wizard in the Tree	•	
American Girls Collection	*Meet Samantha*		•
	Meet Addy		•
	Meet Kirsten		•
	Meet Felicity		•
	Meet Molly		•
Armer, Laura Adams	*Waterless Mountain*	•	
Armstrong, William H.	*Sounder*	•	
Atwater, Richard and Florence	*Mr. Popper's Penguins*	•	
AVI	*Blue Heron*		•
	Punch With Judy		•
	The True Confessions of Charlotte Doyle		•
	Who Was That Masked Man, Anyway?		•
Babbitt, Natalie	*The Eyes of the Amaryllis*	•	
	Goody Hall	•	
	Knee-Knock Rise	•	
Bailey, Carolyn	*Miss Hickory*	•	
Banks, Lynne Reid	*The Indian in the Cupboard*		•
	The Mystery of the Cupboard		•
	One More River		•
	The Return of the Indian		•
	The Secret of the Indian		•
Barnouw, Victor	*Dream of the Blue Heron*	•	
Bauer, Marion Dane	*Face to Face*		•
	On My Honor		•
Bellairs, John	*The House With a Clock in Its Walls*		•
	The Letter, the Witch, and the Ring		•
	The Mansion in the Mist		•
Blos, Joan	*A Gathering of Days*	•	
Blume, Judy	*Are You There God? It's Me, Margaret*		•
	Fudge-A-Mania		•
	Here's to You, Rachel Robinson		•
	Otherwise Known as Sheila the Great	•	
	Superfudge	•	
	Tales of a Fourth Grade Nothing	•	
	Then Again, Maybe I Won't		•
Brink, Carol Ryrie	*Caddie Woodlawn*	•	
Burnett, Frances Hodgson	*The Secret Garden*	•	
Byars, Betsy	*A Blossom Promise*		•
	The Blossoms and the Green Phantom		•
	The Blossoms Meet the Vulture Lady		•

Cumulative Listing

Author	Title	Vol. I	Vol. II
Byars, Betsy (continued)	*The Cartoonist*	•	
	The Computer Nut	•	
	Cracker Jackson	•	
	The Cybil War	•	
	Good-bye, Chicken Little.	•	
	The House of Wings	•	
	The Night Swimmers	•	
	The Not-Just-Anybody Family		•
	The Pinballs	•	
	The Summer of the Swans	•	
	The TV Kid	•	
	The Two-Thousand-Pound Goldfish	•	
	Wanted . . . Mud Blossom		•
Carlson, Natalie Savage	*A Brother for the Orphelines*	•	
	The Empty Schoolhouse	•	
	The Happy Orpheline	•	
	The Letter on the Tree	•	
	The Orphelines in the Enchanted Castle	•	
	A Pet for the Orphelines	•	
	School Bell in the Valley	•	
Cassedy, Sylvia	*Behind the Attic Wall*		•
	Lucie Babbidge's House		•
Christopher, Matt	*Front Court Hex*		•
	Johnny Long Legs		•
	No Arm in Left Field		•
	Red-Hot Hightops		•
Clark, Ann Nolan	*Santiago*	•	
	Secret of the Andes	•	
Cleary, Beverly	*Dear Mr. Henshaw*	•	
	Ellen Tebbits	•	
	Henry and Beezus	•	
	Henry and Ribsy	•	
	Henry and the Clubhouse	•	
	Henry and the Paper Route	•	
	Henry Huggins	•	
	The Mouse and the Motorcycle	•	
	Muggie Maggie		•
	Ralph S. Mouse	•	
	Ramona and Her Mother	•	
	Ramona and Her Father	•	
	Ramona Forever	•	
	Ramona Quimby, Age 8	•	
	Ramona the Brave	•	
	Ramona the Pest	•	
	Ribsy	•	
	Runaway Ralph	•	
	Socks	•	
	Strider		•
Clemens, Samuel L.	*The Adventures of Huckleberry Finn*	•	
	The Adventures of Tom Sawyer	•	

Cumulative Listing

Author	Title	Vol. I	Vol. II
Collier, James Lincoln and Christopher	*My Brother Sam Is Dead*	•	
Cooper, James Fenimore	*The Last of the Mohicans*	•	
Cooper, Susan	*The Dark Is Rising*	•	
	The Grey King	•	
Coville, Bruce	*The Ghost in the Big Brass Bed*		•
	The Ghost Wore Gray		•
	My Teacher Flunked the Planet		•
	My Teacher Is an Alien		•
Dahl, Roald	*Charlie and the Chocolate Factory*		•
	Charlie and the Great Glass Elevator		•
	James and the Giant Peach		•
	The Witches		•
Defoe, Daniel	*Robinson Crusoe*	•	
DeJong, Meindert	*Hurry Home, Candy*	•	
	Puppy Summer	•	
	The Wheel on the School	•	
Dickens, Charles	*Oliver Twist*	•	
	A Tale of Two Cities	•	
Dorris, Michael	*Morning Girl*		•
DuBois, William	*The Twenty-One Balloons*	•	
Eckert, Allan W.	*Incident at Hawk's Hill*	•	
Edmonds, Walter D.	*The Matchlock Gun*	•	
	Two Logs Crossing	•	
Enright, Elizabeth	*Thimble Summer*	•	
Estes, Elizabeth	*The Alley*	•	
	The Coat-Hanger Christmas Tree	•	
	Ginger Pye	•	
	The Hundred Dresses	•	
	The Lost Umbrella of Kim Chu	•	
	The Middle Moffat	•	
	Rufus M.	•	
Fitzhugh, Louise	*Harriet the Spy*	•	
Fleischman, Sid	*Jim Ugly*		•
	The Midnight Horse		•
	The Whipping Boy		•
Forbes, Esther	*Johnny Tremain*	•	
Fox, Paula	*Monkey Island*		•
	One-Eyed Cat	•	
	Slave Dancer	•	
Freedman, Russell	*Franklin Delano Roosevelt*		•
	Lincoln: A Photobiography		•
	The Wright Brothers		•
Gates, Doris	*Blue Willow*	•	
	The Elderberry Bush	•	
	A Morgan for Melinda	•	
George, Jean Craighead	*Coyote in Manhattan*	•	
	Julie of the Wolves	•	
	The Missing 'Gator of Gumbo Limbo		•
	My Side of the Mountain	•	
	River Rats, Inc.	•	

Cumulative Listing

Author	Title	Vol. I	Vol. II
George, Jean Craighead (continued)	*Shark Beneath the Reef*		•
	Who Really Killed Cock Robin?	•	
Gipson, Fred	*Old Yeller*	•	
	Savage Sam	•	
Graeber, Charlotte Towner	*Fudge*		•
Greene, Bette	*Philip Hall Likes Me, I Reckon Maybe.*	•	
Greene, Constance C.	*A Girl Called Al*	•	
Hahn, Mary Downing	*Wait Till Helen Comes: A Ghost Story*		•
Hamilton, Virginia	*Cousins*		•
	M. C. Higgins the Great	•	
	The Planet of Junior Brown	•	
	Zeely		•
Harris, Rosemary	*The Bright and Morning Star*	•	
	The Moon in the Cloud	•	
	The Shadow on the Sun	•	
Haywood, Carolyn	*Back to School With Betsy*	•	
	"B" Is for Betsy	•	
	Betsy and Mr. Kilpatrick	•	
	Eddie's Happenings	•	
	Snowbound With Betsy	•	
Henry, Marguerite	*Born to Trot*	•	
	Brighty of the Grand Canyon	•	
	Justin Morgan Had a Horse	•	
	King of the Wind	•	
	Misty of Chincoteague	•	
	Mustang — Wild Spirit of the West	•	
	Stormy, Misty's Foal	•	
Hinton, S. E.	*The Outsiders*		•
	Tex		•
	That Was Then, This Is Now		•
Howe, James	*Bunnicula: A Rabbit Tale of Mystery*		•
	The Celery Stalks at Midnight		•
	Howliday Inn		•
	Return to Howliday Inn		•
Hunt, Irene	*Across Five Aprils*	•	
	Up a Road Slowly	•	
Ish-Kishor, Sulamith	*Our Eddie*	•	
Kelly, Eric P.	*The Trumpeter of Krakow*	•	
King-Smith, Dick	*Harry's Mad*		•
Konigsburg, E. L.	*Father's Arcane Daughter*	•	
	From the Mixed-Up Files of Mrs. Basil E. Frankweiler	•	
	Jennifer, Hectate, Macbeth, William McKinley and Me, Elizabeth	•	
	T-Backs, T-Shirts, COAT and Suit		•
Krumgold, Joseph	*And Now Miguel*	•	
	Onion John	•	
Lasky, Kathryn	*Beyond the Divide*	•	
	The Night Journey		•
	Shadows in the Water		•
Latham, Jean Lee	*Carry On, Mr. Bowditch*	•	

Cumulative Listing

Author	Title	Vol. I	Vol. II
Lawson, Robert	*Ben and Me*	•	
	Rabbit Hill	•	
	Robbut	•	
	The Tough Winter	•	
L'Engle, Madeleine	*A Swiftly Tilting Planet*	•	
	A Wind in the Door	•	
	A Wrinkle in Time	•	
Lenski, Lois	*Strawberry Girl*	•	
Lewis, C. S.	*The Horse and His Boy*	•	
	The Last Battle	•	
	The Lion, the Witch and the Wardrobe	•	
	The Magician's Nephew	•	
	Prince Caspian	•	
	The Silver Chair	•	
	Voyage of the "Dawn Treader"	•	
Lindgren, Astrid	*Pippi Goes on Board*		•
	Pippi in the South Seas		•
	Pippi Longstocking		•
Lively, Penelope	*Astercote*	•	
	The Ghost of Thomas Kempe	•	
London, Jack	*The Call of the Wild*	•	
Lowry, Lois	*All About Sam*		•
	Attaboy, Sam!		•
	The Giver		•
	Number the Stars		•
MacBride, Roger Lea	*Little House on Rocky Ridge*		•
MacDonald, Betty	*Mrs. Piggle-Wiggle*		•
	Mrs. Piggle-Wiggle's Farm		•
MacLachlan, Patricia	*Baby*		•
	Journey		•
	Sarah, Plain and Tall	•	
Magorian, Michelle	*Good Night, Mr. Tom*		•
Martin, Ann M.	*Ten Kids, No Pets*		•
McKinley, Robin	*Beauty*	•	
	The Blue Sword	•	
	The Hero and the Crown	•	
McKissack, Patricia C.	*The Dark-Thirty: Southern Tales of the Supernatural*		•
McKissack, Patricia C. and Fredrick	*A Long Hard Journey: The Story of Pullman Porter*		•
Meigs, Cornelia	*Invincible Louisa*	•	
Montgomery, L. M.	*Anne of Avonlea*		•
	Anne of Green Gables		•
Naylor, Phyllis Reynolds	*The Agony of Alice*		•
	Beetles, Lightly Toasted		•
	The Boys Start the War		•
	The Grand Escape		•
	Shiloh		•
Neville, Emily	*It's Like This, Cat.*	•	
Nixon, Joan Lowery	*The Kidnapping of Christina Lattimore*		•
	The Other Side of Dark		•

Cumulative Listing

Author	Title	Vol. I	Vol. II
North, Sterling	*Rascal*	•	
	The Wolfling	•	
Norton, Mary	*The Borrowers*	•	
	The Borrowers Afield	•	
	The Borrowers Afloat	•	
	The Borrowers Aloft	•	
	The Borrowers Avenged	•	
O'Brien, Robert C.	*Mrs. Frisby and the Rats of NIMH*	•	
O'Dell, Scott	*Island of the Blue Dolphins*	•	
	My Name Is Not Angelica		•
	Sarah Bishop	•	
	Sing Down the Moon	•	
Paterson, Katherine	*Bridge to Terabithia*	•	
	Jacob I Have Loved	•	
	Lyddie		•
	Of Nightingales That Weep		•
	Park's Quest		•
Paulson, Gary	*Hatchet*		•
	Nightjohn		•
	The Voyage of the Frog		•
	The Winter Room		•
Pearce, Philippa	*Tom's Midnight Garden*	•	
Peck, Richard	*Are You in the House Alone?*		•
	Don't Look and It Won't Hurt		•
	The Ghost Belonged to Me		•
Raskin, Ellen	*The Mysterious Disappearance of Leon (I Mean Noel)*	•	
	The Westing Game	•	
Rawlings, Marjorie Kinnan	*The Yearling*	•	
Reeder, Carolyn	*Shades of Gray*		•
Robertson, Keith	*Henry Reed, Inc.*	•	
	Henry Reed's Babysitting Service	•	
Rodowsky, Colby F.	*What About Me?*	•	
Rylant, Cynthia	*Missing May*		•
Sachar, Louis	*There's a Boy in the Girls' Bathroom*		•
Sawyer, Ruth	*Roller Skates*	•	
Sebestyen, Ouida	*Words By Heart*	•	
Selden, George	*The Cricket in Times Square*	•	
Seredy, Kate	*The White Stag*	•	
Shannon, Monica	*Dobry*	•	
Smith, Doris Buchanan	*The First Hard Times*	•	
	Kelly's Creek	•	
	Kick a Stone Home	•	
	Last Was Lloyd	•	
	A Taste of Blackberries	•	
Smith, Robert Kimmel	*The War with Grandpa*		•
Sobol, Donald J.	*Encyclopedia Brown Carries On*	•	
	Encyclopedia Brown—The Case of the Dead Eagles	•	
	Encyclopedia Brown Solves Them All	•	
Sorensen, Virginia	*Miracles on Maple Hill*	•	

Cumulative Listing

Author	Title	Vol. I	Vol. II
Speare, Elizabeth George	*The Bronze Bow*	•	
	Calico Captive	•	
	Sign of the Beaver	•	
	The Witch of Blackbird Pond	•	
Sperry, Armstrong	*Call It Courage*	•	
Spinelli, Jerry	*Maniac Magee*		•
	Space Station Seventh Grade		•
Steig, William	*Abel's Island*	•	
	The Real Thief	•	
Stevenson, Robert Louis	*Kidnapped*	•	
	Treasure Island	•	
Stolz, Mary	*Cat Walk*	•	
	The Noonday Friends	•	
	Stealing Home		•
Stowe, Harriet Beecher	*Uncle Tom's Cabin*	•	
Taylor, Mildred D.	*Let the Circle Be Unbroken*		•
	The Road to Memphis		•
	Roll of Thunder, Hear My Cry	•	
Trevino, Elizabeth Borton de	*I, Juan de Pareja*	•	
Voigt, Cynthia	*Building Blocks*	•	
	Dicey's Song	•	
	Homecoming	•	
	A Solitary Blue	•	
Warner, Gertrude Chandler	*The Boxcar Children (Boxcar Mystery #1)*		•
	Surprise Island (Boxcar Mystery #2)		•
	The Yellow House Mystery (Boxcar Mystery #3)		•
White, E. B.	*Charlotte's Web*	•	
	Stuart Little	•	
	The Trumpet of the Swan	•	
Wiggin, Kate Douglas	*Rebecca of Sunnybrook Farm*	•	
Wilder, Laura Ingalls	*By the Shores of Silver Lake*	•	
	Farmer Boy	•	
	The First Four Years	•	
	Little House in the Big Woods	•	
	Little Town on the Prairie	•	
	The Long Winter	•	
	On the Banks of Plum Creek	•	
	These Happy Golden Years	•	
Wojciechowska, Maia	*Shadow of a Bull*	•	
Wright, Betty Ren	*Christina's Ghost*		•
	The Dollhouse Murders		•
	Ghosts Beneath Our Feet		•
Wyss, Johann	*The Swiss Family Robinson*	•	
Yates, Elizabeth	*With Pipe, Paddle, and Song*	•	

PART
II

Album of Tests

221
Meet Samantha
Susan S. Adler. (American Girls Collection)

True or False. Decide whether each statement is true or false. Mark your answer sheet accordingly.

1. Samantha had to spend two hours every day cleaning the kitchen.
2. Uncle Gard would only ride in a horse and buggy.
3. Grandmary stayed in bed all the time.
4. Jessie had to leave because she stole some of Grandmary's jewels.
5. Nellie's family was rich.
6. Grandmary said that Samantha could sell boomerangs door-to-door to earn money to buy a doll.
7. Nellie and Samantha went to look for Jessie.
8. Nellie and Samantha didn't like each other.
9. Samantha was in love with Eddie.
10. Grandmary said Jessie could never come to the house again.
11. Nellie had worked in a factory.

Multiple Choice. Read each question. Decide which statement best answers the question. Mark your answer sheet accordingly.

12. Jessie left because
    A. The police took her away
    B. She hated Grandmary
    C. She was having a baby
    D. Grandmary fired her

13. Samantha was shocked to learn that
    A. Nellie's family was cold and hungry
    B. Her parents lived in Chicago
    C. Eddie was really her cousin
    D. Grandmary knew how to fly an airplane

14. Samantha wanted the doll because
    A. She collected dolls
    B. The doll looked like her mother
    C. The doll could say Mama and Papa
    D. The doll could walk and wet

222
Meet Addy
Connie Porter. (American Girls Collection)

True or False. Decide whether each statement is true or false. Mark your answer sheet accordingly.

1. Addy worked in the tobacco fields.

2. Master Stevens sold Addy's father and brother to a different plantation.

3. Addy carried Esther when her family ran away.

4. Slave children didn't go to school.

5. Children didn't have to work on the plantation.

6. The Underground Railroad helped slaves escape to the North.

7. Addy and her mother were rescued by Union soldiers.

8. Poppa ran away after Master Stevens said he was lazy.

9. Momma left Esther with Auntie Lula and Uncle Solomon.

10. Addy was captured by Confederate soldiers.

11. Addy saved her mother from drowning.

Multiple Choice. Read each question. Decide which statement best answers the question. Mark your answer sheet accordingly.

12. Who helped Addy escape?

    A. Master Stevens

    B. Miss Caroline

    C. A Confederate soldier

    D. A Union soldier

13. What was Addy's punishment for not picking off all the tobacco worms?

    A. She was whipped

    B. She was not given any supper

    C. She had to run around the field holding a worm

    D. The overseer made her eat some worms

14. When Addy escaped, she

    A. Took a train

    B. Traveled only at night

    C. Used Mr. Steven's wagon

    D. Dressed like an Indian

223
Meet Kirsten
Janet Shaw. (American Girls Collection)

True or False. Decide whether each statement is true or false. Mark your answer sheet accordingly.

1. The Larson family came to America on a ship.

2. The journey from Sweden to America took the Larson family only five days.

3. The Larson family was planning to live in New York City.

4. A thief took all Mr. Larson's money.

5. The Larsons traveled from New York to Chicago on a noisy, dirty train.

6. Lars broke his leg when he fell from the covered wagon.

7. Kirsten was the only member of her family who could speak English.

8. Kirsten's friend Marta died of cholera on the riverboat *Redwing*.

9. Kirsten's cousins, Anna and Lisbeth, made fun of her Swedish accent.

10. Peter decided to stay in Chicago and work in a factory.

11. On the voyage to America, the Larsons had to share one small cabin with many other families.

Multiple Choice. Read each question. Decide which statement best answers the question. Mark your answer sheet accordingly.

12. What made the journey from Sweden to Minnesota dangerous for Kirsten?

    A. Many pirates sailed the Atlantic Ocean

    B. Indians attacked the trains

    C. Diseases killed many people

    D. There were many outlaws in America

13. Why did the Larsons emigrate to America?

    A. They were trying to make a better life for themselves

    B. Papa was running away from the Swedish army

    C. Mama had always hated Sweden

    D. Peter had insulted the crown prince of Sweden

14. Who was Sari?

    A. Kirsten's doll

    B. Kirsten's dog

    C. Peter's kitten

    D. Kirsten's little sister

224
Meet Felicity
Valerie Tripp. (American Girls Collection)

True or False. Decide whether each statement is true or false. Mark your answer sheet accordingly.

1. Felicity lived in Concord, New Hampshire.
2. Mr. Merriman owned a general store.
3. Jiggy Nye drank rum.
4. Felicity loved to sew.
5. It was hard for Felicity to run in petticoats.
6. Ben never learned that Felicity was wearing his breeches.
7. Felicity named Jiggy Nye's new horse "Indian."
8. Ben was Mr. Merriman's apprentice.
9. Jiggy Nye said he would sell his horse for 10 silver dollars.
10. Jiggy Nye told Felicity to stay away from his horse.
11. Felicity sneaked out early in the morning to see Jiggy Nye's horse.

Multiple Choice. Read each question. Decide which statement best answers the question. Mark your answer sheet accordingly.

12. Felicity heard Jiggy Nye say that he
    A. Bought the horse from George Washington
    B. Would trade the horse for two cows
    C. Would give the horse to anyone who could ride it
    D. Was going to give the horse to a little blind boy

13. Felicity named the horse
    A. Indian
    B. Penny
    C. Cooper
    D. Lightning

14. Felicity
    A. Set the horse loose
    B. Talked her parents into buying the horse
    C. Returned the horse to George Washington
    D. Told Jiggy Nye she would sew him a jacket if he was nice to the horse

225
Meet Molly
Valerie Tripp. (American Girls Collection)

True or False. Decide whether each statement is true or false. Mark your answer sheet accordingly.

1. Molly loved cooked turnips.

2. Mrs. Gilford said Molly had to sit at the table until she finished her turnips.

3. Mrs. Gilford refused to buy canned vegetables.

4. Mrs. McIntire said the children didn't have to eat anything they didn't like.

5. Molly wanted to be Cinderella for Halloween.

6. Molly, Linda, and Susan went trick-or-treating together.

7. Ricky had a crush on Delores.

8. Molly, Linda, and Susan dressed up as the tree people for Halloween.

9. Alison dressed up as an angel.

10. Mrs. McIntire worked in a tank factory.

11. Linda, Susan, and Molly all teased Ricky for liking Delores.

Multiple Choice. Read each question. Decide which statement best answers the question. Mark your answer sheet accordingly.

12. Ricky

    A. Sprayed the girls with the water

    B. Put frogs in the girls' beds

    C. Put a mouse in Molly's room

    D. Locked the girls in a dark basement

13. Susan, Linda, and Molly

    A. Put Ricky's basketball in the outhouse

    B. Painted Ricky's hair orange while he was sleeping

    C. Dumped Ricky's underwear out the window

    D. Put a snake in Ricky's bed

14. Mrs. McIntire

    A. Made everyone stop fighting because there was too much fighting in the world

    B. Spanked the children and sent them to bed

    C. Put mice in everyone's beds

    D. Made everyone write a letter to the president to apologize

226
Blue Heron
AVI

True or False. Decide whether each statement is true or false. Mark your answer sheet accordingly.

1. Joanna was Maggie's stepmother.

2. Maggie's father, Mr. Lavchek, was a quiet and relaxed man.

3. Maggie got up every morning to watch the heron.

4. Mr. Lavchek wanted to capture the heron so he could give it to the local zoo.

5. Tucker was trying to shoot the blue heron with a bow and arrow.

6. Mr. Lavchek did not pay much attention to his baby daughter, Linda.

7. Mr. Lavchek refused to take his heart medicine.

8. Joanna was afraid to talk with her husband about his heart medicine.

9. Tucker accidentally shot Maggie in the arm with an arrow.

10. At the end of the story, Tucker decided not to try to kill the heron.

Multiple Choice. Read each question. Decide which statement best answers the question. Mark your answer sheet accordingly.

11. Tucker

    A. Had a secret hideout on a little island

    B. Lived in an orphanage on the other side of the marsh

    C. Had an old, mangy dog named Butterball

    D. All of the above

12. Mr. Lavchek was always on the telephone because

    A. He worked for the government

    B. He was making deals on the stock market

    C. He was trying to find a job

    D. He sold real estate

13. Joanna asked Maggie to

    A. Go back to Seattle at once

    B. Be nice to Tucker because he was an orphan

    C. Ask her father to take his medicine

    D. Chase away the heron before Mr. Lavchek caught it

14. After yelling at Maggie and ordering her out of the car, Mr. Lavchek

    A. Said he was sorry

    B. Had a heart attack while driving and was involved in an accident

    C. Drove over the blue heron

    D. Was arrested for drunken driving

227
Punch with Judy
AVI

True or False. Decide whether each statement is true or false. Mark your answer sheet accordingly.

1. Punch worked as a servant for the show.
2. Ne-Nip was a drink that was supposed to cure almost anything.
3. Joe McSneed had Punch do magic tricks with Dr. F. X. Pudlow.
4. Joe McSneed's troupe was called "The Ne-Nip Traveling Show."
5. Joe McSneed told Punch that he must marry Judy.
6. New Moosup's parson was angry because his son was in love with Judy.
7. Sheriff Oxnard jailed Judy and Mrs. McSneed.
8. Punch was afraid that Judy was angry with him.
9. Mrs. McSneed went out of her head after her husband died.
10. All four Merry Men abandoned the troupe.
11. Judy insisted that the show switch to comedy.

Multiple Choice. Read each question. Decide which statement best answers the question. Mark your answer sheet accordingly.

12. Punch was finally happy when
    A. Judy told him she loved him like a brother
    B. Judy told him she would marry him
    C. Mr. McSneed adopted him
    D. Mrs. McSneed said that he reminded her of her son

13. The sheriff agreed not to arrest Punch if
    A. Judy would marry him
    B. The troupe would pay him $100
    C. The troupe could make him laugh
    D. They promised never to sell Ne-Nip again

14. Punch learned that
    A. Judy was madly in love with him
    B. Ne-Nip was poisoned
    C. He was Sheriff Oxnard's long-lost son
    D. Mr. McSneed left half interest in the show to him

228
The True Confessions of Charlotte Doyle
AVI

True or False. Decide whether each statement is true or false. Mark your answer sheet accordingly.

1. It took about two months for a ship to sail from England to the United States in 1832.

2. Charlotte stayed in the captain's cabin because she was the only girl on board.

3. Zachariah was the only black man on the ship.

4. Captain Jaggery forced Charlotte to work as a member of the crew.

5. Charlotte was only allowed to work in the galley.

6. Captain Jaggery tried to kill Charlotte.

7. Charlotte told the captain that the crew was going to mutiny.

8. Captain Jaggery shot and killed Mr. Barlow.

9. The captain sailed the *Seahawk* into a hurricane.

10. Charlotte's knife was found in the back of Mr. Hollybrass's body.

11. Charlotte tried to save Zachariah by grabbing the whip as he was being lashed.

Multiple Choice. Read each question. Decide which statement best answers the question. Mark your answer sheet accordingly.

12. Charlotte showed her remorse after Zachariah's burial by

    A. Killing Mr. Hollybrass

    B. Serving as a member of the crew

    C. Working in the galley

    D. Writing letters to his family to describe his death

13. After reading Charlotte's diary, Mr. Doyle

    A. Expressed relief that the man who tried to kill his daughter was dead

    B. Called Charlotte a liar and pointed out her poor spelling

    C. Demanded that his company protect sailors from cruel captains

    D. Announced to the community that Charlotte was a hero

14. Why did Charlotte run away and rejoin the *Seahawk*?

    A. Her father acted much like the late Captain Jaggery

    B. She missed the freedom of being at sea

    C. She was a virtual prisoner in her own home

    D. All of the above

229
Who Was That Masked Man, Anyway?
AVI

True or False. Decide whether each statement is true or false. Mark your answer sheet accordingly.

1. Franklin usually copied Mario's homework.

2. Frankie liked to pretend he was Chet Barker.

3. Mario was the leader in the make-believe games he and Frankie played.

4. Mr. Swerdlow was Frankie's uncle.

5. Mr. Swerdlow kept a skeleton in his closet.

6. Frankie wanted to get in trouble at school so Miss Gomez would come to his house.

7. Tom had been wounded in the war.

8. Frankie's Uncle Charley was mayor of New York City.

9. One of Frankie's favorite radio shows was "The Lone Ranger."

10. Frankie's room was in the basement.

11. Miss Gomez's boyfriend was killed in the war.

Multiple Choice. Read each question. Decide which statement best answers the question. Mark your answer sheet accordingly.

12. Frankie believed that Mr. Swerdlow was

    A. An evil scientist

    B. His long-lost uncle

    C. The Green Hornet

    D. An FBI agent

13. The real reason for Frankie's plot was to

    A. Save the world from evil

    B. Make sure he passed sixth grade

    C. Get Miss Gomez to fall in love with him

    D. Get his room back

14. Grown-ups were upset with Frankie because

    A. He kept getting Mario in trouble

    B. He would only walk backwards

    C. He lived in a world of radio shows

    D. He wrote down everything they said

230
The Indian in the Cupboard
Lynne Reid Banks

True or False. Decide whether each statement is true or false. Mark your answer sheet accordingly.

1. Omri bought the magic cupboard from a wizard.

2. Any toy put in the cupboard would come to life.

3. Little Bear was an Iroquois Indian.

4. Little Bear's people usually lived in teepees.

5. Omri found it difficult to take care of Little Bear.

6. Omri made a whole toy hospital come to life.

7. Patrick used the cupboard to bring his plastic policeman to life.

8. Boone was a fearless cowboy.

9. Boone drew a picture in Omri's art class.

10. Little Bear wanted Omri to bring him a wife.

11. Boone retrieved the magic key from Omri's cat.

Multiple Choice. Read each question. Decide which statement best answers the question. Mark your answer sheet accordingly.

12. When Mr. Johnson saw Little Bear and Boone he

    A. Called the police

    B. Demanded to know the secret of the magic cupboard

    C. Thought he was sick and seeing things that weren't there

    D. Asked Omri and Patrick to bring his plastic knight to life

13. The magic cupboard would bring any toy to life if

    A. It was made of plastic

    B. It had been touched by a wizard

    C. The moon was full

    D. It had been loved by a child

14. At the end of the story, Omri and Patrick

    A. Decided to create an entire city of miniature people

    B. Made a little park for their miniature people to live in

    C. Told Mr. Johnson the secret of the magic cupboard

    D. Decided to send the miniature people back to their own time

---

231
The Mystery of the Cupboard
Lynne Reid Banks

True or False. Decide whether each statement is true or false. Mark your answer sheet accordingly.

1. The house in the country was brand new and very modern.

2. Omri put the magic cupboard in the bank.

3. Omri told Gillan all about the magic cupboard.

4. Jessica Charlotte had very little contact with her family.

5. Jessica could sometimes predict the future.

6. Jessica's son, Fredrick, made the magic cupboard.

7. Jessica had no idea what the cupboard could do.

8. Tom refused to talk to Omri because he was related to Jessica.

9. Jessica stole some earrings from her sister, Maria.

10. Omri brought Jessica Charlotte into his own time with the magic cupboard.

11. Fredrick hated things made with plastic.

Multiple Choice. Read each question. Decide which statement best answers the question. Mark your answer sheet accordingly.

12. Jessica Charlotte

    A. Was terribly spoiled by her parents and her sister

    B. Was shunned because she was involved in the theater

    C. Married Boone

    D. Was a TV and movie star

13. Jenny was

    A. A woman from the past who chose to stay in Jessica's time

    B. Omri's cat

    C. The witch who cast the magic spell on the cupboard

    D. Gillan's girlfriend

14. Who did Omri finally share the secret of the cupboard with?

    A. His mother

    B. His father

    C. Gillan

    D. None of the above

232
One More River
Lynne Reid Banks

True or False. Decide whether each statement is true or false. Mark your answer sheet accordingly.

1. Lesley's father wanted to move to Israel because he thought it would be the safest place for his family to live.

2. Lesley's brother, Noah, had been disowned because he married a Roman Catholic girl.

3. Lesley had lived an easy life in Canada because her family was wealthy.

4. Lesley's roommates were amazed at how quickly she learned Hebrew.

5. Shula was a girl in the kibbutz who befriended Lesley.

6. Gadi was proud of his ability to quickly learn and speak Arabic.

7. When she looked across the Jordan River, Lesley could often see a farmer, his son, and their donkey.

8. Jordanian Arabs frequently crossed the border to visit their Israeli friends who lived in Kibbutz Kfar Orde.

9. Kibbutz Kfar Orde was fortunate that none of its members died in the Six Day War.

10. Children on the kibbutz only stayed with their parents a few hours each day.

11. Lesley asked Mustapha not to hurt his donkey.

Multiple Choice. Read each question. Decide which statement best answers the question. Mark your answer sheet accordingly.

12. Noah restored the relationship with his parents by

    A. Becoming an Orthodox Jew

    B. Divorcing his Roman Catholic wife

    C. Coming to the kibbutz during the war

    D. Giving up his career as a movie actor

13. The other children in the kibbutz didn't like Lesley at first because

    A. They thought she was stuck-up

    B. She had an Arab boyfriend

    C. She was an Orthodox Jew and they were atheists

    D. They were jealous of her good looks and nice clothes

14. Lesley hoped that

    A. Her family would quickly return to Chicago

    B. There would be peace between Arabs and Jews

    C. Noah would marry Shula

    D. Ofer would fall in love with her

233
The Return of the Indian
Lynne Reid Banks

True or False. Decide whether each statement is true or false. Mark your answer sheet accordingly.

1. Omri won a writing contest with his story about Little Bear.

2. Omri's family had moved to a rough neighborhood.

3. Patrick threw his plastic cowboy away.

4. Tommy, the medic from World War I, delivered Bright Stars's baby.

5. Omri and Patrick sent a squad of German soldiers back to Little Bear's village.

6. Boone showed Little Bear's warriors how to use modern weapons.

7. The skinheads asked Omri to be the leader of their gang.

8. Little Bear's village had been attacked by the French.

9. Matron refused to take care of Little Bear unless Omri brought her two more nurses.

10. Omri went back to Little Bear's village.

11. Boone's horse was badly hurt by a cat.

Multiple Choice. Read each question. Decide which statement best answers the question. Mark your answer sheet accordingly.

12. Omri and Patrick brought a plastic corporal to life so that he could

    A. Keep Little Bear from running away

    B. Put Boone in jail

    C. Train Little Bear's warriors

    D. Organize British soldiers to rescue Little Bear's village

13. Omri and Patrick chased away the skinhead burglars by

    A. Fighting them with a squad of British soldiers

    B. Having Little Bear's warriors attack their toes

    C. Having some miniature policemen yell at them

    D. None of the above

14. At the end of the story

    A. Little Bear and Bright Stars had a son

    B. Omri brought Little Bear's whole village into his room

    C. Boone married Bright Stars

    D. Matron married Boone

234
The Secret of the Indian
Lynne Reid Banks

True or False. Decide whether each statement is true or false. Mark your answer sheet accordingly.

1. Omri's parents saw Boone.

2. Emma helped Omri get some toy doctors from Tamsin.

3. Patrick traveled through time and went to France.

4. Emma used the magic cupboard to send Boone's horse to Patrick.

5. Ruby Lou was Boone's mother.

6. Omri read his story about Little Bear and Boone out loud to the whole school.

7. Mr. Johnson tried to make Omri tell him everything about the miniature people.

8. In Boone's world, Patrick was a giant.

9. Matron hated Omri and kept demanding that she be returned to her world at once.

10. Little Bear fell in love with Ruby Lou.

11. Omri decided that he should stop using the magic cupboard.

Multiple Choice. Read each question. Decide which statement best answers the question. Mark your answer sheet accordingly.

12. What did Omri accidentally bring into England with the magic key?

    A. A tribe of Zulus

    B. A Texas cyclone

    C. Little Bear's father

    D. Billy the Kid and the James Gang

13. Omri's parents and Mr. Johnson

    A. Saw the miniature people and called the police

    B. Were distracted by the cyclone and never learned Omri's secret

    C. Were captured by Zulus and taken to Africa

    D. Told Omri and Patrick that they should tell everyone about the cupboard

14. Omri decided

    A. To make it so he could never use the cupboard again

    B. That he would marry Emma when he grew up

    C. To keep Boone, Little Bear, and Ruby Lou in Emma's house

    D. To give the cupboard and magic key to Patrick

235
Face to Face
Marion Dane Bauer

True or False. Decide whether each statement is true or false. Mark your answer sheet accordingly.

1. Michael often dreamed about shooting people.

2. Michael lived on a dairy farm.

3. Michael's father had called him once a week, on Thursdays, ever since the divorce.

4. Dave was very quiet.

5. Kari hated Michael.

6. Cil was Bert Hensley's girlfriend.

7. Michael's father lived in a huge log cabin next to a river.

8. Michael's father wanted to make him tougher.

9. Michael's father was an experienced rafting guide.

10. Michael's father kept Michael by his side the entire time they were together.

11. Michael's father begged Michael to live with him.

Multiple Choice. Read each question. Decide which statement best answers the question. Mark your answer sheet accordingly.

12. While rafting down a river, Michael's father

    A. Drowned

    B. Rescued Cil from certain death

    C. Deliberately caused Michael to be swept into the river

    D. Risked his own life to save two children who fell off a bridge

13. When Michael's father's raft washed up onto a large rock, Michael

    A. Climbed out onto the rock, causing the raft to flip over

    B. Pulled both his father and Cil onto the rock and out of the raft

    C. Began screaming

    D. Was thrown into the river

14. At the end of the story, Michael realized that

    A. His mother had prevented his real father from seeing him

    B. His father, Bert Hensley, was the kind of man he wanted to grow up to be

    C. Dave loved him

    D. Being tough and violent was the best way to get respect

236
On My Honor
Marion Dane Bauer

True or False. Decide whether each statement is true or false. Mark your answer sheet accordingly.

1. Joel was hoping that his father wouldn't let him go with Tony.

2. Tony liked to do foolish and dangerous things.

3. Joel promised his father he would be careful while he and Tony were riding to Starved Rock.

4. Tony and Joel had just met.

5. Tony's mother, Mrs. Zabrinsky, had been Joel's baby-sitter.

6. The Vermillion River was a dirty river.

7. It was Tony who first decided to swim in the Vermillion.

8. Tony dared Joel to swim out to a sandbar in the river.

9. Joel didn't know that Tony couldn't swim.

10. When Tony disappeared in the river, Joel went to get the police immediately.

11. Joel hid Tony's body under the bridge.

Multiple Choice. Read each question. Decide which statement best answers the question. Mark your answer sheet accordingly.

12. Joel and Tony had first planned to go to Starved Rock Park to

    A. Swim in the Vermillion River

    B. Jump off the bluff

    C. Climb up the bluff

    D. Steal radios from tourists

13. At first, Joel told his father that Tony had

    A. Gone on to Starved Rock by himself

    B. Gone down the Vermillion River in a canoe

    C. Run away

    D. Hitched a ride to Chicago

14. Joel felt that

    A. His father shouldn't have let him go to Starved Rock

    B. It was his fault Tony died

    C. He smelled like the Vermillion River

    D. All of the above

237
The House with a Clock in Its Walls
John Bellairs

True or False. Decide whether each statement is true or false. Mark your answer sheet accordingly.

1. After his parents died, Lewis went to live with Uncle Jonathan.

2. Mrs. Zimmermann's favorite color was purple.

3. Isaac Izard and his wife were evil sorcerers.

4. Uncle Jonathan turned Tarby into a white rat.

5. Mrs. Zimmermann locked Lewis in her attic for two days.

6. Uncle Jonathan and Lewis could hear a clock ticking behind every wall in the house.

7. Isaac Izard's goal was to end the world.

8. Uncle Jonathan and Mrs. Zimmermann killed a rat to bring Isaac Izard back to life.

9. Lewis defeated Mrs. Izard by using a gold cross.

10. The hidden clock was in Mr. Izard's tomb.

11. Uncle Jonathan's only magical skill was the ability to pull white rabbits out of hats.

Multiple Choice. Read each question. Decide which statement best answers the question. Mark your answer sheet accordingly.

12. Mrs. Izard came out of her tomb because

    A. On Halloween night, Lewis chanted a spell for raising the dead outside her tomb

    B. Mr. Izard had placed a spell on her to bring her to life after 20 years

    C. She wasn't really dead

    D. Mrs. Zimmermann wished for something unexpected to happen

13. Lewis was able to destroy the clock while the others were held motionless because

    A. He wore a lucky rabbit's foot

    B. He had a bad cold, so he couldn't hear the witch's curse

    C. He was holding Mrs. Zimmermann's magic umbrella

    D. He was the only one who didn't look at the Hand of Glory

14. The clock had to be stopped because

    A. It gave evil witches their power

    B. It was going to end the world

    C. It would send everyone back in time

    D. None of the above

238
The Letter, the Witch, and the Ring
John Bellairs

True or False. Decide whether each statement is true or false. Mark your answer sheet accordingly.

1. Rose hated the idea of learning to act feminine.
2. Uncle Jonathan went with Mrs. Zimmermann to look at Cousin Oley's farm.
3. Rose found Oley's ring hidden in his shaving cream.
4. Gert Bigger hated Mrs. Zimmermann.
5. Gert Bigger was a witch.
6. Gert Bigger took Cousin Oley's ring.
7. Rose Rita drove the car after Mrs. Zimmermann suddenly became ill.
8. Aggie Sipes and Rose Rita both went into Gert Bigger's room.
9. The magic ring could let its user change his or her shape.
10. The demon Asmodai could be called by anyone using the magic ring.
11. Rose was rescued from the power of the ring by Mrs. Zimmermann.

Multiple Choice. Read each question. Decide which statement best answers the question. Mark your answer sheet accordingly.

12. Mrs. Zimmermann

    A. Was turned into a chicken by Gert Bigger

    B. Married Uncle Jonathan

    C. Decided to move out to Cousin Oley's farm

    D. Adopted Rose Rita

13. When Gert Bigger wished to be young and beautiful and to live for 1,000 years

    A. Nothing happened

    B. She was transformed into a beautiful young woman

    C. She was transformed into a young, slender willow tree

    D. She became old and ugly and soon died

14. The magic ring lost its power when

    A. Uncle Jonathan put a charm on it

    B. Gert Bigger used it selfishly

    C. Rose Rita threw it in the lake

    D. Mrs. Zimmermann melted it down

239
The Mansion in the Mist
John Bellairs

True or False. Decide whether each statement is true or false. Mark your answer sheet accordingly.

1. Anthony worked in the library with Miss Eells.
2. Miss Eells told Anthony that she had been to Mars twice.
3. The trunk wasn't always in the room at the end of the corridor.
4. The dimension of the Autarchs was a gloomy and evil place.
5. The Autarchs wanted to drag the earth into their dimension.
6. Anthony accidentally took the Logos Cube back to Minnesota with him.
7. To protect themselves, Anthony and Emerson wore four-leaf clovers on their wrists.
8. The trunk was the only entrance to the Autarchs' dimension.
9. The Grand Autarch disguised himself as a fisherman to fool Emerson and Anthony.
10. The Autarchs turned Miss Eells and Anthony into statues.

Multiple Choice. Read each question. Decide which statement best answers the question. Mark your answer sheet accordingly.

11. The magic desk would go to the Autarchs' dimension if

    A. The moon was full

    B. The blood of a bluebird was sprinkled on it

    C. The ace, three, seven, and nine of spades were arranged on it in the right way

    D. A man, woman, and child were holding hands around it on Halloween night

12. To keep themselves safe while in the Autarchs' dimension, the three friends

    A. Wore special amulets

    B. Carried swords blessed by a Moslem monk

    C. Took guns

    D. Dressed completely in black

13. The Autarchs needed to find the Logos Cube because

    A. It was turning them into humans

    B. It was beginning to change their world

    C. They knew it would soon explode

    D. It held all the secrets of the universe

14. Nathaniel Wabe

    A. Was trying to stop the Autarchs' evil plan

    B. Turned Anthony and Miss Eells into statues

    C. Was the head librarian

    D. Put the Logos Cube in Anthony's lunch box

240
Are You There God? It's Me, Margaret.
Judy Blume

True or False. Decide whether each statement is true or false. Mark your answer sheet accordingly.

1. Margaret's grandparents lived in the basement of Margaret's house.

2. Margaret joined a club called the New Jersey Beauties.

3. The club members all agreed to wear bras.

4. Both of Margaret's parents were Roman Catholic.

5. Margaret was the first girl in her club to have her period.

6. After going to temple, Margaret decided she wanted to become Jewish.

7. Margaret asked God to make her physically mature.

8. The sixth-grade class played kissing games at Norman Fishbein's party.

9. Nancy lied to Margaret about her period.

10. Grandma Simon wanted Margaret to become a Baptist.

11. Margaret begged Grandma and Grandpa Hutchins to stay longer.

Multiple Choice. Read each question. Decide which statement best answers the question. Mark your answer sheet accordingly.

12. Margaret's parents

    A. Were FBI agents

    B. Were letting her decide which religion she wanted to follow

    C. Were upset when they learned that she went to church

    D. Adopted a set of twins from Russia

13. Margaret

    A. Did not choose any particular religion

    B. Ran away to live with Grandma Simon in New York

    C. Told Nancy she could never be her friend

    D. Accidentally tipped over the teacher's desk

14. What happened to Margaret?

    A. She had her first period

    B. Her parents divorced

    C. Grandma Simon adopted her

    D. She flunked the sixth grade

241
Fudge-A-Mania
Judy Blume

True or False. Decide whether each statement is true or false. Mark your answer sheet accordingly.

1. Fudge said that he was going to marry Sheila Tubman.

2. Fudge often called Sheila "honey."

3. Peter's mother hired Sheila to baby-sit Fudge.

4. Fudge took Uncle Feather with him to Maine.

5. Uncle Feather couldn't talk.

6. Peter took his dog, Turtle, with him to Maine.

7. Fudge looked blue because he had eaten all the blueberries.

8. Peter became a member of the I.S.A.F.

9. Sheila's friend, Mouse, didn't come to Maine because she got chicken pox.

10. Grandma Muriel and Buzzy Senior decided to get married.

Multiple Choice. Read each question. Decide which statement best answers the question. Mark your answer sheet accordingly.

11. Fudge was upset when he found out that the library:

    A. Was closed on Saturdays

    B. Didn't have a book called *Tell Me a Fudge*

    C. Didn't have any books about dinosaurs

    D. Was going to be torn down

12. What happened when Peter was riding bikes with Jimmy and Sheila?

    A. Peter swallowed a fly

    B. Jimmy and Sheila got off their bikes and Jimmy kissed Sheila

    C. Jimmy and Sheila both got flat tires

    D. None of the above

13. When Peter's dad fell out of the boat, Peter and Mrs. Tubman

    A. Jumped in after him

    B. Yelled for help

    C. Tossed him some beef jerky

    D. Pointed at him

14. What did Fudge do with his mother's Oil of Olay?

    A. He hid it

    B. He used it to clean Sheila's puppy

    C. He put the whole bottle on his *mitt-sy*

    D. He gave it to Mitzi for her birthday

From *More Quizzes for Great Children's Books*. © 1996. Teacher Ideas Press. (800) 237-6124.

242
Here's to You, Rachel Robinson
Judy Blume

True or False. Decide whether each statement is true or false. Mark your answer sheet accordingly.

1. Charles was quiet and shy.

2. Alison and Stephanie hated Charles.

3. Rachel and Charles went to the same school.

4. Mrs. Robinson was relaxed and easygoing.

5. Rachel and Jessica fought with each other constantly.

6. Rachel liked things to be neat and orderly.

7. Mrs. Robinson believed that there were no problems, just obstacles.

8. Rachel felt that her mother caused all the family's problems.

9. Rachel bragged that she had been invited to take a college-level math course.

10. Jeremy Dragon kissed Rachel.

11. Jessica had very bad cystic acne.

Multiple Choice. Read each question. Decide which statement best answers the question. Mark your answer sheet accordingly.

12. Charles acted the way he did because he

    A. Felt he was smarter than the rest of his family

    B. Felt that he didn't fit in with the rest of the family

    C. Was brain-damaged

    D. Didn't want his parents to get a divorce

13. Rachel

    A. Kept most of her feelings to herself

    B. Loudly tried to get attention

    C. Hated her family so much that she spent most of her time with Tarren

    D. Was angry because she didn't do well in school

14. Tarren

    A. Admired Mrs. Robinson

    B. Was in love with Charles

    C. Was Mr. Robinson's ex-wife

    D. Was Rachel's hero

243
Then Again, Maybe I Won't
Judy Blume

True or False. Decide whether each statement is true or false. Mark your answer sheet accordingly.

1. Tony's grandmother couldn't speak.

2. Tony's family became rich when Mr. Miglione invented an electrical cartridge.

3. Joel was a drug dealer.

4. Grandma loved the new house in Rosemont.

5. The Migliones hired a maid.

6. Grandma cooked all the family's meals in Rosemont.

7. Mr. and Mrs. Miglione were concerned about what their neighbors in Rosemont thought of them.

8. Tony didn't have any friends in Long Island.

9. Tony called the police to tell them about Joel's prank phone calls.

10. Ralph gave up being a teacher to work with his father.

11. Lisa was madly in love with Tony.

Multiple Choice. Read each question. Decide which statement best answers the question. Mark your answer sheet accordingly.

12. Tony wanted binoculars for Christmas so that

    A. He could watch for rare birds

    B. He could see his old house

    C. He could better see into Lisa's bedroom

    D. He could study the airplanes that flew over his house

13. Tony got stomach pains if

    A. He was tense or stressed

    B. He smoked cigarettes

    C. He ran quickly

    D. He ate french fries

14. Joel's father decided to send Joel to a military school after

    A. Joel and Tony stole a car

    B. Joel was arrested for selling L.S.D.

    C. Joel was expelled from junior high school

    D. Joel was caught shoplifting

244
A Blossom Promise
Betsy Byars

True or False. Decide whether each statement is true or false. Mark your answer sheet accordingly.

1. Junior was waiting for Pap to take him to see Mad Mary so he could spend the night in her cave.

2. Junior helped Vern and Michael build their raft.

3. Pap told Vern that rafting down the flooded river would be safe if the raft was big enough.

4. Maggie was upset to discover that her mother was dating someone.

5. Dump was bitten by the snake under the Blossom's house.

6. Pap pulled Vern and Michael out of the flooded river after throwing a lasso around them.

7. Mud dove into the river and dragged both Vern and Michael to safety.

8. Mad Mary took charge of things after Pap had a heart attack.

9. Junior died after he stepped on a rattlesnake in his bare feet.

10. Maggie and her mother couldn't visit Pap in the hospital because they weren't able to leave the rodeo.

11. Maggie told Richie she blamed him for Junior's death.

Multiple Choice. Read each question. Decide which statement best answers the question. Mark your answer sheet accordingly.

12. How did Richie help the Blossoms?

    A. He smuggled Mud into the hospital to see Pap

    B. He got Pap out of the hospital

    C. He took Mad Mary's vultures to the zoo

    D. He made a new sail for Vern's raft

13. What was the Blossom promise made in this story?

    A. Pap promised that he would get well again and come home

    B. Vicki Blossom promised that they would always remember Junior

    C. Vern promised that he would never do anything dangerous again

    D. Maggie promised herself that she would make the Blossom family settle down

14. Why did Vern and Michael take their raft onto the river?

    A. It was an accidental launch and they couldn't get back to shore

    B. Junior was watching and Vern was ashamed to show he was scared

    C. Richie called them yellow bellies

    D. They were trying to rescue Mud

245
The Blossoms and the Green Phantom
Betsy Byars

True or False. Decide whether each statement is true or false. Mark your answer sheet accordingly.

1. Mrs. Blossom was teaching Maggie to trick-ride.

2. The Green Phantom was a submarine.

3. Mud dragged Pap out of a flooded river.

4. Dump was a cat.

5. Michael wanted to meet Vern's family.

6. Ralphie liked Maggie.

7. Junior was sad because none of his inventions ever worked.

8. No one came to rescue Pap when he called for help.

9. Mr. Benson was the Blossoms' dearest friend.

10. Mud took loving care of Dump.

11. The Green Phantom landed on Mr. Benson's chicken house.

Multiple Choice. Read each question. Decide which statement best answers the question. Mark your answer sheet accordingly.

12. Who was able to get Junior's secret ingredient?

    A. Michael

    B. Ralphie

    C. Mad Mary

    D. Pap

13. Where was Pap?

    A. In a dumpster

    B. In jail

    C. In Mad Mary's cave

    D. Trapped under a seesaw

14. Pap was finally rescued by

    A. Mud

    B. The police

    C. The fire department

    D. Mad Mary

246
The Blossoms Meet the Vulture Lady
Betsy Byars

True or False. Decide whether each statement is true or false. Mark your answer sheet accordingly.

1. Mad Mary ate animals killed by cars and trucks.

2. Vern and Maggie made a coyote trap.

3. Pap had gone to school with Mad Mary.

4. Junior, Vern, and Maggie set the coyote trap in the woods.

5. Mud loved raw hamburger.

6. Ralphie had a crush on Maggie.

7. Maggie and Vern had heard that Mad Mary was a witch.

8. Mad Mary carried Junior to her cave.

9. The coyote bit Junior's leg.

10. Pap collected cans.

11. Junior was found tied to Mad Mary's rocking chair.

Multiple Choice. Read each question. Decide which statement best answers the question. Mark your answer sheet accordingly.

12. Who got caught in the coyote trap?

    A. Junior

    B. Junior and Mud

    C. The coyote

    D. Vern and Maggie

13. Mad Mary

    A. Had boxes of books

    B. Took care of Junior

    C. Had avoided people for years

    D. All of the above

14. At the end of the book

    A. Junior went back to visit Mad Mary

    B. Vern caught the coyote

    C. The coyote followed Mud into the house

    D. Pap married Mad Mary

247
The Not-Just-Anybody Family
Betsy Byars

True or False. Decide whether each statement is true or false. Mark your answer sheet accordingly.

1. When Junior saw a police car driving up the road, Vern and Maggie hid.

2. When Junior fell off the barn roof, he broke both his legs.

3. Maggie and Vern carried Junior all the way to the hospital.

4. Ralphie liked to tell wild stories.

5. Vern signaled to Pap in jail by singing Polish marching songs.

6. Vern broke into the jail by climbing through a vent.

7. None of the guards noticed Vern in Pap's cell.

8. The story of Vern breaking into jail was covered by many newspapers.

9. Mud was sprayed by a skunk.

10. The judge sentenced Pap to jail for one year.

11. Maggie and Ralphie smuggled Junior out of the hospital.

Multiple Choice. Read each question. Decide which statement best answers the question. Mark your answer sheet accordingly.

12. Why was Ralphie in the hospital?

    A. He was getting a new artificial leg

    B. He had been hit by a car

    C. He had cancer

    D. He was pretending to be sick

13. Mud was

    A. The Blossoms' dog

    B. The Blossoms' cat

    C. Ralphie's pet snake

    D. Junior's pet mouse

14. Vern was a hero for

    A. Breaking into the jail

    B. Breaking his grandfather out of jail

    C. Saving Junior's life

    D. Saving Maggie's life

248
Wanted . . . Mud Blossom
Betsy Byars

True or False. Decide whether each statement is true or false. Mark your answer sheet accordingly.

1. Junior thought Mad Mary was trying to kill him.

2. When Pap found Mad Mary's cane, he laughed and said that Mad Mary was probably playing a joke on him.

3. Ralphie said that Maggie was an "ogrette."

4. Junior's teacher came to his house to see how Scooty was doing.

5. Junior's dog, Dump, ate Scooty.

6. Mud ate Scooty.

7. During the trial, Mud was made to come out from under the porch so that he could sit on the witness stand.

8. When Pap found out what Vern and Michael had done with Scooty, he drew a circle on the ground and told Junior that he could try and hit Vern.

9. When Mad Mary woke up, she was in a hospital.

10. Ralphie accidentally said "I love you" to Maggie's mother, Violet Blossom.

11. At the end of the book, Ralphie kissed Maggie.

Multiple Choice. Read each question. Decide which statement best answers the question. Mark your answer sheet accordingly.

12. Ralphie went into Maggie's room because he wanted to

    A. Look for the flower he had given Maggie

    B. Hide Scooty in Maggie's closet

    C. Put a fake spider under Maggie's pillow

    D. Read Maggie's diary

13. When Maggie found Ralphie in her room, Ralphie said that he was

    A. Taking a nap

    B. Looking for a Bible

    C. Lost

    D. Playing hide-and-seek

14. Where did Mad Mary live?

    A. In a large, brick house next to the Blossoms

    B. In a nursing home

    C. In a cave

    D. None of the above

249
Behind the Attic Wall
Sylvia Cassedy

True or False. Decide whether each statement is true or false. Mark your answer sheet accordingly.

1. Uncle Morris lived with Aunt Lillian and Aunt Harriet.

2. Maggie did not like the doll Aunt Lillian gave her.

3. Maggie told Aunt Lillian that she didn't play with dolls.

4. Maggie liked to play solitaire.

5. Maggie had a habit of sucking her hair.

6. The Backwoods Girls were very smart.

7. Aunt Harriet invited the Backwoods Girls to dinner.

8. The Backwoods Girls were not real people.

9. Maggie took Timothy John and Miss Christabel to school.

10. Timothy John liked to read in his newspaper about a fire and a washtub.

11. At the end of the book, Uncle Morris died.

Multiple Choice. Read each question. Decide which statement best answers the question. Mark your answer sheet accordingly.

12. Before coming to live with Aunt Harriet and Aunt Lillian, Maggie had been

    A. Kicked out of a lot of other places

    B. Living with Uncle Morris

    C. Living on a farm in Connecticut

    D. Living with her sister in Chicago

13. Timothy John and Miss Christabel

    A. Had a garden that was really just wallpaper

    B. Asked Maggie to water their roses

    C. Pretended to eat pretend pieces of bread

    D. All of the above

14. Uncle Morris told Maggie that

    A. The Greens had died in a fire

    B. She must never visit the attic

    C. Aunt Lillian was really Maggie's mother

    D. Aunt Harriet and Aunt Lillian were ghosts

From *More Quizzes for Great Children's Books*. © 1996. Teacher Ideas Press. (800) 237-6124.

250
Lucie Babbidge's House
Sylvia Cassedy

True or False. Decide whether each statement is true or false. Mark your answer sheet accordingly.

1. Lucie Babbidge was Miss Pimm's favorite student.
2. As the story unfolds, the reader discovers that Lucie is now an old woman writing about her childhood.
3. Lucie lived in an orphanage for girls called Norwood Hall.
4. The other girls in the school disliked Lucie and called her Goosey-Loosey.
5. Mumma, Olive, Emmett, Dadda, and Mr. Broome were all dolls in a dollhouse.
6. Delia Hornsby was Lucie's pen pal.
7. Emmett was a smart aleck and always pretended to misunderstand people.
8. The other students were jealous of Lucie because she was so smart.
9. Mr. Broome and Olive got married.
10. Lucie had dim memories of being at the beach with her father.
11. Delia Hornsby and some of her family were mysteriously kidnapped and then later returned home in an equally mysterious way.

Multiple Choice. Read each question. Decide which statement best answers the question. Mark your answer sheet accordingly.

12. Lucie learned from Delia that

    A. Whatever Lucie did in her dollhouse really happened in Delia's house

    B. She and Delia were twins who had been separated at birth

    C. The other girls would like Lucie more if she didn't act like she knew everything

    D. She and Delia both lived in the same house at different times

13. What probably happened to Lucie's family?

    A. They were on a trip to Europe

    B. They died in a train crash

    C. They were stranded on a desert island in the Pacific Ocean

    D. None of the above

14. How did Lucie change?

    A. She finally spoke up for herself against Miss Pimm's ridicule

    B. She stopped trying to be a know-it-all

    C. She stopped playing cruel practical jokes on the girls in her class

    D. She ran away from home to live with her grandmother

From *More Quizzes for Great Children's Books.* © 1996. Teacher Ideas Press. (800) 237-6124.

251
Front Court Hex
Matt Christopher

True or False. Decide whether each statement is true or false. Mark your answer sheet accordingly.

1. No matter how hard he tried, Jerry couldn't score any points.

2. Jerry's team was the Foxfires.

3. Freddie was mean to Jerry.

4. Lin Foo was Jerry's best friend.

5. Jerry was often lazy and dishonest.

6. Danny seemed to know all about Jerry.

7. Danny said he was Jerry's relative.

8. Danny said that Jerry wouldn't score points unless Jerry paid him $100.

9. Jerry didn't believe that Danny was a warlock.

10. When Jerry was obeying his parents and being honest, he scored points.

11. Danny wanted Jerry to learn to be a good person.

Multiple Choice. Read each question. Decide which statement best answers the question. Mark your answer sheet accordingly.

12. Jerry played for the

    A. Bulls

    B. Chariots

    C. Foxfires

    D. Peacocks

13. Danny could put a spell on Jerry because

    A. Jerry had the evil eye

    B. He and Jerry were related

    C. Danny was the most powerful warlock in the universe

    D. Freddie had paid him to cast a spell

14. Danny wanted Jerry to

    A. Live decently, not steal, and obey his parents

    B. Pay him $100

    C. Become his brother warlock

    D. Learn to be the best basketball player in the world

From *More Quizzes for Great Children's Books.* © 1996. Teacher Ideas Press. (800) 237-6124.

252
Johnny Long Legs
Matt Christopher

True or False. Decide whether each statement is true or false. Mark your answer sheet accordingly.

1. Johnny and Toby were stepbrothers.

2. Johnny and Toby played on different teams.

3. Johnny was from New York City.

4. Jim Sain was rude to Johnny when Johnny first arrived in Lansburg.

5. Johnny was hit by a snowplow.

6. Jim Sain's father came to all Jim's games.

7. Johnny practiced his jumping in front of the garage.

8. Johnny asked Jim's coach not to kick Jim off the team after Jim scared the horses pulling sleds.

9. Johnny and Jim were in Jim's house when it caught fire.

10. Johnny was never able to outjump Jim.

11. Johnny punched anybody who called him Johnny Long Legs.

Multiple Choice. Read each question. Decide which statement best answers the question. Mark your answer sheet accordingly.

12. Johnny played for the

    A. Astrojets

    B. Hornets

    C. Red Foxes

    D. White Cats

13. Jim Sain played for the

    A. Astrojets

    B. Hornets

    C. Red Foxes

    D. White Cats

14. Jim Sain

    A. Lived alone with his father

    B. Was Toby's best friend

    C. Was Johnny's cousin

    D. Was sent to jail

253
No Arm in Left Field
Matt Christopher

True or False. Decide whether each statement is true or false. Mark your answer sheet accordingly.

1. Tony disliked Terry because Terry was black.

2. Terry was easily fooled into swinging at high, outside pitches.

3. The coach told Terry that only white boys could play on his team.

4. Terry had trouble throwing in the ball from left field.

5. Terry couldn't catch fly balls.

6. Tony, Terry, and Mick all played for the Roadrunners.

7. Mr. Delaney told Terry to stay away from white children.

8. Terry didn't go to the world series movie because Tony didn't call him.

9. Tony told Terry that his father had played big-league baseball.

10. Terry and Mick rode in Harry Casterline's dune buggy.

11. Terry hit a home run.

Multiple Choice. Read each question. Decide which statement best answers the question. Mark your answer sheet accordingly.

12. Which team did Terry play for?

    A. The Roadrunners

    B. The Forest Lakers

    C. The Thunderheads

    D. The Boilers

13. Tony and Terry ran into each other when

    A. Terry ran around the bases the wrong way

    B. They both tried to catch the same ball

    C. Tony was trying to steal third base

    D. Terry hit a home run

14. Terry told Tony that

    A. If they pulled together they could win

    B. The coach was going to marry his sister

    C. His father had played professional basketball

    D. He hated him

From *More Quizzes for Great Children's Books*. © 1996. Teacher Ideas Press. (800) 237-6124.

254
Red-Hot Hightops
Matt Christopher

True or False. Decide whether each statement is true or false. Mark your answer sheet accordingly.

1. Ester was Kelly's best friend.

2. Ester and Kelly played on the same basketball team.

3. Anthony was a boy who Kelly liked.

4. Kelly froze when she played basketball in front of a crowd.

5. Kelly bought the red hightops at Wal-Mart.

6. Coach Tina Kosloski wouldn't let Kelly wear the red hightops during games.

7. Kelly became much more spunky when she wore the red shoes.

8. The red shoes made Kelly jump above the rim.

9. Sandi Hendrix had a way of getting people to give her things.

10. Sandi put a magic flower on the red shoes.

11. Kelly sometimes fouled other players.

Multiple Choice. Read each question. Decide which statement best answers the question. Mark your answer sheet accordingly.

12. How did Kelly get the red hightops?

    A. Ester secretly put them in her locker

    B. Her father bought them in Africa

    C. Sandi gave them to her

    D. Kelly and Anthony bought them at Wal-Mart

13. The red hightops changed the way Kelly played because

    A. Sandi put a spell on them

    B. She thought they were magic and just played better

    C. An inventor put a special chemical on them

    D. They had special bouncing rubber soles

14. At the end of the story

    A. The red hightops disappeared

    B. Kelly went to New York City

    C. Kelly gave the hightops to Sandi

    D. Kelly had the red shoes burned

From *More Quizzes for Great Children's Books*. © 1996. Teacher Ideas Press. (800) 237-6124.

255
Muggie Maggie
Beverly Cleary

True or False. Decide whether each statement is true or false. Mark your answer sheet accordingly.

1. Maggie was in the third grade.

2. Kisser was Maggie's dog.

3. Maggie noticed that her parents did not write cursive correctly.

4. Maggie's mother went to school to talk to Maggie's teacher.

5. Maggie was sent to the principal's office because she wouldn't write in cursive.

6. Maggie thought she was gifted and talented.

7. Maggie's father said she couldn't use the computer until she learned cursive.

8. The school psychologist thought Maggie needed to go to a hospital.

9. Many other students knew that Maggie wouldn't write cursive.

10. Maggie couldn't read cursive writing.

11. Kirby and Maggie pushed the table back and forth into each other's stomachs.

Multiple Choice. Read each question. Decide which statement best answers the question. Mark your answer sheet accordingly.

12. Who started calling Maggie "Muggie Maggie"?

    A. Kelly

    B. Courtney

    C. Jo Ann

    D. Kirby

13. Why did Maggie refuse to learn cursive?

    A. She hated Mrs. Leeper

    B. She wanted to learn, but she was too proud to admit it

    C. She was secretly afraid she would not be smart enough to learn

    D. She was scared of cursive

14. Why did Maggie finally learn to read cursive?

    A. She wanted to read the notes she was carrying for the teachers

    B. Kirby told her that he was smarter than she was

    C. Her father said he would pay her $10 if she learned it

    D. Her mother wouldn't let her watch TV until she learned it

256
Strider
Beverly Cleary

True or False. Decide whether each statement is true or false. Mark your answer sheet accordingly.

1. Mr. President was the local dog catcher.

2. Leigh and Barry found Strider on the beach.

3. Barry and Leigh agreed to have joint custody of Strider.

4. Mrs. Smerling raised the Botts' rent as soon as she saw Strider.

5. Strider liked to run.

6. Leigh taught Strider to read the words "roll over."

7. Mr. Botts lost his rig.

8. Leigh liked to talk about his future plans.

9. Leigh gave his new shirt to Kevin.

10. Kevin and Leigh were both on the track team.

11. It was difficult for Leigh to talk with his father.

Multiple Choice. Read each question. Decide which statement best answers the question. Mark your answer sheet accordingly.

12. Leigh and Barry nearly ended their friendship when

    A. They both liked Geneva

    B. They argued about who was Kevin's best friend

    C. They argued about Strider

    D. Barry called Leigh's house a shack

13. Mrs. Smerling said

    A. Strider could stay if the Botts paid more rent

    B. Strider could stay if Leigh built a fence

    C. Strider couldn't stay with them

    D. Strider could stay at her house

14. Leigh thought the most important part of running track was

    A. Winning the race

    B. The fact that it might get his parents back together

    C. Beating his own time

    D. Being around Geneva

257
The Ghost in the Big Brass Bed
Bruce Coville

True or False. Decide whether each statement is true or false. Mark your answer sheet accordingly.

1. Norma Bliss ran an antique store.

2. *Early Harvest* was a silent movie made by Ms. Bond.

3. Cornelius Fletcher's personality had changed after his experiences in World War I.

4. Chris and Nina saw a ghost the first time they went into Phoebe's house.

5. The ghost of the little girl kept saying, "Where's my mommy?"

6. Cornelius Fletcher's ghost told Nina and Chris to burn down Phoebe's house.

7. Cornelius saved Jimmy's life during World War I.

8. Ms. Bond wanted to buy Phoebe's house.

9. The ghost of Cornelius Fletcher gave Nina a metal box filled with letters.

10. Byron Fletcher wanted to become a war hero like his relative Cornelius.

11. Cornelius hid the *Lost Masterpiece* under the bathtub.

Multiple Choice. Read each question. Decide which statement best answers the question. Mark your answer sheet accordingly.

12. Who rescued Nina and Chris from Ms. Bond?

    A. Mr. Tanleven

    B. Phoebe

    C. The ghost of the little girl

    D. The ghost of Cornelius Fletcher

13. Why did Alida Fletcher die of influenza?

    A. Cornelius got drunk and forgot to bring her medicine

    B. Cornelius was badly beaten and couldn't return home with the medicine

    C. No one knew she was sick until it was too late

    D. None of the above

14. What was the relationship between Jimmy and Cornelius?

    A. Jimmy was Cornelius's only brother

    B. Jimmy helped Cornelius work on his *Lost Masterpiece*

    C. Jimmy was Cornelius's son

    D. Jimmy killed Cornelius

From *More Quizzes for Great Children's Books.* © 1996. Teacher Ideas Press. (800) 237-6124.

258
The Ghost Wore Gray
Bruce Coville

True or False. Decide whether each statement is true or false. Mark your answer sheet accordingly.

1. The ghost of Jonathan Gray was horribly ugly.

2. Mr. Tanleven was going to restore the Quackadoodle.

3. The Quackadoodle had been a stop on the Underground Railroad.

4. Both Nina and Chris saw the ghost of Jonathan Gray.

5. Samson Carter was a Confederate agent who tried to kill Abraham Lincoln.

6. The ghost of Jonathan Gray wanted his body properly buried.

7. Jonathan Gray was trying to smuggle jewels into Canada when he died at the Quackadoodle.

8. Baltimore Cleveland tried to kill Nina and Chris.

9. Porter Markson wanted Nina to write a book on ghosts for him.

10. Jonathan Gray kept trying to scare everyone out of the hotel.

11. Samson Carter was a former slave who helped other slaves escape.

Multiple Choice. Read each question. Decide which statement best answers the question. Mark your answer sheet accordingly.

12. Jonathan Gray willed his fortune to

    A. Samson Carter

    B. Any member of the Markson family

    C. Baltimore Cleveland's great-grandfather

    D. None of the above

13. Who else was interested in the secret of Jonathan Gray?

    A. Baltimore Cleveland

    B. Mrs. Cleveland

    C. Arnie and Meg

    D. Porter Markson

14. Jonathan Gray's ghost was able to leave the Quackadoodle when

    A. His bones were buried

    B. The treasure was sent back to Virginia

    C. Chris and Nina gave it a hug

    D. The ghost of Samson Carter guided it out

259
My Teacher Flunked the Planet
Bruce Coville

True or False. Decide whether each statement is true or false. Mark your answer sheet accordingly.

1. The Interplanetary Council was trying to decide the fate of the planet Earth.
2. The Interplanetary Council was worried about the violence on Earth.
3. The aliens named Peter "Krepta."
4. Big Julie drank swamp water.
5. Many of the aliens wanted to destroy Earth.
6. The aliens thought that humans were the most intelligent species in the galaxy.
7. Duncan, Susan, and Peter had to make a report on why the Earth should be saved.
8. Broxholm and Hoo-Lan both agreed that television was wonderful.
9. Peter found his father and Ms. Schwartz working together in a shelter.
10. The aliens showed Duncan, Susan, and Peter how awful life was for many of the world's people.
11. The poots were the police of the galaxy.

Multiple Choice. Read each question. Decide which statement best answers the question. Mark your answer sheet accordingly.

12. What did Hoo-Lan do to slow down human progress and prevent humans from developing space travel?
    A. He ruined the school system
    B. He kidnapped all the rocket scientists
    C. He helped humans invent television
    D. None of the above

13. What unusual fact did Hoo-Lan tell the Interplanetary Council?
    A. Humans were the most intelligent species in the galaxy
    B. All humans were part of the same organism
    C. Humans had ruled the galaxy 10,000 years ago
    D. Humans had almost no intelligence

14. Peter asked the Interplanetary Council to
    A. Send teachers to Earth
    B. Scatter humans on planets all around the galaxy
    C. Make it so televisions would never function on Earth again
    D. Leave so that humanity could decide its own future

260
My Teacher Is an Alien
Bruce Coville

True or False. Decide whether each statement is true or false. Mark your answer sheet accordingly.

1. Peter and Duncan had been best friends since kindergarten.

2. Susan Simmons was very smart and very popular too.

3. The sixth-grade class loved their substitute teacher, Mr. Smith.

4. Mr. Smith seemed to hate almost all music.

5. Susan learned that Ms. Schwartz was in love with Mr. Smith.

6. Duncan was the first to realize that Mr. Smith was an alien.

7. Peter wouldn't tell anyone else in the class that Mr. Smith was an alien.

8. Mr. Smith/Broxholm was planning to kidnap five sixth-grade students.

9. Ms. Schwartz was trapped by a force field in Mr. Smith/Broxholm's attic.

10. Susan was able to pull off Mr. Smith/Broxholm's mask.

11. The rumor that Mr. Smith was an alien spread through the whole school.

Multiple Choice. Read each question. Decide which statement best answers the question. Mark your answer sheet accordingly.

12. How did the sixth-grade class react to the news that five of them were going to be taken into space?

    A. The best students began acting bad, and the worst students began acting good

    B. No one would come to class anymore

    C. They all thought that Susan and Peter were telling lies

    D. The whole class jumped on Mr. Smith/Broxholm and pulled off his mask

13. How was Mr. Smith/Broxholm exposed?

    A. He wasn't exposed

    B. The police found Ms. Schwartz in his house

    C. Susan and Peter took Mr. Smith/Broxholm's communicator to the police station

    D. None of the above

14. At the end of the story

    A. Mr. Smith/Broxholm took Susan, Peter, Duncan, Mike, and Stacey into outer space

    B. Mr. Smith/Broxholm decided to stay on Earth because he was in love with Ms. Schwartz

    C. Peter went with Mr. Smith/Broxholm into outer space

    D. Susan woke up and found out the whole adventure was a dream

261
Charlie and the Chocolate Factory
Roald Dahl

True or False. Decide whether each statement is true or false. Mark your answer sheet accordingly.

1. The Bucket family was very poor.

2. Grandpa Joe said that no one had been seen going in or out of Wonka's factory for many years.

3. Charlie's grandparents all stayed on the same bed all day.

4. Grandma Josephine bought the candy bar with the golden ticket and gave it to Charlie.

5. Mrs. Bucket went with Charlie to visit Wonka's factory.

6. The Oompa-Loompas were very small.

7. Veruca Salt and her parents were put into a garbage chute by squirrels.

8. Augustus Gloop became a giant blueberry.

9. There was a river of chocolate in Wonka's factory.

10. The Oompa-Loompas lived in Wonka's factory.

11. Charlie disobeyed Mr. Wonka and drank some Fizzy Lifting Drink.

Multiple Choice. Read each question. Decide which statement best answers the question. Mark your answer sheet accordingly.

12. What happened to Mike Teavee?

    A. He shrank after sending himself into a TV set

    B. He fell into a chocolate river

    C. He was captured by Oompa-Loompas

    D. He ate a chocolate tree and became ill

13. Every time a child disobeyed Willy Wonka

    A. The child was yelled at by 10 Oompa-Loompas

    B. Willy Wonka would cry

    C. Something terrible would happen to the child

    D. The Oompa-Loompas would give the child a chocolate bar

14. At the end of the story

    A. Willy Wonka gave his chocolate factory to Charlie

    B. Charlie and his family went to live in Mr. Wonka's factory

    C. Charlie was the only child who didn't disobey Mr. Wonka

    D. All of the above

262
Charlie and the Great Glass Elevator
Roald Dahl

True or False. Decide whether each statement is true or false. Mark your answer sheet accordingly.

1. Mr. Wonka wanted to take his Great Glass Elevator to the Moon.

2. There were more than 100 Oompa-Loompas riding in the Great Glass Elevator.

3. Showler, Shuckworth, and Shanks were small Oompa-Loompas.

4. The president thought that the people in the Great Glass Elevator might be from Mars or Venus.

5. The Space Hotel was full of Vermicious Knids.

6. The Great Glass Elevator was Knid-proof.

7. When Grandma Georgina took a Wonka-Vite, she became as strong as 10 men.

8. When Grandpa George took too many Wonka-Vite pills, he turned into an Oompa-Loompa.

9. The vice-president was the president's nanny.

10. Knids were very dangerous.

11. The Gnoolies lived in Minusland.

Multiple Choice. Read each question. Decide which statement best answers the question. Mark your answer sheet accordingly.

12. Why did Grandpa George, Grandma Georgina, and Grandma Josephine finally get out of bed?

    A. The Oompa-Loompas kept tickling their feet

    B. They wanted to go see the president

    C. They wanted some of Mr. Wonka's chocolate

    D. Charlie said he would cry if they didn't

13. A person who took too many Wonka-Vite pills would

    A. End up in Minusland

    B. Turn into an Oompa-Loompa

    C. Become as strong as 10 men

    D. Smell like a Knid

14. The riders in the Great Glass Elevator were heroes because

    A. They gave the president a lifetime supply of chocolate

    B. They rescued the Commuter Capsule from the Knids

    C. They brought the Space Hotel back to Earth

    D. All of the above

From *More Quizzes for Great Children's Books.* © 1996. Teacher Ideas Press. (800) 237-6124.

263
James and the Giant Peach
Roald Dahl

True or False. Decide whether each statement is true or false. Mark your answer sheet accordingly.

1. Both Aunt Spiker and Aunt Sponge loved and spoiled James.

2. Aunt Spiker and Aunt Sponge never let James play with other children.

3. The peach began to grow after James spilled magic crystals around the tree.

4. Centipede was proud of being a pest.

5. Earthworm and Centipede were best friends.

6. The giant creatures inside the peach were afraid of James because he was a human.

7. The giant peach was invisible to everyone but James.

8. The Cloud-Men threw hailstones at the giant peach.

9. James and his friends used spider-web ropes to tie the peach to an ocean liner.

10. Ladybug was crushed to death when the peach rolled down the hill.

Multiple Choice. Read each question. Decide which statement best answers the question. Mark your answer sheet accordingly.

11. The Cloud-Men threw things at the peach because

    A. The peach wrecked their favorite cloud

    B. They thought Glowworm was an out-of-control lightning bolt

    C. The peach smelled like spoiled syrup

    D. Centipede yelled insults at them

12. How did James make the peach fly?

    A. He tied ropes of silk and spider web to hundreds of seagulls

    B. He made a balloon out of silkworm silk

    C. He asked his aunts to cast a spell on it

    D. He pumped the peach full of hot air so that it floated

13. When the peach reached New York City

    A. It sank in the middle of New York Harbor

    B. It landed on the top of the Empire State Building

    C. Millions of rats swarmed out of the sewers and ate it

    D. Spider, Ladybug, Centipede, and Earthworm were put in the New York City Zoo

14. The creatures in the peach grew to enormous size because

    A. Aunt Sponge cast a spell on them

    B. The Cloud-Men poured rainbow paint on them

    C. The magic crystals touched them

    D. The peach was full of special vitamins

264
The Witches
Roald Dahl

True or False. Decide whether each statement is true or false. Mark your answer sheet accordingly.

1. The narrator learned that real witches hate children.

2. Grandmamma said that witches liked to destroy children magically.

3. Grandmamma told the narrator that both men and women could be witches.

4. Grandmamma was a retired witch.

5. Grandmamma was an expert on witches.

6. Grandmamma said that it was easy to spot a real witch.

7. The Grand High Witch of the World always flew on a broomstick.

8. To a witch, a clean child smelled like dog droppings.

9. The narrator and his grandmother were both turned into frogs.

10. The plan of the Grand High Witch was to turn thousands of English children into mice.

11. Bruno loved to eat.

Multiple Choice. Read each question. Decide which statement best answers the question. Mark your answer sheet accordingly.

12. The Grand High Witch was going to destroy the children of England by

    A. Buying candy shops and feeding them enchanted chocolate

    B. Buying toy stores and selling them enchanted toys

    C. Putting disappearing ink on the most popular comic books

    D. Poisoning all Halloween candy

13. The narrator destroyed all the English witches by

    A. Shining a light on them

    B. Sawing their brooms in half

    C. Putting their own magic potion in their soup

    D. Chanting backwards in Latin

14. In this book, witches

    A. Wore wigs

    B. Had blue spit

    C. Always wore gloves

    D. All of the above

265
Morning Girl
Michael Dorris

True or False. Decide whether each statement is true or false. Mark your answer sheet accordingly.

1. Morning Girl had three sisters.

2. Morning Girl was the first person in her family to get up every day.

3. Star Boy was given his name because he loved starfish.

4. A tribe of cannibals captured Morning Girl.

5. A bear ruined the village's food supply.

6. There were biting bugs on Morning Girl's island.

7. Morning Girl's father caught a shark with his bare hands.

8. Names were very special to Morning Girl's people.

9. Star Boy liked to be out at night.

10. Morning Girl's family lived in a log cabin.

11. Star Boy sometimes acted like a child.

Multiple Choice. Read each question. Decide which statement best answers the question. Mark your answer sheet accordingly.

12. Which disaster put Star Boy in danger?

    A. A tidal wave

    B. An earthquake

    C. A hurricane

    D. A thunderstorm

13. Morning Girl lived in

    A. A hut with her parents and Star Boy

    B. A teepee with her mother

    C. A log cabin with her mother and three sisters

    D. A giant lodge with the entire village

14. The strangers Morning Girl saw arriving were

    A. Her great-grandfather, chief of all the Taino

    B. Christopher Columbus and his men

    C. The Pilgrims

    D. The Vikings

266
Jim Ugly
Sid Fleischman

True or False. Decide whether each statement is true or false. Mark your answer sheet accordingly.

1. Aurora wanted to kill Jim Ugly because he bit her.

2. Axie was trying to raise chickens.

3. A bounty hunter was looking for Jake's dad.

4. Jake's father was an actor.

5. Jim Ugly could follow a scent almost anywhere.

6. Wilhelmina and Mr. Cornelius were looking for Jake's father.

7. Jake got a job in the traveling play *Romeo and Juliet*.

8. D. D. Skeats kept following Jake and Jim Ugly.

9. Mr. Cornelius hired D. D. Skeats to capture Sam Bannock.

10. Jim Ugly killed the bounty hunter.

11. Axie didn't really bury Sam Bannock; he buried a casket full of ice instead.

Multiple Choice. Read each question. Decide which statement best answers the question. Mark your answer sheet accordingly.

12. How did Jake warn his father about the bounty hunter?

    A. He left a note on his father's grave

    B. He tied a note to one of Aurora's chickens

    C. He put a note on Jim Ugly's collar

    D. None of the above

13. What was unusual about the diamonds that Sam Bannock took?

    A. They were junk diamonds

    B. Cornelius had planted them around a mine to make it seem valuable

    C. They were all eaten by chickens

    D. All of the above

14. At the end of the story, Jim Ugly

    A. Was loyal to Jake instead of Jake's father

    B. Joined a wolf pack in the mountains of Montana

    C. Was killed by D. D. Skeats

    D. Ate all of Aurora's chickens

267
The Midnight Horse
Sid Fleischman

True or False. Decide whether each statement is true or false. Mark your answer sheet accordingly.

1. The Great Chaffalo could turn straw into a horse.

2. Judge Wigglesforth was Touch's only relative.

3. Judge Wigglesforth started a rumor that the Red Raven Inn was infested with small pox.

4. Judge Wigglesforth tried to cheat Touch out of his inheritance.

5. Otis Cratt was the village blacksmith.

6. Mr. Hobbs told Sally not to sell the inn to the judge.

7. Otis Cratt worked with Judge Wigglesforth.

8. Touch asked the Great Chaffalo to turn the judge into stone.

9. Judge Wigglesforth had some pearls that belonged to Touch.

10. Otis Cratt had many gold teeth.

11. There were no guests at the Red River Inn.

Multiple Choice. Read each question. Decide which statement best answers the question. Mark your answer sheet accordingly.

12. Touch made Otis Cratt think that

    A. The judge would put Otis in jail if he hurt Sally

    B. Otis was invisible as long as he had an oak leaf in his hatband

    C. The Great Chaffalo was haunting the Red River Inn

    D. The sheriff had gone to Boston

13. Otis Cratt was captured when

    A. The Great Chaffalo turned his horse into straw

    B. Touch locked him in the basement of the Red River Inn

    C. He accidentally put on Sally's clothes instead of his own

    D. He drove his cart into some quicksand

14. At the end of the story

    A. The Great Chaffalo came back to life

    B. Touch married Sally

    C. Judge Wigglesforth apologized

    D. None of the above

268
The Whipping Boy
Sid Fleischman

True or False. Decide whether each statement is true or false. Mark your answer sheet accordingly.

1. Prince Brat couldn't read or write.

2. Jemmy was Prince Brat's younger brother.

3. Prince Brat decided to run away from the palace.

4. Hold-Your-Nose Billy wanted the king to pay a ransom for the prince.

5. Cutwater and Hold-Your-Nose Billy let Jemmy go, but they kept the prince.

6. Prince Brat wouldn't cooperate with Jemmy's plan to outwit the villains.

7. Prince Horace was proud that his people called him Prince Brat.

8. Petunia was a lovely woman who took Jemmy and the prince into the city.

9. No one was supposed to touch the prince.

10. The prince didn't want to return to the castle.

11. Jemmy and the prince went into the sewers to hide from the villains.

Multiple Choice. Read each question. Decide which statement best answers the question. Mark your answer sheet accordingly.

12. Prince Brat's behavior began to change after

    A. He was whipped by Cutwater and Hold-Your-Nose Billy

    B. Petunia told him she loved him

    C. Jemmy nearly died

    D. He felt hunger for the first time

13. Cutwater and Hold-Your-Nose Billy thought Jemmy was the prince because

    A. Prince Brat acted like a baby and Jemmy didn't

    B. Prince Brat told them that Jemmy was the prince

    C. Jemmy knew how to write and the prince couldn't

    D. Jemmy and Prince Brat had switched clothes

14. A whipping boy's job was to

    A. Be whipped in place of the prince when the prince misbehaved

    B. Punish the prince

    C. Drive the royal coach

    D. Teach the prince how to defend himself

269
Monkey Island
Paula Fox

True or False. Decide whether each statement is true or false. Mark your answer sheet accordingly.

1. Clay went to live on the streets because he hated his parents.

2. The hotel where Clay and his mother lived was very run-down.

3. Clay's mother was pregnant when she left Clay.

4. Buddy and Calvin sold drugs to buy food.

5. Buddy and Calvin robbed Clay's mother.

6. A group of teenagers chased homeless people out of the park.

7. Buddy was Clay's cousin.

8. After living on the streets for a month, Clay caught pneumonia.

9. Clay and his mother didn't know where Clay's father was living.

10. Clay never saw his mother again.

11. Clay's father found him living in the park and took him home.

Multiple Choice. Read each question. Decide which statement best answers the question. Mark your answer sheet accordingly.

12. When Clay found Buddy again, Buddy was

    A. Living in a box in the park

    B. Working as a messenger

    C. Selling drugs

    D. Robbing a store with Calvin

13. Why did Clay leave the foster home?

    A. Social Services found his mother

    B. Buddy talked him into running away

    C. His foster parents hated him

    D. He hated his new school

14. How did Calvin, Buddy, and Clay earn money on the streets?

    A. They sold drugs in the park

    B. They robbed stores

    C. They picked pockets

    D. Clay and Buddy sold cans that they found

270
Franklin Delano Roosevelt
Russell Freedman

True or False. Decide whether each statement is true or false. Mark your answer sheet accordingly.

1. Franklin flunked the second grade because he was hyperactive.
2. Franklin's family was very rich.
3. Franklin admired his cousin, Teddy Roosevelt.
4. Eleanor was a distant relative of Franklin.
5. Franklin was depressed after he was soundly defeated the first time he ran for public office.
6. Sara Roosevelt completely avoided Franklin after he married Eleanor.
7. Franklin Roosevelt was willing to use new and untested methods to solve problems.
8. The Supreme Court ruled that some of Roosevelt's New Deal programs were unconstitutional.
9. Franklin was the governor of Virginia before he was elected president.
10. Franklin disliked being president.
11. Franklin was crippled by polio when he was an adult.

Multiple Choice. Read each question. Decide which statement best answers the question. Mark your answer sheet accordingly.

12. Franklin and Eleanor's marriage changed forever after Franklin
    A. Was crippled by polio
    B. Was elected governor
    C. Was elected president
    D. Had an affair with Lucy Mercer

13. Roosevelt could best be described as
    A. Complicated and difficult to understand
    B. Simple and easygoing
    C. Open and honest
    D. A workaholic, a perfectionist, and extremely temperamental

14. Which of the following Roosevelt plans was a failure?
    A. The Lend-Lease Program
    B. The Supreme Court packing plan
    C. The Tennessee Valley Authority (TVA)
    D. The New Deal

271
Lincoln: A Photobiography
Russell Freedman

True or False. Decide whether each statement is true or false. Mark your answer sheet accordingly.

1. Lincoln and Mary Todd often fought and quarreled.

2. Lincoln's friends called him Abe.

3. Abraham Lincoln was weak and sickly most of his life.

4. By the standards of his time, Lincoln was thought a handsome man.

5. Immediately after being elected president, Lincoln announced his intention to free every slave.

6. The first political party that Lincoln belonged to was the Republican Party.

7. Stephen Douglas was one of Lincoln's major rivals.

8. Many people in the North disagreed with Lincoln's decision to free the slaves.

9. At first, Lincoln had trouble finding good generals to lead the Union armies.

10. Lincoln wanted to punish the South for starting the Civil War.

11. Lincoln was a wealthy man when he married Mary Todd.

Multiple Choice. Read each question. Decide which statement best answers the question. Mark your answer sheet accordingly.

12. Lincoln always looked stiff and formal in pictures because

    A. He was a sober and serious person

    B. It was considered undignified to smile at a camera

    C. Mary Todd had told him that he was ugly when he smiled

    D. None of the above

13. Lincoln's first political party was

    A. The Democrats

    B. The Federalists

    C. The Republicans

    D. The Whigs

14. Lincoln waited to free the slaves until

    A. The Union army won a major victory

    B. A majority of voters in the North wanted the slaves freed

    C. The South surrendered

    D. He won the election of 1864

272
The Wright Brothers
Russell Freedman

True or False. Decide whether each statement is true or false. Mark your answer sheet accordingly.

1. Both Wilbur and Orville graduated from the Chicago School of Engineering.
2. Wilbur and Orville worked in a bicycle shop.
3. The Wright brothers carefully studied all existing information on gliders and flight.
4. The Wright brothers were the first to build a glider that could carry a person.
5. The Wright brothers were the first to solve the problem of controlling a plane in flight.
6. The War Department helped the Wright Brothers invent their first airplane.
7. The Wright brothers built a wind tunnel to study wing and tail design.
8. The Wright brothers were famous in France before they were famous in America.
9. The airplane design used today is basically the design developed by the Wright brothers.
10. Both Wilbur and Orville died in airplane crashes.
11. After their successful flight at Kitty Hawk, the Wright brothers stopped designing and making airplanes.

Multiple Choice. Read each question. Decide which statement best answers the question. Mark your answer sheet accordingly.

12. The Wright brothers tested their airplanes at Kitty Hawk because it
    A. Was one of the windiest spots in the United States
    B. Had miles of sandy beaches for soft landings
    C. Was isolated, which allowed the brothers to experiment in secret
    D. All of the above

13. As the brothers worked on the airplane, they discovered that
    A. They had to design and create everything they needed themselves
    B. Learning to fly was so easy that they were amazed no one had done it before
    C. They didn't like each other very much
    D. None of the above

14. When the Wright brothers first announced their first successful flight
    A. Hardly anyone noticed
    B. They became instantly famous
    C. The United States government declared their work top secret
    D. A mob attacked them for breaking the laws of nature

273
The Missing 'Gator of Gumbo Limbo
Jean Craighead George

True or False. Decide whether each statement is true or false. Mark your answer sheet accordingly.

1. Travis was trying to kill Dajun because Dajun was killing people's dogs.

2. Many rare and endangered species lived on Gumbo Limbo Hammock.

3. The "woods people" were outlaws.

4. Liza K and James James wanted to hide Dajun from Travis.

5. Dajun cleaned the weeds out of Gumbo Limbo Hole.

6. Liza K and James James found Dajun hiding in a culvert.

7. James James discovered that salt water was killing the freshwater fish.

8. Travis accidentally shot James James in the leg.

9. Dajun was discovered hiding in the lake by the golf course.

10. Dajun would rest on the beach in the sunshine to warm himself.

11. Priscilla told Travis where Dajun was hiding so she could collect the reward.

Multiple Choice. Read each question. Decide which statement best answers the question. Mark your answer sheet accordingly.

12. Priscilla collected mini gin bottles because she

    A. Thought they were diamonds

    B. Used them to feed hummingbirds

    C. Liked to drink gin and get drunk

    D. Put flowers in them

13. Where was Dajun hiding?

    A. Underneath the royal palm that floated on Gumbo Limbo Hammock

    B. In the cyprus swamp west of Gumbo Limbo Hammock

    C. In the canal next to the toxic waste disposal plant

    D. In the sink in the middle of Gumbo Limbo Hammock

14. At the end of the book

    A. Priscilla talked Travis into leaving Dajun alone

    B. Gumbo Limbo Hammock was made into a protected area

    C. Developers bought Gumbo Limbo to use as a parking lot

    D. Travis killed Dajun

274
Shark Beneath the Reef
Jean Craighead George

True or False. Decide whether each statement is true or false. Mark your answer sheet accordingly.

1. Tomás enjoyed being with his grandfather and uncle.
2. Japanese factory ships were wiping out the fish in the Sea of Cortez.
3. Miguel and Ramón didn't trust the *oficiales*.
4. Tomás wanted to live with his father in Texas.
5. José liked making his own fireworks.
6. Miguel and Ramón caught sharks in the Sea of Cortez.
7. The shark that Tomás saw beneath the reef was a whale shark.
8. The *oficiales* threw Miguel and Tomás in jail for trespassing on government land.
9. José was killed by a giant firecracker on Christmas Eve.
10. Tomás never caught the shark beneath the reef.

Multiple Choice. Read each question. Decide which statement best answers the question. Mark your answer sheet accordingly.

11. The *oficiales* told Miguel and Ramón that
    A. Tomás had to go back to school at once
    B. They would have to start paying rent for their island
    C. Sharks were an endangered species and could no longer be caught
    D. It was illegal to shoot homemade fireworks on Christmas Eve

12. The Baja region of Mexico is
    A. A tropical rain forest
    B. An enormous swamp
    C. A mountainous desert
    D. A dusty grassland

13. Why was it difficult for Tomás to catch the shark?
    A. It was a hammerhead shark, not a whale shark
    B. His rifle jammed
    C. The shark bit off his hand
    D. The *oficiales* took his net

14. Tomás decided to
    A. Go to high school
    B. Go fishing with Ramón and Miguel
    C. Become an *oficiale*
    D. Run away to Texas to live with his father

275
Fudge
Charlotte Towner Graeber

True or False. Decide whether each statement is true or false. Mark your answer sheet accordingly.

1. Fudge was the biggest puppy in Biggie's litter.

2. Leslie wanted the puppy named Bear.

3. Chad's mother was going to have twins.

4. The Garcias said that they would keep all the puppies.

5. Chad's parents thought he wouldn't be able to take care of a puppy.

6. Fudge wet on the kitchen floor.

7. Fudge howled and cried at night.

8. Leslie's parents said she couldn't have one of Biggie's puppies.

9. Chad sold Fudge to Leslie.

10. Fudge slept with Chad's parents.

11. Leslie baby-sat Fudge for Chad.

Multiple Choice. Read each question. Decide which statement best answers the question. Mark your answer sheet accordingly.

12. Chad's parents

    A. Bought Biggie, Bear, and Fudge

    B. Said that he could have Fudge on a seven-day trial

    C. Said that he would have to keep Fudge at the Garcias

    D. Said that he should buy a fish instead of a dog

13. When Chad took Fudge to bed with him

    A. Fudge cried all night

    B. Fudge ripped Chad's pillow apart

    C. Chad accidentally kicked Fudge

    D. Fudge wet on the bed

14. Chad learned that

    A. Leslie wanted goldfish

    B. Fudge could read

    C. His father was allergic to dogs

    D. Taking care of a puppy was hard work

276
Wait Till Helen Comes: A Ghost Story
Mary Downing Hahn

True or False. Decide whether each statement is true or false. Mark your answer sheet accordingly.

1. Heather seemed to enjoy causing fights in her family.

2. Molly was uncomfortable with having a graveyard close to her house.

3. Molly, Michael, and Heather all saw Helen's ghost.

4. Molly and Michael learned that several children had drowned in Harper Pond.

5. Helen destroyed Michael's room.

6. Mr. Simmons took care of St. Swithin's Graveyard.

7. The Harper House had been destroyed by a tornado.

8. Heather would tell lies to get Molly and Michael in trouble.

9. Helen wanted Heather to die so that Heather would always be with her.

10. Helen couldn't leave St. Swithin's Graveyard.

11. Helen gave Heather a locket.

Multiple Choice. Read each question. Decide which statement best answers the question. Mark your answer sheet accordingly.

12. What did Helen and Heather have in common?

    A. They both liked TV

    B. Both of their mothers had died in fires

    C. They both hated their mothers

    D. They each liked dogs and hated cats

13. Heather's secret was

    A. She started the fire that killed her mother

    B. She had been Helen in a past life

    C. She accidentally drowned her father's dog

    D. She was afraid of heights

14. Helen's ghost found peace when

    A. Heather died and the two spirits left together

    B. Molly buried Helen's bones

    C. She was reunited with her mother

    D. The Harper House was destroyed

277
Cousins
Virginia Hamilton

True or False. Decide whether each statement is true or false. Mark your answer sheet accordingly.

1. Gram Tut was in a nursing home.

2. Cammy's parents were divorced.

3. Patty Ann seemed to do everything perfectly.

4. Andrew tried to help Richie find a job.

5. Cammy was embarrassed to be around Elode (L.O.D.) because L.O.D. was rich.

6. Cammy thought that Aunt Effie was the nicest woman she knew.

7. Gram Tut was an active and energetic woman.

8. Cammy, L.O.D., and Patty Ann went to the same day camp.

9. Cammy didn't like Patty Ann.

10. Patty Ann drowned saving L.O.D.

11. Andrew never let Cammy ride in his truck.

Multiple Choice. Read each question. Decide which statement best answers the question. Mark your answer sheet accordingly.

12. After Patty Ann's death, Cammy

    A. Was secretly happy

    B. Tried to kill herself

    C. Moved into Aunt Effie's house

    D. None of the above

13. What helped Cammy deal with Patty Ann's death?

    A. Andrew and her father brought Gram Tut to see her

    B. She spent the night in Patty Ann's room

    C. Her mother took her to see Patty Ann's grave

    D. She moved in with Gram Tut

14. Richie and Patty Ann were

    A. Going to get married

    B. Brother and sister

    C. Killed in a car wreck

    D. Students from Mexico visiting the United States

278
Zeely
Virginia Hamilton

True or False. Decide whether each statement is true or false. Mark your answer sheet accordingly.

1. Geeder and Toeboy spent the summer on their uncle's farm.

2. Geeder and Toeboy often slept outside.

3. Zeely and Nat Tayber raised prize hogs.

4. Uncle Ross asked Zeely to marry him.

5. Geeder believed that there was a night traveler moving on the road after dark.

6. Geeder only told Uncle Ross and Toeboy that she thought Zeely was a queen.

7. Zeely never spoke to Geeder.

8. Zeely told Geeder that she was a Watutsi queen and would soon return to Africa.

9. Zeely always seemed beautiful and calm.

10. Geeder agreed to return to Africa with Zeely.

11. Toeboy was Geeder's brother.

Multiple Choice. Read each question. Decide which statement best answers the question. Mark your answer sheet accordingly.

12. Zeely told Geeder that

   A. She was going to marry Uncle Ross

   B. She was the last of the royal family of the Watutsi tribe

   C. When she was young, she had wanted to believe she had royal blood

   D. Night travelers kidnapped young children

13. Geeder

   A. Was moody and liked to daydream

   B. Was very interested in boys

   C. Hated her parents and wanted to run away

   D. None of the above

14. Geeder decided that

   A. She was of royal blood just like Zeely

   B. Zeely's actions and attitudes made her a queen

   C. Zeely was just an ordinary person

   D. She would dress, act, and talk like Zeely for the rest of her life

279
The Outsiders
S. E. Hinton

True or False. Decide whether each statement is true or false. Mark your answer sheet accordingly.

1. Ponyboy and his friends called themselves "Greasers."

2. Johnny's parents abused him.

3. Socs were the rich kids who lived on the other side of town.

4. Dally Winston helped Johnny and Ponyboy hide out.

5. Darry was very strict with his brother, Ponyboy.

6. Cherry Valance was Sodapop's girlfriend.

7. The Socs often attacked or threatened Ponyboy and his friends.

8. Ponyboy dropped out of school to work with his brothers.

9. Johnny killed a Soc named Bob.

10. Two-Bit died in a rumble.

11. Ponyboy learned that Socs had problems of their own.

Multiple Choice. Read each question. Decide which statement best answers the question. Mark your answer sheet accordingly.

12. Johnny died because

    A. He was injured while saving some children from a fire

    B. He was caught in the crossfire during a rumble

    C. His parents slowly poisoned him

    D. Dally gave him uncut heroine

13. Ponyboy realized that Darry

    A. Really did love him

    B. Was going to join the army

    C. Would end up as a criminal in a few years

    D. Was just like him

14. Ponyboy learned that Sodapop

    A. Liked him more than he liked Darry

    B. Wanted to join the Shepard gang

    C. Felt torn apart when he and Darry fought

    D. Was deeply ashamed that he had dropped out of school

280
Tex
S. E. Hinton

True or False. Decide whether each statement is true or false. Mark your answer sheet accordingly.

1. Mason sold the horses to punish Tex for being expelled from school.

2. Mason was a star basketball player.

3. Tex and Mason lived by themselves most of the time.

4. Most girls thought Tex was ugly.

5. Mr. Collins thought Tex was a bad influence on his son, Johnny.

6. Pop seemed to care more about Mason than he did about Tex.

7. Mason and Tex picked up a hitchhiker who was an escaped convict.

8. Tex was arrested for stealing horses.

9. Lem was an old friend of Mason and Tex.

10. Tex was often in trouble at school.

11. Tex and Mason's mother had been dead for many years.

Multiple Choice. Read each question. Decide which statement best answers the question. Mark your answer sheet accordingly.

12. Tex was shot when

    A. He was with Lem when Lem was making a drug deal

    B. He, Mason, and Pop were hunting quail

    C. He was trying to teach Jamie how to shoot

    D. The store he was buying a comic book in was robbed

13. Tex went away with Lem after Mason told him that

    A. He had to sell Tex's horse, Negrito

    B. Mr. Collins had forbidden him to ever see Jamie again

    C. Pop wasn't Tex's father

    D. After Mason went to college, Tex would live in a foster home

14. Mason often yelled at Tex and scolded him because

    A. He loved him and felt responsible for him

    B. He was upset that Tex was irresponsible

    C. Mason yelled at everyone

    D. Tex did everything he possibly could to hurt Mason

281
That Was Then, This Is Now
S. E. Hinton

True or False. Decide whether each statement is true or false. Mark your answer sheet accordingly.

1. Mark and Byron were twin brothers.

2. M&M was a 13-year-old hippie.

3. Mark saw nothing wrong with stealing.

4. Mark and Byron knew Ponyboy Curtis.

5. Cathy was M&M's sister.

6. Byron and Mark robbed liquor stores for cash.

7. Two Shepards beat up Byron after Mark cut off their sister's hair.

8. Byron began to change after Charlie was killed.

9. Mark and Cathy didn't like each other.

10. M&M was stabbed to death by the Shepard gang.

11. Mark and Byron lived in a rough part of town.

Multiple Choice. Read each question. Decide which statement best answers the question. Mark your answer sheet accordingly.

12. When Byron learned that Mark was selling drugs, he

    A. Told him never to do it again

    B. Asked him if he could have a piece of the action

    C. Hit him over the head with a bottle

    D. Called the police

13. Byron and Cathy found M&M

    A. In jail

    B. Having a bad L.S.D. trip

    C. Dead in a parked car

    D. Lying stabbed to death in the Shepard's house

14. At the end of the story

    A. Byron married Cathy

    B. Mark hated Byron

    C. Ponyboy moved into Mark and Byron's house

    D. Both Byron and Mark were in reform school

282
Bunnicula: A Rabbit Tale of Mystery
Deborah Howe and James Howe

True or False. Decide whether each statement is true or false. Mark your answer sheet accordingly.

1. Both Chester and Harold could read.

2. Chester started staying up all night to watch Bunnicula.

3. Chester was sure that Bunnicula was able to open the refrigerator door.

4. Harold wanted to eat Bunnicula.

5. Chester used garlic to keep Bunnicula out of the kitchen at night.

6. After Bunnicula was brought home, the Monroes began finding white vegetables in their house.

7. The Monroes thought that something was wrong with Chester.

8. Harold loved chocolate.

9. Bunnicula never talked to Harold and Chester.

10. Bunnicula was able to get out of his cage.

11. Chester tried to warn the Monroes about Bunnicula by wearing a towel around his neck and acting like a vampire.

Multiple Choice. Read each question. Decide which statement best answers the question. Mark your answer sheet accordingly.

12. Chester tried to stop Bunnicula by

    A. Putting a sirloin steak on him and pounding it over his heart

    B. Spreading garlic around the house

    C. Throwing water on him

    D. All of the above

13. The vet told the Monroes that

    A. Bunnicula was a deadly vampire

    B. Chester was a vampire cat

    C. Bunnicula needed a liquid diet

    D. Harold was so intelligent, he should be on TV

14. The vet told the Monroes that Chester was

    A. Emotionally overwrought and should see a cat psychiatrist

    B. A hero for saving them from Bunnicula

    C. The most unusual cat he had ever seen

    D. Afraid of mice

283
The Celery Stalks at Midnight
James Howe

True or False. Decide whether each statement is true or false. Mark your answer sheet accordingly.

1. Chester believed that Bunnicula was a vampire rabbit.

2. Howie loved Harold but disliked Chester.

3. Howie called Chester "Pop."

4. Chester, Harold, and Howie found white vegetables all over town.

5. Chester wanted Howie and Harold to sprinkle catnip on the vampire vegetables.

6. Bunnicula bit Howie.

7. Snowball was a cat.

8. Chester thought that Toby and Pete had been turned into vampires.

9. Toby and Pete sold Chester to a mad scientist.

10. Harold, Chester, and Howie rode in the back of a truck filled with garbage.

11. Chester fell in love with Snowball.

Multiple Choice. Read each question. Decide which statement best answers the question. Mark your answer sheet accordingly.

12. What did Chester think Bunnicula was doing?

    A. Creating vampire vegetables

    B. Trying to kill Howie

    C. Turning into a werewolf

    D. Teaching himself to drive a car

13. Howie, Chester, and Harold saw

    A. Bunnicula biting vegetables and sucking out the juice

    B. Snowball riding in a car that Bunnicula was driving

    C. Toby and Pete dressed up as vampires

    D. None of the above

14. Whenever Chester, Howie, and Harold saw a white vegetable, they

    A. Stabbed it with a toothpick

    B. Sprinkled catnip on it

    C. Ran away and hid

    D. Had Bunnicula bite it

284
Howliday Inn
James Howe

True or False. Decide whether each statement is true or false. Mark your answer sheet accordingly.

1. Both Harold and Chester spent a week at the Chateau Bow-Wow.

2. Chester was sure both Heather and Howard were werewolves.

3. Only dogs could stay at the Chateau Bow-Wow.

4. All the animals at the Chateau knew how to open their cages and get out.

5. Taxi wasn't very smart.

6. The first animal to disappear was Lyle.

7. Jill kidnapped all of the animals at the Chateau Bow-Wow.

8. Chester thought that Louise had been murdered.

9. Howard was a large cat.

10. Heather and Howard had puppies.

Multiple Choice. Read each question. Decide which statement best answers the question. Mark your answer sheet accordingly.

11. Which animal disappeared first?

    A. Howard

    B. Max

    C. Lyle

    D. Louise

12. Georgette and Louise were

    A. Interested in Max

    B. Cats that acted very strangely

    C. Rabbits

    D. The girls who took care of the animals at the Chateau Bow-Wow

13. When Chester disappeared

    A. Harold was sure that Chester had been poisoned

    B. Harold ran to get the police

    C. Max and Taxi dug an escape tunnel

    D. Lyle was so scared he flew up into a tree and wouldn't come down

14. At the end of the story Chester told Harold that

    A. Jill had murdered Louise

    B. Harrison had kidnapped the animals

    C. Max was really a giant hamster

    D. Lyle was only pretending be crazy

285
Return to Howliday Inn
James Howe

True or False. Decide whether each statement is true or false. Mark your answer sheet accordingly.

1. Chester was delighted to learn that he was returning to the Chateau Bow-Wow.

2. Hamlet believed that his master was in Europe.

3. Chester was terrified to learn that he would have to share a cage with Bunnicula.

4. Bob and Linda were snobbish and never spoke to the other animals.

5. Howie accidentally let the parrot out of its cage.

6. Ditto, the parrot, could speak only Russian and Turkish.

7. The voice of Rosebud said that a dog had been murdered.

8. The cats were given the job of digging a tunnel so all the animals could escape.

9. Felony and Miss Demeanor stopped the Weasel from stealing food.

10. The animals disliked the food at the Chateau Bow-Wow.

11. Ditto pried open the front gate with her beak to help the other animals escape.

Multiple Choice. Read each question. Decide which statement best answers the question. Mark your answer sheet accordingly.

12. The spirit of Rosebud turned out to be

    A. Hamlet using ventriloquism

    B. Bunnicula

    C. Howie playing practical jokes

    D. Chester trying to prove he could make Harold believe anything

13. The animals found Hamlet's master

    A. In the hospital

    B. In a nursing home

    C. Living next door to the Chateau Bow-Wow

    D. In jail

14. How did the animals know where to look for Hamlet's master?

    A. Chester looked up his address in the files

    B. Hamlet's keen sense of smell found him

    C. Miss Demeanor overheard a worker talking about him

    D. Howie found a postcard he had mailed to Hamlet from jail

286
Harry's Mad
Dick King-Smith

True or False. Decide whether each statement is true or false. Mark your answer sheet accordingly.

1. Madison, the parrot, ate only peanuts.

2. Harry's parents never learned that Madison could talk.

3. Madison liked American food.

4. When Madison played Monopoly, he usually won.

5. Madison helped Harry with his homework.

6. The Holdsworths' dog hated Madison and kept trying to bite him.

7. Harry often took Madison to school with him.

8. Madison knew how to use a telephone.

9. Madison could read.

10. When a burglar came to the house, Madison scared him away by sounding like a policeman.

11. A garbage man found Madison in an old box.

Multiple Choice. Read each question. Decide which statement best answers the question. Mark your answer sheet accordingly.

12. Madison could

    A. Tell the future

    B. Become invisible

    C. Travel in time

    D. None of the above

13. The parrot, Fweedy

    A. Never talked

    B. Was a girl parrot

    C. Attacked Madison

    D. Liked to dance to rock and roll

14. Madison escaped from Silver Ware by

    A. Going up the chimney

    B. Crashing through a window

    C. Talking like a police officer

    D. Playing dead

287
T-Backs, T-Shirts, COAT and Suit
E. L. Konigsburg

True or False. Decide whether each statement is true or false. Mark your answer sheet accordingly.

1. Bernadette and Nick had lived on a commune together.
2. Bernadette had a cat named Peace Child.
3. Chlöe worked with Bernadette in the commissary van.
4. Chlöe let Tyler think that Bernadette was a witch.
5. Business for Bernadette and Chlöe picked up after the other women started wearing T-backs.
6. The COAT organization said anyone should be able to wear a T-back.
7. Reverend Butler believed that Bernadette was a witch.
8. Wanda and Velma quit wearing T-backs as soon as the protests began.
9. Chlöe didn't like living with Bernadette.
10. Daisy had been a police drug dog.
11. Bernadette was a member of the Church of the Endless Horizon.

Multiple Choice. Read each question. Decide which statement best answers the question. Mark your answer sheet accordingly.

12. What was strange about Zack claiming that Bernadette had a witchcraft tattoo?
    A. Zack was blind
    B. Bernadette had never been tattooed
    C. Zack had the same tattoo
    D. None of the above

13. COAT wanted Bernadette to sign their petition because she was
    A. The first driver to wear a T-back
    B. The only female driver not wearing a T-back
    C. A leader of the Church of the Endless Horizon
    D. Famous and respected by the whole community

14. When Chlöe was with Bernadette and Daisy, she
    A. Always felt afraid
    B. Felt she was part of a three-in-one
    C. Kept wishing that she was at home
    D. Felt like she was in a trance

288
The Night Journey
Kathryn Lasky

True or False. Decide whether each statement is true or false. Mark your answer sheet accordingly.

1. Nana Sashie was still good at fixing things even though she was old.

2. A pogrom was an anti-Jewish riot.

3. It was very difficult for Jews to leave Russia.

4. Rachel and Nana Sashie would talk at 2:30 in the morning.

5. Wolf helped Sashie's family escape.

6. Sashie's family disguised themselves as members of the czar's family.

7. Sashie's family bribed a guard with gold to get across the border.

8. Rachel's parents thought it wasn't good for Nana Sashie to talk about the past.

9. Sashie was the one who thought of an escape plan.

10. Nana Sashie died soon after telling Rachel about her escape from Russia.

11. The samovar was used to hold the money while Sashie's family escaped.

Multiple Choice. Read each question. Decide which statement best answers the question. Mark your answer sheet accordingly.

12. What is a samovar?

    A. A glass piggy bank

    B. A case for holding scrolls

    C. A cloth suitcase

    D. A brass urn used to make tea

13. What is Purim?

    A. The Russian holiday celebrating the czar's birthday

    B. A Jewish holiday remembering Queen Esther

    C. The first day of Passover

    D. The Russian New Year

14. How did the family sneak out of town?

    A. They rode in boxcars on a freight train

    B. They rode in a wagon underneath a load of chickens

    C. They pretended they were going on a picnic

    D. They floated down the Bug River on a raft

289
Shadows in the Water
Kathryn Lasky

True or False. Decide whether each statement is true or false. Mark your answer sheet accordingly.

1. No one knew about the Starbuck twins' ability to communicate telepathically.

2. Honey wanted to put the twins in military school.

3. Robbie had purple hands.

4. Mr. Starbuck was in the Florida Keys to look for toxic waste dumpers.

5. The Starbucks lived in a trailer on Pelican Key.

6. The dolphins wanted Liberty and July to help them catch tuna.

7. Moon Spirit was a white dolphin.

8. Liberty and July helped baby turtles on Lonely Key.

9. The twins were able to talk to the dolphins telepathically.

10. Cuda and his gang were illegally hunting sea turtles.

11. Molly and Charly accidentally drowned a rare sea turtle.

Multiple Choice. Read each question. Decide which statement best answers the question. Mark your answer sheet accordingly.

12. The twins escaped Cuda's gang by

    A. Riding away on the backs of dolphins

    B. Making the gang members think they were seeing double

    C. Calling in crocodiles to bite the gang's boat

    D. None of the above

13. The Starbuck children and Robbie rescued Charly from the crocodile by

    A. Blinding it with their flashbulbs

    B. Tossing a can of toxic waste into the crocodile's mouth

    C. Telling a dolphin to ram the crocodile's stomach

    D. Hitting it with their boat

14. The twins learned that dolphins

    A. Wanted the sea turtles to leave

    B. Were as intelligent as humans

    C. Hated all humans

    D. Were scared to death of whales

290
Pippi Goes on Board
Astrid Lindgren

True or False. Decide whether each statement is true or false. Mark your answer sheet accordingly.

1. Pippi lived alone in Villa Villekulla with a horse and a monkey.

2. Pippi bought toys and candy for a large group of children.

3. Tommy was the only boy as strong as Pippi.

4. Pippi was scared by the snakes at the fair.

5. Annika, Tommy, and Pippi pretended to be stranded on an island.

6. The teacher said Pippi couldn't go to the school picnic.

7. Pippi threw a man into the air after he whipped his horse.

8. Pippi had bad table manners.

9. Captain Longstocking had become a cannibal king.

10. Captain Longstocking said Pippi had to go to school.

11. The only person stronger than Pippi was Captain Longstocking.

Multiple Choice. Read each question. Decide which statement best answers the question. Mark your answer sheet accordingly.

12. Pippi told lies because

    A. She didn't know the difference between true and false

    B. She thought it was fun to tell wild stories

    C. Captain Longstocking had told her, "Never tell the truth"

    D. She was under a magic spell

13. Pippi decided to stay at Villa Villekulla because

    A. The ship wasn't big enough for her horse

    B. She always got seasick

    C. Her father wanted her to go to school

    D. She knew Tommy and Annika would miss her

14. Pippi's hair was

    A. Brown

    B. Black

    C. Red

    D. Bright yellow

291
Pippi in the South Seas
Astrid Lindgren

True or False. Decide whether each statement is true or false. Mark your answer sheet accordingly.

1. Pippi sold Villa Villekulla.

2. Pippi decided that a spink was a giant tree.

3. Miss Rosenblom decided that Pippi was the smartest girl in the school.

4. The ship *Hoptoad* came to take Pippi to Kurrekurredutt Island.

5. Tommy and Annika's mother said it was okay for them to go with Pippi.

6. Tommy and Annika ran away to go with Pippi.

7. Pippi's father was king of Kurrekurredutt Island.

8. Pippi, Annika, Tommy, and the native children were left alone on the island.

9. Tommy was killed by a shark.

10. All the toys on Kurrekurredutt Island were made of gold.

11. The people of Kurrekurredutt Island could make themselves invisible.

Multiple Choice. Read each question. Decide which statement best answers the question. Mark your answer sheet accordingly.

12. Jim and Buck wanted

    A. The gold toys on the island

    B. The children's pearls

    C. Food

    D. To be the kings of the island

13. Tommy and Annika celebrated a late Christmas

    A. On Kurrekurredutt Island

    B. With their parents

    C. In Villa Villekulla

    D. On board the *Hoptoad*

14. Pippi, Tommy, and Annika took pills so that they would

    A. Never grow up

    B. Never forget Kurrekurredutt Island

    C. Not get seasick

    D. Turn into monkeys

292
Pippi Longstocking
Astrid Lindgren

True or False. Decide whether each statement is true or false. Mark your answer sheet accordingly.

1. Pippi was unusually strong.

2. Pippi kept a horse on her front porch.

3. Pippi lived at Villa Villekulla.

4. Pippi had a monkey named Mr. Nilsson.

5. Tommy and Annika lived with Pippi.

6. Annika, Tommy, and Pippi went to school together every day.

7. Five sailors from her father's ship lived with Pippi.

8. No one ever rode Pippi's horse.

9. Pippi was stronger than the circus strong man.

10. Pippi liked her kitchen neat and clean.

11. Pippi's father had been lost at sea.

Multiple Choice. Read each question. Decide which statement best answers the question. Mark your answer sheet accordingly.

12. Pippi liked to

    A. Tell unbelievable stories

    B. Go to school

    C. Stay neat and clean

    D. Wrestle with pigs

13. Pippi told Tommy and Annika that

    A. There were ghosts in her attic

    B. Mr. Nilsson was a genie

    C. Her horse could sing and dance

    D. Her mother was the Queen of Russia

14. Pippi

    A. Was the smartest child in school

    B. Picked up the hospital and carried it one mile

    C. Rescued two children from a fire

    D. Caught a wild lion by herself

293
All About Sam
Lois Lowry

True or False. Decide whether each statement is true or false. Mark your answer sheet accordingly.

1. Anastasia named Sam.

2. Sam could understand and think as soon as he was born.

3. Sam only understood baby talk.

4. Sam tried to talk as a baby, but nobody understood him.

5. Sam was afraid of the terrible twos.

6. Sam flushed the goldfish down the toilet because he wanted to kill it.

7. Anastasia cut off all of Sam's hair.

8. Sam felt bad after he stole the gum from the store.

9. Sam never said the word "no."

10. Gertrude Stein signaled "hi" to Sam with a flashlight.

11. Sam had a pet lightning bug.

Multiple Choice. Read each question. Decide which statement best answers the question. Mark your answer sheet accordingly.

12. Sam's pet won a prize for being the

    A. Fastest pet

    B. Most invisible pet

    C. Pet with the biggest ears

    D. Pet with the worst smell

13. What did Sam take to Show-and-Tell?

    A. The King of Worms

    B. Anastasia's dead goldfish

    C. His father's pipe

    D. Anastasia

14. Why did Sam put the goldfish in the toilet?

    A. To kill it

    B. To clean it

    C. To potty train it

    D. To make it rain goldfish

294
Attaboy, Sam!
Lois Lowry

True or False. Decide whether each statement is true or false. Mark your answer sheet accordingly.

1. When Anastasia baby-sat Alexander, Sam went with her.
2. When Anastasia baby-sat Alexander, he never woke up.
3. Sam climbed a tree at nursery school and then couldn't get down.
4. Sam cut off a little of his hair at nursery school.
5. Mrs. Sheehan was giving her kittens away for free.
6. Mrs. Sheehan was selling her kittens for $10 each.
7. Sam brought home a kitten without first asking his mother.
8. Anastasia was knitting a sweater for her mother's birthday.
9. Anastasia was writing a poem for her mother's birthday.
10. Mr. Krupnik loved his car.

Multiple Choice. Read each question. Decide which statement best answers the question. Mark your answer sheet accordingly.

11. Sam's homemade perfume
    A. Smelled bad
    B. Made noises
    C. Exploded
    D. All of the above

12. What did Mrs. Krupnik do to make herself feel better?
    A. She bought herself a new car
    B. She bought Mr. Krupnik a new car
    C. She got her hair cut
    D. She sold their house

13. What did Sam do to make himself feel better?
    A. He went scuba diving
    B. He drove his father's car
    C. He bought a bottle of perfume for his mother
    D. He brought home a kitten

14. At the end of the book, Sam, Anastasia, and Mr. Krupnik decided to
    A. Go on a trip so that Mrs. Krupnik could have some peace and quiet for her birthday
    B. Give Mrs. Krupnik a kitten for her birthday
    C. Plant a beautiful garden for Mrs. Krupnik's birthday
    D. Take Mrs. Krupnik to the county fair for her birthday

295
The Giver
Lois Lowry

True or False. Decide whether each statement is true or false. Mark your answer sheet accordingly.

1. The community where Jonas lived had no crime, unemployment, or divorce.

2. In the community, children were allowed to misbehave until they reached age eight.

3. The most important ceremony was the Ceremony of Two.

4. A young person's occupation was decided for him or her by the Committee of Elders.

5. Children were raised by Nurturers until they were given to a family.

6. The strongest punishment the community gave was to release a citizen.

7. Jonas and Asher were chosen to become Defenders.

8. Only the Giver and Receiver could remember the past and feel real emotion.

9. Jonas had occasionally seen objects in color, not just black and white.

10. There was only one Receiver of Memories in the Community.

11. Once a memory had been transferred from Giver to Receiver, it was lost forever to the Giver.

Multiple Choice. Read each question. Decide which statement best answers the question. Mark your answer sheet accordingly.

12. Jonas discovered that when a person was released, he was

    A. Sent to another settlement in the community

    B. Required to work as a slave in caves under the community

    C. Put to death by lethal injection

    D. Banished to the wilderness beyond the zone of climate control

13. The job of the Receiver was to

    A. Make sure everyone in the community was constantly aware of the past

    B. Use the wisdom and pain of the past to advise the Committee of Elders

    C. Make sure the climate control and life support systems functioned properly

    D. Protect the community from attack by groups of people who had been banished

14. Why did Jonas flee the community?

    A. He couldn't stand the pain that the memories of starvation and death caused him

    B. He learned that little Gabriel was going to be released because he was fussy at night

    C. He wanted to experience things like snow, rain, and hunger

    D. The Giver told him that he was a failure

296
Number the Stars
Lois Lowry

True or False. Decide whether each statement is true or false. Mark your answer sheet accordingly.

1. Copenhagen seemed to be filled with German soldiers.

2. Annemarie and Kirsti were Jewish.

3. The Resistance tried to smuggle Danish Jews to England.

4. Ellen Rosen lived in Annemarie's room for two years.

5. Henrik was a fisherman who helped smuggle Jews out of Denmark.

6. The Danes blew up their own navy so the Germans couldn't use it.

7. Mrs. Johansen broke her ankle after leading the Rosens to a fishing boat.

8. The German soldiers tried to use dogs to find hiding Jews.

9. The Jews waiting in Henrik's house pretended they were having a birthday party.

10. Both Lise and Peter died in the Resistance.

11. Mr. and Mrs. Rosen were arrested before they could escape Denmark.

Multiple Choice. Read each question. Decide which statement best answers the question. Mark your answer sheet accordingly.

12. Why were the handkerchiefs that Annemarie carried to Henrik important?

    A. Henrik needed them because he had a cold

    B. The Resistance sewed messages in the lining

    C. The handkerchiefs were treated to destroy a dog's sense of smell

    D. The handkerchiefs belonged to the King of Denmark

13. The Resistance knew that the roundup of Jews was coming because

    A. Some Germans warned them

    B. Danish spies heard Hitler give the order

    C. Dutch Jews had seen the empty trains headed for Denmark

    D. All of the above

14. What happened to the Rosens?

    A. They were captured

    B. They stayed with the Johansens in Copenhagen

    C. They stayed with Henrik

    D. They escaped to Sweden

297
Little House on Rocky Ridge
Roger Lea MacBride

True or False. Decide whether each statement is true or false. Mark your answer sheet accordingly.

1. The Wilders left the prairies because the rain flooded their farm.

2. Grandma and Grandpa Ingalls went to Missouri with the Wilders.

3. The Wilders traveled with the Cooleys.

4. Rose was captured by outlaws.

5. A bear killed Rose's dog.

6. Mrs. Wilder had $1,000 in silver coins sewn into her bonnet.

7. Mr. Wilder bought a farm in Missouri.

8. Mr. Wilder wanted to run a hotel.

9. Alva Stubbins liked to act ladylike.

10. The Wilders saw many people traveling in covered wagons.

11. At first, the chickens wouldn't go into the henhouse.

Multiple Choice. Read each question. Decide which statement best answers the question. Mark your answer sheet accordingly.

12. Who found the missing $100 bill?

   A. Fido

   B. Rose

   C. Alva

   D. George

13. Why was Paul mad at Rose?

   A. Rose got him in trouble with his father

   B. Rose took his Indian arrowhead

   C. Paul's dog liked Rose better than it liked him

   D. His brother, George, said he'd rather play with Rose

14. How did Mr. Wilder get his barn built before winter?

   A. He built it himself

   B. He paid some Russians with apples and potatoes

   C. His neighbors all helped him

   D. He dragged a barn from the farm next door

298
Mrs. Piggle-Wiggle
Betty MacDonald

True or False. Decide whether each statement is true or false. Mark your answer sheet accordingly.

1. Mrs. Piggle-Wiggle's house was upside-down.

2. Mrs. Piggle-Wiggle had 10 sons and 10 daughters.

3. Children loved to visit Mrs. Piggle-Wiggle's house.

4. Mrs. Piggle-Wiggle said that Mr. Piggle-Wiggle had been a pirate.

5. Mothers would ask Mrs. Piggle-Wiggle for advice about their children.

6. Mrs. Piggle-Wiggle taught Mary Lou to enjoy cleaning the kitchen.

7. In the "Answer-Backer Cure," Mrs. O'Toole spanked Mary every time she talked back.

8. Penelope Parrot was rude.

9. In the "Selfishness Cure," Mrs. Piggle-Wiggle told Dick Thompson's parents to give away all his toys.

10. The "Radish Cure" was for a girl who wouldn't take a bath.

11. Bobby, Larry, and Susan Gray were allowed to stay up all night in "The Never-Want-to-Go-to-Bedders Cure."

Multiple Choice. Read each question. Decide which statement best answers the question. Mark your answer sheet accordingly.

12. In the "Won't-Pick-Up-the-Toys-Cure," Mrs. Prentiss

    A. Let Hubert's toys pile up until he was trapped in his room

    B. Sold every toy that Hubert left out

    C. Gave every toy she found to Mrs. Piggle-Wiggle

    D. Bought Hubert more toys every time he left out his old toys

13. In the "Radish Cure," Patsy's mother

    A. Made Patsy eat one radish every day

    B. Planted radishes in the dirt on Patsy's skin

    C. Gave radishes to Penelope Parrot

    D. Made Patsy dress up like a giant radish

14. In the "Fighter-Quarreler's Cure," Mrs. Piggle-Wiggle told the twins' parents to

    A. Lock the twins in the same room until they stopped fighting

    B. Act just like the twins

    C. Tell the twins they had to fight; they weren't allowed to like each other

    D. Give the twins radishes

299
Mrs. Piggle-Wiggle's Farm
Betty MacDonald

True or False. Decide whether each statement is true or false. Mark your answer sheet accordingly.

1. Penelope, the parrot, lived on the farm with Mrs. Piggle-Wiggle.

2. Fetlock told people that his father was a thief.

3. Fetlock liked to tell people that he was a cowboy.

4. After a month at Mrs. Piggle-Wiggle's farm, Fetlock wasn't small and puny.

5. Arbutus was Mrs. Piggle-Wiggle's horse.

6. In the "Pet-Forgetter Cure," Mrs. Piggle-Wiggle made Rebecca give away all her pets.

7. Rebecca never forgot to feed Mrs. Piggle-Wiggle's animals.

8. Mrs. Piggle-Wiggle let Rebecca think she had been forgotten so she would learn how it felt not to be cared for.

9. In the "Destructiveness Cure," Jeffie liked to break things.

10. Jeffie took things apart, but he never put them back together.

11. Fanny, the sow, chased Jeffie.

Multiple Choice. Read each question. Decide which statement best answers the question. Mark your answer sheet accordingly.

12. Phoebe learned not to be a "fraidy-cat" after

    A. An apple barrel fell on Mrs. Piggle-Wiggle's foot

    B. Mrs. Piggle-Wiggle gave her a magic pill

    C. She saved Mrs. Piggle-Wiggle from a bear

    D. She pulled Arbutus out of the well

13. What did Morton find in the "Can't-Find-It-Cure"?

    A. Penelope

    B. Lester

    C. A calf

    D. Wags

14. Which animal could talk?

    A. Penelope

    B. Lester

    C. Arbutus

    D. Trotsky

300
Baby
Patricia MacLachlan

True or False. Decide whether each statement is true or false. Mark your answer sheet accordingly.

1. Larkin's parents hadn't named their baby son, who only lived one day.

2. Larkin's father was afraid to love Sophie because he knew they wouldn't be able to keep her.

3. The island where Larkin's family lived was a popular year-round tourist attraction.

4. Sophie learned to talk while she stayed with Larkin's family.

5. Grandma Byrd wanted to give Sophie to the police because she felt keeping her would hurt the family emotionally.

6. Even though at first she didn't want to, Larkin grew to love Sophie.

7. Ms. Minifred was Lalo's stepmother.

8. Sophie always cried when Papa tap-danced.

9. The people who lived on the island loved Sophie.

10. Mama was horrified to learn that Sophie's father was the school janitor, Rebel.

11. Papa said that poetry was for fools and wouldn't allow poetry books in the house.

Multiple Choice. Read each question. Decide which statement best answers the question. Mark your answer sheet accordingly.

12. What finally happened with Sophie and Larkin's family?

    A. Sophie's mother, Julia, let Sophie stay with Mama, Papa, and Larkin

    B. Julia and Sophie moved next door to Larkin

    C. Julia came and took Sophie away

    D. The authorities were unable to locate Julia so Mama and Papa adopted Sophie

13. How did having Sophie help Larkin's family?

    A. Sophie helped the family deal with the loss of Larkin's brother

    B. The other islanders finally accepted the family

    C. Because of Sophie, Mama and Papa began speaking again

    D. All of the above

14. What did Sophie gain from her time on the island?

    A. A loving family to stay with forever

    B. A loving and happy experience to begin her life

    C. A new home next to Larkin's family

    D. None of the above

301
Journey
Patricia MacLachlan

True or False. Decide whether each statement is true or false. Mark your answer sheet accordingly.

1. Journey's mother promised to write to him every day.

2. Cat was Journey's sister.

3. Grandfather took pictures of almost everything.

4. Grandma kept telling Journey that his mother would come back soon.

5. Grandfather always told Journey the truth.

6. Journey tried to fix the family pictures that his mother tore.

7. Grandma made the cat, Bloom, stay out in the barn.

8. Only Cat and Journey were upset that their mother was gone.

9. Grandpa liked to take family pictures.

10. Cooper was Journey's little brother.

11. Grandfather believed that things had to be perfect.

Multiple Choice. Read each question. Decide which statement best answers the question. Mark your answer sheet accordingly.

12. Journey's mother

    A. Dreamed of being a Hollywood movie star

    B. Always wanted to be somewhere else

    C. Let everyone know where she was all the time

    D. Wanted to be a model in New York City

13. Grandfather took lots of pictures because

    A. He wanted Journey to have memories of his family

    B. He was trying to win a magazine photography contest

    C. He was trying to get a job as a photographer

    D. Grandmother told him to find a hobby

14. Grandfather's secret was that he

    A. Set up a photography studio in the barn

    B. Knew where Journey's mother was

    C. Set up a darkroom in the barn

    D. Bought a puppy for Cooper

From *More Quizzes for Great Children's Books.* © 1996. Teacher Ideas Press. (800) 237-6124.

302
Good Night, Mr. Tom
Michelle Magorian

True or False. Decide whether each statement is true or false. Mark your answer sheet accordingly.

1. Many children from London were sent to Little Weirwold to keep them safe.

2. Tom Oakley isolated himself after his wife and son died.

3. Both Willie and Zach were sent from London to live with Tom Oakley.

4. Tom could tell from Willie's behavior and bruises that he had been abused.

5. Willie was desperately homesick for London and ran away five times.

6. Zacharias Wrench was almost as quiet and shy as Willie.

7. The local children avoided Willie because they thought he was conceited.

8. Miss Thorne discovered that Willie had an amazing ability to become the character he was portraying in a drama.

9. Mr. Tom encouraged Willie to develop his natural ability to draw.

10. Carrie was killed when a R.A.F. fighter plane was shot down and crashed into her school.

11. Willie's mother beat him and locked him in a closet after she made him return to London from Little Weirwold.

Multiple Choice. Read each question. Decide which statement best answers the question. Mark your answer sheet accordingly.

12. How did Mr. Tom get Willie back to Little Weirwold?

    A. He told the authorities that Willie was being abused

    B. He kidnapped Willie from the hospital

    C. He promised Willie's mother that he would make sure Willie went to school

    D. He told Willie's mother that Willie was dead

13. How did Willie change Tom Oakley?

    A. Tom became more outgoing and social

    B. Tom grew to love Willie

    C. Tom became happier and much less gruff

    D. All of the above

14. How did Zach die?

    A. He was killed in a bombing raid after he returned to London

    B. He drowned in the ocean while on vacation with Tom and Willie

    C. He was run over by an army truck

    D. He died from the measles

303
Ten Kids, No Pets
Ann M. Martin

True or False. Decide whether each statement is true or false. Mark your answer sheet accordingly.

1. Mrs. Rosso said that 10 kids were enough, so the family couldn't have any pets.
2. The Rosso children were all homesick for New York City.
3. Ira was the neatest of all the Rosso children.
4. Ira lied to his second-grade class and told them that his family had all sorts of unusual animals on their farm.
5. Gardenia and Faustine tried to hide Goliath, the turkey, in Candy's secret room.
6. Jan was positive that her father was giving the family a dog for Christmas because she heard him say he was working on a doghouse.
7. Hardy liked to be a detective and try to solve mysteries.
8. Hannah accidentally gave her pet-hint valentines to her class at school.
9. Dinnie decided that she didn't ever want another animal after the injured bird, Sally, died.
10. The Rossos had a Halloween party with 30 kids.
11. Abigail hid a pet deer, which she named Bambi, two weeks before she told her mother about it.

Multiple Choice. Read each question. Decide which statement best answers the question. Mark your answer sheet accordingly.

12. Why didn't the Rossos eat Goliath for Thanksgiving?
    A. He was so big that he scared Jan
    B. The children liked him too much
    C. Hardy helped him escape to the woods
    D. Someone else accidentally picked him up for their dinner

13. Why did the Rossos finally get a pet?
    A. Mr. Rosso said that he had always secretly wanted a dog
    B. They needed a cat to kill the mice
    C. Mrs. Rosso loved the way the bird sang
    D. None of the above

14. Which type of pet did the Rossos get?
    A. A dog
    B. A cat
    C. A tame fawn
    D. A canary

304
The Dark-Thirty: Southern Tales of the Supernatural
Patricia C. McKissack

True or False. Decide whether each statement is true or false. Mark your answer sheet accordingly.

1. In "The Legend of Pin Oak," Harper McAvoy and Henri were both black.

2. Harper tried to sell his own brother into slavery.

3. In, "We Organized," a group of slaves all ran away together.

4. The slaves in "We Organized" put a curse on their master until he set them free.

5. In "Justice," Hooper Granger was a member of the Ku Klux Klan.

6. Chief Baker arrested Alvin Tinsley because Hooper told him to.

7. Alvin punished Hooper for murdering him by making Hooper see his crimes in the windows of his house.

8. In "The Sight," Esau Mayes could sometimes see the future.

9. Esau's family died, even though Esau tried to avoid the disaster.

10. In the "Woman in the Snow," the white driver refused to let a woman and her sick baby ride because she didn't have the fare.

11. The ghost of the woman and her baby were seen at the first snowfall of each year.

Multiple Choice. Read each question. Decide which statement best answers the question. Mark your answer sheet accordingly.

12. In "The Conjure Brother," when Josie tried to magically create a little brother

    A. Nothing happened

    B. She got an older brother instead of a younger brother

    C. She found herself in a totally different family

    D. She suddenly had a little brother but her older sister disappeared

13. In "Boo Mama," little Nealy disappeared into the woods for a year. It turned out that Nealy

    A. Had been raised by wolves

    B. Had been cared for by a hidden group of the descendants of runaway slaves

    C. Had become a zombie

    D. Had been cared for by the Sasquatch people

14. If a porter heard a train whistle at 11:59, it meant he would

    A. See a ghost that night

    B. Have bad luck for 12 days

    C. Die in 24 hours

    D. Lose his job in two days

From *More Quizzes for Great Children's Books.* © 1996. Teacher Ideas Press. (800) 237-6124.

305
A Long Hard Journey: The Story of Pullman Porter
Patricia C. McKissack and Fredrick McKissack

True or False. Decide whether each statement is true or false. Mark your answer sheet accordingly.

1. George Pullman worked hard to make sure that his workers were treated fairly.

2. The Pullman sleeping car was often said to be as luxurious as a hotel.

3. For nearly 100 years, every single Pullman porter was black.

4. Porters depended on tips because their wages were so low.

5. George Pullman made it very clear that his porters had to be treated respectfully.

6. If a passenger stole a towel, the porter had to pay for it.

7. The Pullman Company raised porters' wages only after they launched a one-month, nationwide strike.

8. Any porter suspected of being part of the union was fired.

9. A. Philip Randolph led the fight against the Pullman Company.

10. The black establishment supported the Brotherhood in its fight against the Pullman Company.

11. President Calvin Coolidge publicly scolded the Pullman Company for the way it treated its porters.

Multiple Choice. Read each question. Decide which statement best answers the question. Mark your answer sheet accordingly.

12. In the 1920s, unions were

    A. Thought to be nesting grounds for radicals and communists

    B. Only for black workers

    C. Against the law

    D. Widely respected

13. The Pullman Company refused to negotiate with the Brotherhood because

    A. It said it wouldn't negotiate with communists

    B. It claimed the company union represented the porters

    C. George Pullman refused to even be in the same room with Randolph

    D. All of the above

14. What finally forced the Pullman Company to negotiate a fair contract with the Brotherhood?

    A. Congress amended the Railway Labor Act of 1934 to include porters

    B. President Coolidge issued a federal decree ordering Pullman to negotiate

    C. Randolph threatened to call a nationwide strike

    D. President Roosevelt called for a boycott unless Pullman negotiated

306
Anne of Avonlea
L. M. Montgomery

True or False. Decide whether each statement is true or false. Mark your answer sheet accordingly.

1. The goal of the Avonlea Village Improvement Society was to improve the behavior of people who were rude or mean.

2. Anne warned all her students that she would whip anyone who misbehaved.

3. Mr. Harrison, Anne's neighbor, had a parrot that cursed and swore terribly.

4. The students of the Avonlea school burned it down.

5. Marilla decided she could only have Dora live at Green Gables.

6. Miss Lavender was as imaginative as Anne.

7. Marilla asked Rachel Lynde to come live at Green Gables after Mr. Lynde died.

8. Anne's dearest friend, Diana Berry, was killed in the hailstorm that unexpectedly swept over Prince Edward Island.

9. No one in Avonlea would cooperate with any of the goals of the Avonlea Village Improvement Society.

10. Miss Lavender turned down Stephen Irving's proposal because he kept her waiting for 25 years.

11. Davy tended to be mischievous.

Multiple Choice. Read each question. Decide which statement best answers the question. Mark your answer sheet accordingly.

12. What went wrong with the project to paint the town hall?

   A. Most of the people liked the town hall just the way it was

   B. Joshua Pye painted the hall a deep, brilliant blue instead of green

   C. Gilbert painted each wall a different color

   D. Mr. Harrison bought the hall and wouldn't let anyone touch it

13. Anne finally won over Anthony Pye after she

   A. Gave him a whipping

   B. Took him to Green Gables

   C. Asked him to help her start the fire each morning

   D. Hugged him

14. Anne discovered that Mr. Harrison was

   A. Her only living relative

   B. A famous author trying to find solitude

   C. Married

   D. Secretly in love with Marilla

From *More Quizzes for Great Children's Books.* © 1996. Teacher Ideas Press. (800) 237-6124.

307
Anne of Green Gables
L. M. Montgomery

True or False. Decide whether each statement is true or false. Mark your answer sheet accordingly.

1. Matthew and Marilla went to the orphanage and picked out Anne to adopt.

2. Anne was an unusually beautiful little girl.

3. Anne had a very active imagination.

4. Matthew was very stern with Anne.

5. Diana Berry was Anne's best friend.

6. Mrs. Rachel Lynde never forgave Anne for throwing a tantrum after she told Anne that her hair looked like carrots.

7. Marilla was often amused by Anne, but she tried not to show it.

8. The boys and girls of Avonlea went to separate schools.

9. Diana and Anne both went to Queen's to study to become teachers.

10. The children of Avonlea disliked Anne because she constantly swore.

11. Marilla died of a heart attack while Anne was away at school.

Multiple Choice. Read each question. Decide which statement best answers the question. Mark your answer sheet accordingly.

12. Why did the relationship between Anne and Gilbert Blythe stay poor for so long?

    A. Gilbert resented Anne because she was so smart

    B. Anne couldn't forgive Gilbert for calling her "carrots"

    C. Gilbert had wanted Matthew and Marilla to adopt him

    D. Anne was jealous of Gilbert's wealthy family

13. How can Matthew and Marilla's feelings toward Anne be summed up?

    A. They felt it was their difficult task to take care of Anne

    B. They loved Anne deeply and felt she was the best thing that had ever happened to them

    C. They liked Anne, but didn't love her

    D. They both resented being forced to raise Anne

14. Anne was skilled at writing and reciting because

    A. She was very creative and expressive

    B. Matthew made her practice her grammar every evening

    C. Marilla told her she would go back to the orphanage if she didn't learn to speak properly

    D. All of the above

308
The Agony of Alice
Phyllis Reynolds Naylor

True or False. Decide whether each statement is true or false. Mark your answer sheet accordingly.

1. Alice felt that she did too many embarrassing things.

2. Mr. McKinley married Miss Cole.

3. Alice saw a boy in his underwear in the clothing store.

4. Alice tried to get transferred from Mrs. Plotkin's class to Miss Cole's class.

5. Miss Cole had Alice clean her room every morning.

6. Miss Cole was in charge of the safety patrol.

7. All the girls liked the perfume Alice wore to school.

8. Lester's girlfriend broke up with him.

9. Alice enjoyed listening to Mrs. Plotkin read books.

10. On Valentine's Day, Alice didn't get any valentines.

11. Alice refused to write in her journal.

Multiple Choice. Read each question. Decide which statement best answers the question. Mark your answer sheet accordingly.

12. Alice wanted to

    A. Be like Miss Cole

    B. Be like Mrs. Plotkin

    C. Sing in the opera when she grew up

    D. Quit school

13. When Alice was in Chicago with her aunt, she

    A. Got lost downtown

    B. Had her first period

    C. Wrote a 12-page letter to Miss Cole

    D. Fell in love with her cousin, Billy

14. Mrs. Plotkin gave Alice

    A. A ring that had been passed down to the women in her family

    B. The globe in her room that Alice wanted so much

    C. A new journal

    D. The bicycle Mrs. Plotkin had as a child

From *More Quizzes for Great Children's Books.* © 1996. Teacher Ideas Press. (800) 237-6124.

309
Beetles, Lightly Toasted
Phyllis Reynolds Naylor

True or False. Decide whether each statement is true or false. Mark your answer sheet accordingly.

1. Andy Moller lived in an apartment in Chicago.

2. Andy was a hearty eater who would eat almost anything.

3. The essay topic for the Roger B. Sudermann contest was "Unusual Foods."

4. Sam Hollins lived on a farm in the country.

5. After fifth-graders first heard the essay topic, they decided to boycott the contest.

6. Andy put beetles in brownies, and many of his classmates unknowingly ate them.

7. Aunt Wanda helped Andy make Butterfly Wing Jello for the church picnic.

8. Andy never ate the worms or beetles, he just pretended to.

9. Only Sam Hollins knew what Andy was going to write about in his essay.

10. Sam Hollins won the Roger B. Sudermann contest.

Multiple Choice. Read each question. Decide which statement best answers the question. Mark your answer sheet accordingly.

11. Who won the Roger B. Sudermann Contest?

    A. Sam Hollins

    B. Aunt Wanda

    C. Dora Kray

    D. None of the above

12. Everyone who tasted the fried worms

    A. Threw up

    B. Thought they tasted like applesauce

    C. Asked for the recipe so they could make them

    D. Said they were too chewy

13. When the teacher read Andy's essay to the fifth-grade class, the class

    A. Was mad

    B. Was so sick that many of them vomited

    C. Laughed

    D. Sung "For He's a Jolly Good Fellow" to Andy

14. The beetles tasted like

    A. Applesauce

    B. Hamburger

    C. Cinnamon

    D. Nuts

310
The Boys Start the War
Phyllis Reynolds Naylor

True or False. Decide whether each statement is true or false. Mark your answer sheet accordingly.

1. The Hatford brothers wanted to make the Malloys move away.

2. Wally thought of dumping a load of dead things in the river by the Malloys.

3. Josh accidentally kissed Caroline.

4. Caroline loved performing.

5. Josh, Wally, and Jake pretended to dump Peter's body in the river.

6. Caroline threw Mrs. Hatford's cake into the river.

7. Eddie hit Jake in the head with a rotten pumpkin.

8. The Hatfords and the Malloys became friends after they washed the Malloys' windows.

9. Beth liked to read scary stories.

10. The Hatfords scared Beth with the floating head trick.

11. The Malloy girls went up on the Hatford roof to scare them.

Multiple Choice. Read each question. Decide which statement best answers the question. Mark your answer sheet accordingly.

12. Who declared the war?

    A. Caroline

    B. Beth

    C. Wally

    D. Jake

13. The Hatford boys and the Malloy girls

    A. Decided that the war between them was sort of fun

    B. Decided that they should be friends

    C. Asked their parents to move

    D. Joined the same baseball team

14. When the Hatfords locked Caroline in the shed

    A. Caroline's sisters kidnapped Jake and offered to exchange him

    B. Caroline pretended to have rabies

    C. They accidentally locked Wally in too

    D. Caroline's parents called the police

311
The Grand Escape
Phyllis Reynolds Naylor

True or False. Decide whether each statement is true or false. Mark your answer sheet accordingly.

1. The Neals threw water on Marco and Polo to teach them to stay in the house.
2. Marco and Polo liked to call people on the telephone and ask them if they were taking good care of their cats.
3. Texas Jake was impressed when he learned that Marco could read.
4. Polo liked to suck on string, shoelaces, and tinsel.
5. Carlotta was Marco and Polo's mother.
6. Elvis brought Marco and Polo to the Club of Mysteries and begged Texas Jake to let them stay.
7. Many neighborhood cats ate the leftovers in the garbage cans behind the Big Burger restaurant.
8. Carlotta was the only cat that Bertram the Bad wouldn't try to kill.
9. The Club of Mysteries met in the loft of an old garage.
10. The first mystery that Marco and Polo had to solve was finding out what was in Bertram the Bad's doghouse.
11. Polo discovered that he loved the taste of fresh mouse.

Multiple Choice. Read each question. Decide which statement best answers the question. Mark your answer sheet accordingly.

12. The second mystery Marco and Polo had to solve was
    A. Why do dogs hate cats?
    B. Where does water go when it rains?
    C. How fast can Bertram the Bad run?
    D. Where does the garbage truck take the trash?
13. What finally made Marco and Polo decide to go home?
    A. Texas Jake was killed by Bertram the Bad
    B. Carlotta told them to go home
    C. The Big Burger put a locked cover on the dumpster
    D. Polo was tired of eating mice
14. What surprise was waiting for Marco and Polo when they returned to the Neals?
    A. The Neals had moved
    B. The Neals had bought a dog
    C. The Neals had two new kittens
    D. There was a trap door so the cats could go in and out

312
Shiloh
Phyllis Reynolds Naylor

True or False. Decide whether each statement is true or false. Mark your answer sheet accordingly.

1. Marty Preston's family was poor.

2. The first time Shiloh came to Marty's house, Marty and his father took him back to Judd.

3. Judd mistreated his dogs.

4. Shiloh was a quiet dog.

5. Marty and Shiloh often went rabbit hunting together.

6. Marty hid Shiloh in his bedroom.

7. Shiloh followed Marty to school every day.

8. Mrs. Preston was the first to learn that Marty was hiding Shiloh.

9. Shiloh was badly hurt by a bear.

10. Judd said that because Marty loved the dog so much, he could have Shiloh for free.

11. Marty felt it was okay to lie to protect Shiloh.

Multiple Choice. Read each question. Decide which statement best answers the question. Mark your answer sheet accordingly.

12. Shiloh was badly hurt when

   A. A snake bit him

   B. He was mauled by a bear

   C. A German shepherd attacked him

   D. He was run over by Judd's pickup truck

13. The deal between Marty and Judd was that

   A. Marty could have Shiloh for free

   B. Shiloh would stay at Marty's house except when Judd used him to hunt

   C. Marty could have Shiloh if he worked for 20 hours around Judd's house

   D. Marty could buy Shiloh for $50

14. What made Judd willing to talk to Marty about Shiloh?

   A. Marty reminded Judd of his own son

   B. Marty saw Judd kill a deer out of season

   C. Judd saw how much all the Prestons loved Shiloh

   D. None of the above

313
The Kidnapping of Christina Lattimore
Joan Lowery Nixon

True or False. Decide whether each statement is true or false. Mark your answer sheet accordingly.

1. Christina often went to the hamburger place run by one of her kidnappers.

2. Christina's grandmother, Cristabel, was a wealthy and powerful woman.

3. Christina learned that Zack's wife, Loretta, was the other kidnapper.

4. When the police arrived, Christina was shocked to find that they thought she might be an accessory to her own kidnapping.

5. Christina was able to learn much about her kidnappers by listening to them through the furnace.

6. Christina's captors never allowed her to leave the basement.

7. Cristabel refused to press charges against Christina's kidnappers.

8. Only Christina's parents believed that Christina wasn't an accomplice in her own kidnapping.

9. Christina learned that Zack used to be her father's best friend.

10. Della warned Christina that trying to solve the kidnapping case could be dangerous.

11. Mr. and Mrs. Lattimore hired a detective to find the kidnappers.

Multiple Choice. Read each question. Decide which statement best answers the question. Mark your answer sheet accordingly.

12. Why was Christina certain that someone besides Zack had planned the kidnapping?

    A. Christina knew that Zack wasn't smart enough to have planned it

    B. Christina thought that she saw three people when she was first kidnapped

    C. Zack kept jokingly talking about a "Mr. Brains"

    D. None of the above

13. Who did Christina discover knew something about her kidnappers?

    A. Della

    B. Cristabel

    C. Her father

    D. Her mother

14. Christina showed that she had matured when she

    A. Told Kelly that she was too young to marry him

    B. Decided to earn her own money and not depend on Cristabel's money

    C. Asked her father not to quit his job

    D. Told Cristabel that she was behind the kidnapping

314
The Other Side of Dark
Joan Lowery Nixon

True or False. Decide whether each statement is true or false. Mark your answer sheet accordingly.

1. When Stacy was in the clinic, a reporter asked her some questions.

2. Stacy's father did not come to see her while she was in the clinic.

3. Stacy's father did not have a job.

4. Detective Markowitz wanted Stacy to live at his house for a while.

5. Stacy's sister, Donna, was expecting a baby.

6. Stacy's sister, Donna, took her shopping for new clothes.

7. Stacy's sister, Donna, refused to see or talk with Stacy because she did not want to be reminded of their mother's death.

8. When Stacy was baby-sitting the three children next door, one of them said that she thought she saw someone in Stacy's yard.

9. When Stacy was at home alone, she received some upsetting telephone calls.

10. Jeff was not at the party that Stacy went to with Jan and B. J.

11. At the party, Stacy unknowingly drank some vodka that Jarrod Tucker gave her.

Multiple Choice. Read each question. Decide which statement best answers the question. Mark your answer sheet accordingly.

12. Jarrod Tucker told Stacy that

    A. He had a friend

    B. His mother was a criminal

    C. Stacy's father gave him some money

    D. Stacy's sister, Donna, was using drugs

13. When Jarrod Tucker came to Stacy's house, she tried to hide from him

    A. In the garage

    B. In the bathroom

    C. In a pile of leaves

    D. In her old tree house

14. At the end of the book, Stacy found out that Jeff

    A. Was her mother's murderer

    B. Worked for the police department

    C. Sold drugs

    D. Was a newspaper reporter

315
My Name Is Not Angelica
Scott O'Dell

True or False. Decide whether each statement is true or false. Mark your answer sheet accordingly.

1. Raisha was captured and sold into slavery by an African king.

2. The captain of the slave ship beat Raisha every day.

3. Raisha and Konje were sold to the same master.

4. There was a shortage of fresh water on the island of St. John.

5. Raisha was a house slave.

6. Runaway slaves hid at Mary Point.

7. Nero did all he could to help slaves escape.

8. The slaves on St. John were planning to revolt.

9. Konje became the leader of the runaways.

10. Governor Gardelin believed that cruel laws would keep slaves from running away.

11. Isaak Gronnewold thought that torturing the slaves would make them obey.

Multiple Choice. Read each question. Decide which statement best answers the question. Mark your answer sheet accordingly.

12. When a slave uprising began on St. John's

    A. The planters formed an army to fight the slaves

    B. Governor Gardelin brought in French soldiers

    C. The slaves killed all the whites on the island

    D. The planters set fire to the island

13. When the runaways were trapped, they

    A. Fought until they were all killed

    B. Surrendered on the condition that they wouldn't be punished

    C. Committed suicide

    D. Escaped by canoes to the island of St. Thomas

14. Isaak Gronnewold

    A. Was killed trying to protect the slaves

    B. Was killed by Konje

    C. Led the governor to the slaves' hideout

    D. Helped the surviving slaves escape to Rhode Island

From *More Quizzes for Great Children's Books.* © 1996. Teacher Ideas Press. (800) 237-6124.

316
Lyddie
Katherine Paterson

True or False. Decide whether each statement is true or false. Mark your answer sheet accordingly.

1. When Lyddie found a black man hiding in her father's cabin, she turned him in to the authorities.

2. Lyddie gave the black man some money.

3. During Lyddie's first week in the weaving room, Diana was kind to her and helped her learn to work the loom.

4. Mrs. Bedlow hired Lyddie's mother to work as a maid in the boardinghouse.

5. Lyddie's father came to visit her while she was living in Mrs. Bedlow's boardinghouse.

6. Lyddie was not able to save any of the money she earned working in the weaving room.

7. Lyddie asked Mrs. Bedlow if she could keep her sister, Rachel, with her for a short time in the boardinghouse.

8. Charlie asked Lyddie if he could live with her in Mrs. Bedlow's boardinghouse.

9. When Lyddie's brother, Charles, came to see her at the boardinghouse, he told her that Mrs. Phinney asked him to bring Rachel back.

10. When Lyddie finally decided to sign the petition, she found out that it was too late and that she would have to wait until next year.

11. Lyddie did not want the family farm to be sold.

12. At the end of the book, Lyddie decided that she would go to college.

Multiple Choice. Read each question. Decide which statement best answers the question. Mark your answer sheet accordingly.

13. Diana told Lyddie that she was leaving her job at the mill because

  A. She was going to become a nun

  B. A long-lost aunt had died and left her a large amount of money

  C. She was dying

  D. She was going to have a child

14. Lyddie became worried when Rachel began to

  A. Cough at night

  B. Sneeze

  C. Tell lies

  D. Talk to herself

317
Of Nightingales That Weep
Katherine Paterson

True or False. Decide whether each statement is true or false. Mark your answer sheet accordingly.

1. Takiko was frightened by Goro's appearance when she first saw him.

2. Goro was a famous samurai general.

3. Takiko's father died fighting the Genji.

4. Takiko was invited to live at the emperor's house because of her musical talent.

5. The emperor was a little boy.

6. Takiko's first job in the capital was to brush Princess Aoi's hair.

7. The emperor's court fled because the Genji were about to capture the city.

8. Hideo was a spy for the Genji.

9. Takiko's mother was killed by the plague.

10. When the Heike fleet was destroyed by the Genji, Takiko tried to kill herself.

11. When the war was over Takiko went back to Goro's farm.

Multiple Choice. Read each question. Decide which statement best answers the question. Mark your answer sheet accordingly.

12. When the samurai Hideo finally found Takiko again, he

    A. Took her to the capital and married her

    B. Asked her to sing for the new emperor

    C. Left her because she was now ugly

    D. Brought her a new *koto*

13. When Goro came to ask Takiko to help her pregnant mother

    A. Takiko went with him at once

    B. Takiko refused to go with him

    C. Goro told everyone that Princess Aoi was a spy

    D. Goro told Takiko not to trust the emperor

14. Eventually, Takiko

    A. Committed suicide because the Heike forces were defeated

    B. Was forced to join a convent

    C. Married Goro

    D. Married Hideo

318
Park's Quest
Katherine Paterson

True or False. Decide whether each statement is true or false. Mark your answer sheet accordingly.

1. Park's mother told him almost nothing about his father.

2. Park liked to daydream about being a knight.

3. Park's father was missing-in-action in Vietnam.

4. Grandpa Broughton lived on a small farm in Vermont.

5. Grandfather Broughton couldn't talk because he had had a stroke.

6. Thanh had never seen Grandfather Broughton.

7. The Broughton family threw a huge welcome-home party for Park when he first arrived.

8. Thanh was furious when Park tried to ride a cow.

9. Park was afraid of his grandfather.

10. Frank was married to Thanh's mother.

11. Park ran home to his mother after Thanh bit him.

Multiple Choice. Read each question. Decide which statement best answers the question. Mark your answer sheet accordingly.

12. Park was shocked to learn that

   A. His mother had divorced his father

   B. He was adopted

   C. He had to live on his grandfather's farm

   D. Milk came from cows

13. Thanh turned out to be

   A. The daughter of the president of Vietnam

   B. A communist spy

   C. Park's half-sister

   D. The daughter of the man who killed his father

14. Park and Thanh had a fight after

   A. Park insulted Frank

   B. Thanh slapped Grandfather Broughton

   C. Park shot a crow

   D. Park tried to kiss Thanh

319
Hatchet
Gary Paulsen

True or False. Decide whether each statement is true or false. Mark your answer sheet accordingly.

1. The pilot of the plane Brian was in had a heart attack and died.

2. Brian's plane crashed into a small field in the middle of a forest.

3. Brian had only one pack of matches with him.

4. Brian made a shelter against a rocky ledge.

5. Brian used the wrecked plane for a house.

6. A moose attacked Brian.

7. At first, Brian found it very difficult to spear fish.

8. Brian had a pet Arctic fox.

9. Brian learned that events could rapidly switch from good to bad in the wilderness.

10. Because he was worried about survival, Brian didn't think about his parents' divorce.

11. The only tool Brian had with him was his hatchet.

Multiple Choice. Read each question. Decide which statement best answers the question. Mark your answer sheet accordingly.

12. Brian had trouble catching foolbirds because

   A. The birds nested in the tops of pine trees

   B. It was impossible to get close to them

   C. The birds swam out in the middle of the lake

   D. Brian was looking for a bird's colors, not the shape of the bird

13. Brian was attacked by

   A. A moose

   B. A wolf

   C. A pelican

   D. A flock of geese

14. The one good thing that the tornado did was to

   A. Bring the plane up to the surface of the lake

   B. Kill the bear

   C. Clear out all the trees so the search planes could see Brian

   D. Kill a reindeer

320
Nightjohn
Gary Paulsen

True or False. Decide whether each statement is true or false. Mark your answer sheet accordingly.

1. Nightjohn was Sarny's younger brother.

2. The slave children on the Waller plantation were raised by Mammy.

3. The slaves all ate out of the same trough.

4. Master Waller often whipped his slaves.

5. Master Waller didn't want his slaves to learn to read.

6. Master Waller would hunt down escaping slaves with dogs.

7. Nightjohn was born on the Waller plantation.

8. Nightjohn was trying to start a slave revolt.

9. Master Waller was always kind to Mammy.

10. Sarny was a maid in the big house.

Multiple Choice. Read each question. Decide which statement best answers the question. Mark your answer sheet accordingly.

11. When Master Waller learned that Nightjohn had taught Sarny some letters

    A. He sold Sarny to a planter in Florida

    B. He whipped Sarny

    C. He sold Nightjohn to a sugar plantation in Louisiana

    D. He chopped off Nightjohn's big toes

12. Why did Nightjohn want to teach slaves to read?

    A. So they could organize a revolt

    B. So they would be able to write about their experiences

    C. Because reading would be a valuable skill when they escaped

    D. Because he wanted them to think like free men and women

13. After running away from the Waller plantation, Nightjohn

    A. Went to the North to tell everyone how horrible slavery was

    B. Was captured and executed

    C. Returned to the area and secretly taught slaves to read

    D. Became the first African American governor of Rhode Island

14. Nightjohn taught Sarny to read because

    A. Sarny wanted to learn

    B. Mammy begged him to teach Sarny

    C. He knew Sarny was about to be sold

    D. Sarny was his older sister

321
The Voyage of the Frog
Gary Paulsen

True or False. Decide whether each statement is true or false. Mark your answer sheet accordingly.

1. Uncle Owen asked David to show him a picture of the *Frog* before he died.

2. David was unable to sail back to port because he forgot how to read the compass.

3. The first warning of the approaching storm was a flock of seagulls flying to shore.

4. An oil tanker didn't see the *Frog* and almost ran it over.

5. While David was adrift on the *Frog*, he ate fish for breakfast, lunch, and supper.

6. There were no emergency flares on board the *Frog*.

7. One night after a storm, a large shark repeatedly attacked the *Frog*.

8. David scared away a group of killer whales by waving a lighted candle at their eyes.

9. A luxury liner rescued David as he was drifting near the Bahamas.

10. David was so hungry that he killed and ate a dolphin.

Multiple Choice. Read each question. Decide which statement best answers the question. Mark your answer sheet accordingly.

11. Uncle Owen's last request was for David to

    A. Sail the *Frog* until he couldn't see land and then throw his ashes into the sea

    B. Sail the *Frog* past his hospital window so he could see it one last time

    C. Sail with him to Cuba so that he could die in his homeland

    D. None of the above

12. The shark attacked the *Frog* because

    A. Blood from David's leg was on the side of the boat

    B. David had been throwing his garbage over the side of the boat

    C. The shark thought the boat was a wounded fish

    D. The shark thought the boat was a killer whale

13. Why didn't David sail home right after the storm?

    A. He still wanted to take his Uncle Owen to Cuba

    B. There was no wind

    C. The sails had been shredded by the high winds

    D. The oil tanker had broken off the *Frog*'s rudder in a collision

14. Why didn't the oil tanker stop and pick David up?

    A. The crew didn't see David

    B. The crew thought David was just out fishing

    C. The tanker was going too fast to stop, so instead, they radioed for help

    D. The captain thought David looked like a drug smuggler

From *More Quizzes for Great Children's Books.* © 1996. Teacher Ideas Press. (800) 237-6124.

322
The Winter Room
Gary Paulsen

True or False. Decide whether each statement is true or false. Mark your answer sheet accordingly.

1. Eldon's family watched TV every night.

2. Eldon thought the farm smelled bad in the spring.

3. Wayne and Eldon were brothers.

4. Nels and Uncle Dave came to Minnesota from Norway.

5. Stacker and Jim were the hired men who worked on the farm.

6. The animals were slaughtered in the winter.

7. Uncle David had never married.

8. Eldon's family never ate in their dining room.

9. Nels and Uncle David lived in a loft in the barn.

10. In the story of "Crazy Alen," Alen liked to play jokes on people.

11. The story of "Orud the Terrible" was about a Viking and the woman he captured.

Multiple Choice. Read each question. Decide which statement best answers the question. Mark your answer sheet accordingly.

12. What did the family do in the winter room?

    A. They listened to Uncle David tell stories

    B. They watched TV

    C. They listened to the radio

    D. They played checkers and Monopoly

13. How did Wayne hurt Uncle David's feelings?

    A. He said that Uncle David was bad at checkers

    B. He said that Uncle David's stories were lies

    C. He called Uncle David a dumb Norwegian

    D. He said he wished that Uncle David would die soon

14. Eldon hated fall because

    A. He didn't like school

    B. Fall was the time that the animals were slaughtered

    C. It meant that winter was coming soon

    D. None of the above

323
Are You in the House Alone?
Richard Peck

True or False. Decide whether each statement is true or false. Mark your answer sheet accordingly.

1. The Lawvers were one of the most powerful families in Oldfield Village.

2. Gail's friend, Alison, was dating Phil Lawver.

3. Many New Yorkers had been moving to Oldfield Village.

4. The first threatening, obscene note that Gail received was tacked to her bedroom door.

5. When Gail showed the second obscene note to the school counselor, the counselor immediately called the police.

6. Gail's mother did not like Gail's boyfriend, Steve.

7. Steve was one of the best students in Oldfield Village High School.

8. Gail knew she was being stalked because whenever she was alone, the phone rang and then went dead.

9. Gail opened the door of Mrs. Montgomery's house because she thought it was Steve.

10. When the police chief learned that Phil had raped Gail, he arrested Phil.

11. Madam Malevich told Gail that she couldn't run from what had happened to her.

Multiple Choice. Read each question. Decide which statement best answers the question. Mark your answer sheet accordingly.

12. The lawyer told Gail and her parents that Phil would not be convicted because

    A. The police chief would do nothing because he didn't believe in rape

    B. Phil was considered an upstanding young citizen with a brilliant future

    C. Gail had been sexually active with Steve

    D. All of the above

13. Which of the following happened after Gail was raped?

    A. Gail went to live with her Aunt Viola in Harrisburg

    B. Steve and Gail's father beat Phil up so badly that he had to be hospitalized

    C. Madam Malevich publicly announced that Phil was a rapist

    D. Phil raped and nearly killed Sonia Slanek

14. Which of the following statements is true?

    A. Phil was finally arrested but plea bargained his way out of jail

    B. Phil left town but never was arrested

    C. Gail moved back to New York City

    D. Gail and Alison never spoke to each other again

324
Don't Look and It Won't Hurt
Richard Peck

True or False. Decide whether each statement is true or false. Mark your answer sheet accordingly.

1. Ellen's boyfriend, Kevin, told her that his work was to help draft dodgers.

2. Ellen found out that Kevin had lied to her about his work.

3. Carol and Mitsy Decker were good friends.

4. Ellen, Carol, and Liz shared the same room.

5. The man who left the quarters on the curb for Carol and Liz turned out to be their father.

6. Carol's friend, Jerry, missed a lot of school.

7. When Ellen's mother heard that Ellen was pregnant, she was happy and excited.

8. Carol's art teacher was a shy, quiet person.

9. Carol found out that Liz was hiding a cat in the bedroom.

10. At the end of the book, Ellen brought her baby home to Claypitts.

11. At the end of the book, Ellen decided to give her baby up for adoption.

Multiple Choice. Read each question. Decide which statement best answers the question. Mark your answer sheet accordingly.

12. Ellen's boyfriend, Kevin

    A. Died in a car accident

    B. Went to jail

    C. Went with his family to Germany

    D. Rode a unicycle

13. While Carol was in the car with Jerry

    A. Another car tried to run them off the road

    B. He tried to get her to take some drugs

    C. He fell asleep and she had to drive the rest of the way home

    D. He told her that he was really a police detective

14. Where did Carol get the money to visit Liz at the Courtneys?

    A. Ellen sent it to her

    B. She found it in one of her mother's old purses

    C. She earned it baby-sitting

    D. None of the above

325
The Ghost Belonged to Me
Richard Peck

True or False. Decide whether each statement is true or false. Mark your answer sheet accordingly.

1. Blossom Culp told Alexander that her mother knew there was a ghost in his barn.

2. The Van Deeters were the leading family of Bluff City.

3. Uncle Miles had buried Inez Dumaine in Alexander's yard.

4. The ghost of Inez wanted revenge for her murder.

5. The loft of the barn was wet and swampy when the ghost appeared.

6. Inez's ghost wanted Blossom to be her friend.

7. Inez's ghost warned Alexander that the trolley was in danger.

8. Tom came to Lucille's coming-out party drunk.

9. Alexander never told anyone about the ghost of Inez Dumaine.

10. Alexander, Uncle Miles, and Blossom went to New Orleans.

11. Inez had been robbed after she died.

Multiple Choice. Read each question. Decide which statement best answers the question. Mark your answer sheet accordingly.

12. The ghost of Inez Dumaine wanted

    A. Revenge for her murder

    B. Her body to be returned to her home and buried

    C. Someone to be her friend

    D. A chance to correct the mistakes she had made

13. The ghost of Inez was accompanied by

    A. The ghost of her dog, Trixie

    B. The ghost of her cat, Bubbles

    C. A torch that burned day and night

    D. An owl with red eyes

14. Blossom was given

    A. A brooch from Inez

    B. A diamond from Inez

    C. The gift of knowing the spirit world

    D. The ability to predict the future

326
Shades of Gray
Carolyn Reeder

True or False. Decide whether each statement is true or false. Mark your answer sheet accordingly.

1. Will's mother's will said that he should live with his relatives.
2. Will Page's family had owned slaves.
3. Some of Jed Jones's neighbors disliked him because he hadn't fought in the war.
4. Will refused to call Mr. Jones "Uncle Jed."
5. Both armies had stolen food and livestock from local farmers.
6. Meg was ashamed that her father hadn't fought in the war.
7. One of Will's chores was to check the trap line.
8. Will had a fight with Hank.
9. Uncle Jed was against slavery.
10. The sick Yankee stayed for several days at the Jones's farm.
11. Will killed a Yankee soldier with his father's sword.

Multiple Choice. Read each question. Decide which statement best answers the question. Mark your answer sheet accordingly.

12. Will learned that

    A. His uncle was a brave man who did what he believed was right

    B. His Uncle Jed was a Yankee spy

    C. Meg was married to a Yankee soldier

    D. He hated farm life

13. Will's brother, Charlie Page

    A. Ran away from home

    B. Was killed by Yankee sentries

    C. Told Will to leave the Jones's place as soon as he could

    D. Beat up Hank

14. Will decided to

    A. Move back to his hometown and live with Dr. Martin

    B. Move to Ohio

    C. Move to Georgia

    D. Stay with his aunt and uncle

327
Missing May
Cynthia Rylant

True or False. Decide whether each statement is true or false. Mark your answer sheet accordingly.

1. Summer and Uncle Ob lived in West Virginia.

2. Uncle Ob and Aunt May were poor.

3. Cletus Underwood liked to collect pictures.

4. Summer was an orphan living with other relatives when Uncle Ob and Aunt May found her and took her home.

5. Summer was in love with Cletus Underwood.

6. Cletus wanted to see the state capitol in Charleston.

7. Ob thought he felt May's spirit.

8. Cletus suggested Ob take up jogging to help him get over May's death.

9. The Reverend Miriam Young refused to help Ob contact May.

10. Summer thought that Cletus was strange.

11. Ob made whirligigs.

Multiple Choice. Read each question. Decide which statement best answers the question. Mark your answer sheet accordingly.

12. When Ob, Summer, and Cletus reached Glen Meadows they found that

    A. Reverend Young was a fraud

    B. Reverend Young was dead

    C. Reverend Young charged $500 to contact the dead

    D. None of the above

13. Summer knew that Ob was giving up on life when he

    A. Didn't wake her up for school

    B. Began crying and couldn't stop

    C. Made out his will

    D. Began shopping for his coffin

14. Ob showed that he had decided to go on with life when he

    A. Got a job in a gas station

    B. Took Summer and Cletus to the state capitol

    C. Flirted with the Reverend Miriam Young

    D. Made a statue of May and put it in the garden

328
There's a Boy in the Girls' Bathroom
Louis Sachar

True or False. Decide whether each statement is true or false. Mark your answer sheet accordingly.

1. Both Bradley and Jeff went into the girls' bathroom.
2. At first, Bradley was rude to Carla.
3. Some of the parents didn't like Carla.
4. The first time Bradley did his homework, he ripped it up.
5. Melinda gave both Bradley and Jeff black eyes.
6. Bradley played with a collection of toy animals.
7. Jeff punched Bradley in the stomach.
8. Carla gave Bradley a book.
9. Bradley's father was happy to help him with his homework.
10. Carla believed that Bradley could be a good student if he wanted to be.
11. Colleen liked Jeff.

Multiple Choice. Read each question. Decide which statement best answers the question. Mark your answer sheet accordingly.

12. Bradley was nervous about going to Colleen's party because he
    A. Would be the only boy there
    B. Was afraid of Colleen
    C. Didn't know what to do at a party
    D. Was afraid that his father would call him a sissy

13. Bradley didn't think he could do well in school because
    A. Everyone thought he was a monster and would never change
    B. He knew he was stupid
    C. Carla said he should go ahead and flunk
    D. His parents didn't care how he did in school

14. Bradley's gift from the heart to Carla was
    A. His pet rat
    B. A promise to not run away from home
    C. His pet spider
    D. His favorite animal, Ronnie

329
The War with Grandpa
Robert Kimmel Smith

True or False. Decide whether each statement is true or false. Mark your answer sheet accordingly.

1. Peter tried to argue with his parents against giving up his room, but their minds were made up.

2. Peter had always shared a room with his sister, Jennifer.

3. Peter was scared at night in his new room.

4. When Grandpa Jack first arrived, he acted very sad and quiet.

5. Grandpa Jack told Peter's parents that Peter had declared war on him.

6. The night that Peter declared war, Grandpa Jack put spiders in Peter's bed.

7. Grandpa Jack wouldn't take Peter fishing because he didn't like the way Peter was behaving.

8. As the war went on, Grandpa Jack became very unhappy.

9. Steve and Billy told Peter not to try to get his room back.

10. Peter set Grandpa Jack's underwear on fire.

11. Grandpa Jack put green food color in Peter's goldfish bowl.

Multiple Choice. Read each question. Decide which statement best answers the question. Mark your answer sheet accordingly.

12. Why was the war difficult for Peter?

    A. It wasn't difficult; Peter thought it was fun and exciting

    B. Peter was angry at his grandfather, but he also loved him very much

    C. Jennifer helped Grandpa Jack so it was two against one

    D. His parents punished him every time he did something to Grandpa Jack

13. What ended the war?

    A. Peter felt bad after he hid Grandpa's false teeth

    B. Grandpa felt bad after he made Peter late for school

    C. Peter's parents told them to stop fighting

    D. Both Peter and Grandpa Jack felt bad after Jennifer was hurt

14. What solution did Grandpa Jack and Peter work out?

    A. Grandpa Jack decided he would move back to Florida

    B. Grandpa Jack and Peter decided to share Peter's room

    C. Peter got his room back and Grandpa made an apartment in the basement

    D. Grandpa Jack moved into the house next door

330
Maniac Magee
Jerry Spinelli

True or False. Decide whether each statement is true or false. Mark your answer sheet accordingly.

1. Maniac avoided the East End because he was afraid to be in the black part of town.

2. The blacks and whites of Two Mills lived in separate sections of town.

3. Maniac left the Beales because Mrs. Beale was afraid to have a white child in her house.

4. When Maniac first arrived in Two Mills, Mars Bar Thompson was unfriendly to him.

5. Maniac ran away from his aunt and uncle because they beat him.

6. For part of the winter, Maniac lived in the buffalo pen at the zoo.

7. Maniac moved out of the bandshell after Grayson died.

8. The McNabs' house was filthy.

9. Maniac taught Grayson how to read.

10. Mars Bar went with Maniac to visit the McNabs.

11. Maniac was adopted by the McNabs.

Multiple Choice. Read each question. Decide which statement best answers the question. Mark your answer sheet accordingly.

12. What was unusual about the McNabs' house?

    A. It was pink

    B. There was a pillbox in the dining room

    C. It was in the middle of a swamp

    D. All of the above

13. Amanda and Mars Bar finally convinced Maniac to

    A. Return to the Beales' house and live with Amanda's family

    B. Stay out of the East End because it caused too much trouble to have him around

    C. Go to the orphanage

    D. Go back and live with his aunt and uncle

14. The relationship between Mars Bar and Maniac began to change after

    A. Mars Bar hit a home run

    B. Mars Bar scored a touchdown

    C. Mars Bar and Maniac began running together

    D. Mars Bar ran away to live in the zoo

From *More Quizzes for Great Children's Books.* © 1996. Teacher Ideas Press. (800) 237-6124.

331
Space Station Seventh Grade
Jerry Spinelli

True or False. Decide whether each statement is true or false. Mark your answer sheet accordingly.

1. Jason's father wanted to join the Jewish faith.

2. When Jason was suspended from school, Ham grounded him for one week

3. Debbie Breen was in love with Jason.

4. Jason played on the junior-high basketball team.

5. Timmy kept taking Jason's dinosaurs.

6. Jason called his sister "cootyhead."

7. Peter and his little brother, Kippy, were often together.

8. Jason went out for track because he had always wanted to be a track star.

9. Jason was the fastest person on the seventh-grade track team.

10. Debbie Breen went to Jason's house every Tuesday during the school year.

11. Richie and Jason put ants in the fudge they made for cooking class.

Multiple Choice. Read each question. Decide which statement best answers the question. Mark your answer sheet accordingly.

12. Jason was suspended from school because he

    A. Made a moose call while Marceline was playing her trombone at a talent show

    B. Pulled the fire alarm after Peter dared him to do it

    C. Put a pail of cow manure in Ralphie's desk

    D. Accidentally broke the window in the principal's office

13. Which character died?

    A. Peter

    B. Richie

    C. Marceline

    D. Kippy

14. Which statement best describes how Jason's feelings changed?

    A. He went from disliking Marceline to liking her

    B. He started out hating Debbie Breen but ended up going steady with her

    C. He went from being best friends with Richie to deciding never to talk to him again

    D. None of the above

332
Stealing Home
Mary Stolz

True or False. Decide whether each statement is true or false. Mark your answer sheet accordingly.

1. Thomas and his grandfather didn't watch TV.
2. Ivan was a duck.
3. Ringo, the cat, hated Aunt Linzy.
4. Grandpa's favorite sport was soccer.
5. Thomas and his grandfather loved to fish.
6. Aunt Linzy was a vegetarian.
7. Thomas took his baseball glove almost everywhere he went.
8. Aunt Linzy painted Grandpa's house red.
9. Thomas had to let Aunt Linzy move into his bedroom.
10. Ivan bit Aunt Linzy every time she came near him.

Multiple Choice. Read each question. Decide which statement best answers the question. Mark your answer sheet accordingly.

11. Aunt Linzy
    A. Was constantly cleaning
    B. Didn't like fishing
    C. Didn't like baseball
    D. All of the above

12. Mr. McCallam
    A. Gave Aunt Linzy a job managing his motel
    B. Fell in love with Aunt Linzy and married her
    C. Played shortstop for the Chicago Cubs
    D. None of the above

13. When did Aunt Linzy quarrel with Grandpa and Thomas?
    A. Whenever Ringo ate her mail
    B. Most of the time
    C. Never
    D. Whenever Ivan bit her

14. Thomas and Grandpa listened to baseball games on the radio because
    A. Grandpa felt that radio made you use your imagination
    B. Their next-door neighbor was a radio announcer
    C. Aunt Linzy hated the sound of the TV
    D. The TV was broken

333
Let the Circle Be Unbroken
Mildred D. Taylor

True or False. Decide whether each statement is true or false. Mark your answer sheet accordingly.

1. Mr. Jamison was unpopular with the white community.
2. Mr. Wheeler wanted to form a farmers' union with both white and Negro members.
3. Wordell was mentally retarded.
4. No Negroes in Cassie's area were allowed to vote.
5. The large landowners were cheating their tenants out of their government money.
6. The Logan family were sharecroppers for Mr. Granger.
7. Dubé was very involved in the union.
8. Suzella wanted to pass as white.
9. Uncle Hammer felt that interracial marriage was a good thing.
10. Moe and Stacey ran away to find work.
11. Negroes were not allowed to use the bathrooms in the courthouse.

Multiple Choice. Read each question. Decide which statement best answers the question. Mark your answer sheet accordingly.

12. After Mr. Jamison proved that T. J. couldn't have been the murderer
    A. The sheriff arrested R. W. and Melvin Simms
    B. The jury returned a verdict of not guilty
    C. The jury couldn't reach a verdict
    D. The jury returned a verdict of guilty

13. When Stacey cut sugar cane, he
    A. Earned more money than his father
    B. Was treated like a slave
    C. Accidentally killed a white man
    D. Lost the use of his right arm

14. What happened when Mrs. Lee Annie tried to register to vote?
    A. She was put in jail
    B. The clerks laughed at her
    C. Mr. Granger threw her and her family out of their home
    D. She was fined $1,000

334
The Road to Memphis
Mildred D. Taylor

True or False. Decide whether each statement is true or false. Mark your answer sheet accordingly.

1. Jeremy Simms fought his cousins to keep them from bothering Harris.
2. Sissy said that Clarence might not be the man who got her pregnant.
3. Cassie wanted to marry Moe before she finished high school.
4. Clarence wasn't sure he wanted to marry Sissy.
5. Mr. Jamison suggested to Cassie and Stacey that it would be better for Moe to go North than to face the law in Mississippi.
6. Some white men yelled at Cassie because she tried to use a "Whites Only" rest room.
7. When Stacey, Cassie, and Moe reached Memphis, they were arrested by the state police.
8. Cassie tried to convince Clarence to talk with Sissy.
9. Leon, Troy, and Statler were publicly humiliating Clarence.
10. Mr. Simms beat up Jeremy for helping Moe.
11. Uncle Hammer crashed his car into Mr. Simms's house.

Multiple Choice. Read each question. Decide which statement best answers the question. Mark your answer sheet accordingly.

12. Jeremy Simms was unusual because
    A. He was nearly seven feet tall
    B. He wasn't prejudiced against Negroes
    C. He was the only Sioux Indian in the state of Mississippi
    D. He wanted to become president of the United States

13. Moe struck out at three white men because
    A. They were insulting him and Cassie
    B. They said his mother was a prostitute
    C. They were trying to burn down his house
    D. They were going to kill Clarence

14. Which statement about Solomon Brady is correct?
    A. He was a black man who owned his own newspaper in Memphis
    B. He was the head of the Mississippi branch of the KKK
    C. He controlled the town of Strawberry
    D. He had made a fortune smuggling drugs from Mexico into the United States

335
The Boxcar Children
Gertrude Chandler Warner. (Boxcar Mystery #1)

True or False. Decide whether each statement is true or false. Mark your answer sheet accordingly.

1. The Boxcar Children thought their grandfather didn't like them.

2. The baker's wife wanted to send Benny to the children's home.

3. Henry robbed people to get money.

4. The Boxcar Children named their dog Rover.

5. The Boxcar Children made beds out of pine needles.

6. Henry won a race.

7. Dr. Moore had Henry work for him.

8. The children made a fireplace of stones.

9. There was a little stream close to the boxcar.

10. Jessie's refrigerator was a hole in a rock behind a little waterfall.

11. Dr. Moore adopted the children.

Multiple Choice. Read each question. Decide which statement best answers the question. Mark your answer sheet accordingly.

12. Jessie, Benny, and Violet found plates and cups for the boxcar in

    A. Dr. Moore's house

    B. An old store

    C. An empty house

    D. A dump

13. The children named their dog

    A. Rover

    B. Fido

    C. Watch

    D. Doggie

14. What finally happened to the boxcar?

    A. It was moved to their grandfather's house

    B. It burned down

    C. It was pulled away by a train

    D. It rolled away during a thunderstorm

336
Surprise Island
Gertrude Chandler Warner. (Boxcar Mystery #2)

True or False. Decide whether each statement is true or false. Mark your answer sheet accordingly.

1. Grandfather Alden sent the children to the island because they were bad in school.

2. The children lived in Captain Daniel's shack.

3. Joe knew a lot about nature.

4. Captain Daniel said that Joe was a handyman.

5. The children found a cat in the yellow house.

6. Violet learned to play the violin.

7. The children made a museum in the barn.

8. Joe was afraid of Henry.

9. Benny found an Indian bone.

10. Jessie was a good cook.

11. Watch was with the children on the island.

Multiple Choice. Read each question. Decide which statement best answers the question. Mark your answer sheet accordingly.

12. The children never visited

   A. The barn

   B. Captain Daniel's shack

   C. Indian Point

   D. The yellow house

13. On the island, the children lived in

   A. The barn

   B. Captain Daniel's shack

   C. Indian Point

   D. The yellow house

14. Joe was

   A. The children's half-brother

   B. The children's cousin

   C. Captain Daniel's father

   D. A bank robber

337
The Yellow House Mystery
Gertrude Chandler Warner. (Boxcar Mystery #3)

True or False. Decide whether each statement is true or false. Mark your answer sheet accordingly.

1. Joe and Alice were married in Grandfather Alden's house.

2. A man was murdered in the yellow house on the island.

3. Bill had disappeared from the island many years ago.

4. Benny found a letter hidden behind a brick on the chimney.

5. The Boxcar Children followed the Bear Trail in a motorboat.

6. Grandfather Alden went with the children on the Bear Trail.

7. Bill sold two racehorses and never gave Mr. Alden the money.

8. Benny never caught any fish.

9. The Boxcar Children thought Bill might be somewhere along the Bear Trail.

10. Violet was carried away by a bear.

11. Alice didn't like Benny.

Multiple Choice. Read each question. Decide which statement best answers the question. Mark your answer sheet accordingly.

12. Who found the missing money?

    A. Henry

    B. Jessie

    C. Violet

    D. Benny

13. Bill was

    A. Living as a hermit

    B. Hiding in an outhouse

    C. The mayor of Old Village

    D. A forest ranger

14. The Boxcar Children knew that Bill must be nearby when

    A. Violet saw him in a dream

    B. They realized the house they were in was the same design as the yellow house

    C. The Indians told them about an old man with two old horses

    D. Watch began to bark

338
Christina's Ghost
Betty Ren Wright

True or False. Decide whether each statement is true or false. Mark your answer sheet accordingly.

1. Christina and Jenny went to stay with Uncle Ralph after Grandma went to the hospital.

2. Uncle Ralph didn't like children.

3. The ghost of the little boy would appear whenever Christina was happy.

4. The first time Uncle Ralph saw the ghost of the little boy, he fainted in terror.

5. Christina learned that there were at least seven ghosts haunting the mansion.

6. Christina learned that a boy and a man had been murdered in the old mansion many years ago.

7. Uncle Ralph asked Christina to tell him scary ghost stories every night.

8. Christina spent much of her time teaching herself to swim in the lake behind the mansion.

9. Even after Uncle Ralph saw the ghost of Russell Charles, he claimed that he didn't believe in ghosts.

10. Whenever the ghost of Dixon appeared, a freezing wind blew.

11. The only person to whom the ghost of Russell Charles spoke was Jenny.

Multiple Choice. Read each question. Decide which statement best answers the question. Mark your answer sheet accordingly.

12. The relationship between Christina and Uncle Ralph began to change after

    A. He saw the ghost of Russell Charles

    B. He saved her from drowning

    C. She began reading riddles to Uncle Ralph

    D. She told him she thought he was brave

13. The ghosts were haunting the mansion because

    A. Their bodies hadn't been properly buried

    B. The identity of their murderer had never been discovered

    C. Before they died, they had promised not to leave until Mr. Charles returned home

    D. The stolen stamps had never been located

14. The haunting of the mansion ended when

    A. Uncle Ralph buried the skulls Christina found in the basement

    B. Uncle Ralph was arrested for the murders

    C. Christina told the ghosts that they were scaring her

    D. Christina and Uncle Ralph took the stamps to the police

339
The Dollhouse Murders
Betty Ren Wright

True or False. Decide whether each statement is true or false. Mark your answer sheet accordingly.

1. Amy's sister, Louann, lived in a group home for retarded children.

2. It was often Amy's job to take care of Louann.

3. Aunt Clare asked Amy to stay with her.

4. The dollhouse in Aunt Clare's attic was a copy of the White House in Washington, D.C.

5. Aunt Clare's grandparents were both murdered in the house Aunt Clare was living in.

6. Amy's friends seemed uncomfortable around Louann.

7. The four dolls in the dollhouse looked like Aunt Clare and Mr. Treloar and their grandparents.

8. Aunt Clare didn't like the dollhouse.

9. When Louann was brought to Amy's birthday party, Ellen and Kathy quietly left.

10. Aunt Clare laughed when she thought Amy was playing with the dolls in the dollhouse.

11. Aunt Clare's fiancé, Tom Keaton, died the night her grandparents were murdered.

Multiple Choice. Read each question. Decide which statement best answers the question. Mark your answer sheet accordingly.

12. Which of the following facts about the dollhouse are true?

    A. The dolls kept moving themselves to where the people they represented were positioned on the night of the murders

    B. The grandmother doll cried and moved miniature books while Amy and Louann watched

    C. The dollhouse lit up by itself

    D. All of the above

13. What did Aunt Clare secretly feel guilty about?

    A. She thought Tom had killed her grandparents

    B. She knew she had left the door unlocked

    C. She felt she should have been there to help her grandparents

    D. She had been bragging in town about how rich her grandparents were

14. What finally happened to the dollhouse?

    A. It collapsed into dust as soon as Aunt Clare found the message

    B. It burst into flames as soon as the murderer walked into the attic

    C. Aunt Clare locked it in the coal bin

    D. Aunt Clare gave it to Louann

340
Ghosts Beneath Our Feet
Betty Ren Wright

True or False. Decide whether each statement is true or false. Mark your answer sheet accordingly.

1. Uncle Frank wanted Katie's family to take care of his house while he was away.

2. Nancy Trelawny told Katie that knackers were the ghosts of dead miners.

3. Jay and Skip were both interested in motorcycles.

4. Jay was glad to be in Newquay because he hated Milwaukee.

5. Katie learned from Gram that Uncle Frank's son had died in a mine accident.

6. The ghost of May Nichols would only appear in the mirror in the upstairs hallway of Uncle Frank's house.

7. Both Jay and Katie were able to see the ghost of May Nichols.

8. Uncle Frank's house was shifting and settling because the hill it was sitting on had been weakened by the mine.

9. Skip Poldeen was widely admired in Newquay because of his honesty and kindness.

10. Jay didn't feel he belonged with Katie and her mother.

11. Uncle Frank warned Katie that Jay was evil and someday would bring heartache and ruin to her family.

Multiple Choice. Read each question. Decide which statement best answers the question. Mark your answer sheet accordingly.

12. What scared both Katie and Joan in the shaft house?

    A. The knackers screaming and yelling down in the pit

    B. A tape recording hidden in the ore car saying, "Help us! Save us!"

    C. A puppy sitting in the ore car

    D. The ghost of Uncle Frank's son

13. What was the ghost of May Nichols trying to communicate?

    A. She wanted everyone to get out of Uncle Frank's house before the hill collapsed

    B. She wanted her body to be buried next to the body of her husband

    C. That the man who caused the mine disaster was still in Newquay

    D. That there was a treasure in stolen diamonds hidden in the attic

14. At the end of the story

    A. Uncle Frank married Nancy Trelawny

    B. Katie, Katie's mother, and Jay decided to stay in Newquay

    C. May Nichols's body was properly buried

    D. Jay felt that he was part of the family

PART
III

Answers

Answer Key

221

Adler, Susan S. *Meet Samantha.* (American Girls Collection)
CATEGORY: A
POINT VALUE: 5

1. F	5. F	9. F	13. A
2. F	6. F	10. F	14. B
3. F	7. T	11. T	
4. F	8. F	12. C	

222

Porter, Connie. *Meet Addy.* (American Girls Collection)
CATEGORY: A
POINT VALUE: 5

1. T	5. F	9. T	13. D
2. T	6. T	10. F	14. B
3. F	7. F	11. T	
4. T	8. F	12. B	

223

Shaw, Janet. *Meet Kirsten.* (American Girls Collection)
CATEGORY: A
POINT VALUE: 5

1. T	5. T	9. F	13. A
2. F	6. F	10. F	14. A
3. F	7. F	11. T	
4. F	8. T	12. C	

224

Tripp, Valerie. *Meet Felicity.* (American Girls Collection)
CATEGORY: A
POINT VALUE: 5

1. F	5. T	9. F	13. B
2. T	6. F	10. T	14. A
3. T	7. F	11. T	
4. F	8. T	12. C	

225

Tripp, Valerie. *Meet Molly.* (American Girls Collection)
CATEGORY: A
POINT VALUE: 5

1. F	5. T	9. T	13. C
2. T	6. T	10. F	14. A
3. T	7. T	11. T	
4. F	8. F	12. A	

226

AVI. *Blue Heron.*
CATEGORY: C
POINT VALUE: 15

1. T	5. T	9. F	13. C
2. F	6. T	10. T	14. B
3. T	7. T	11. A	
4. F	8. T	12. C	

227

AVI. *Punch with Judy.*
CATEGORY: D
POINT VALUE: 10

1. T	5. F	9. T	13. C
2. T	6. T	10. F	14. D
3. F	7. F	11. T	
4. F	8. T	12. A	

228

AVI. *The True Confessions of Charlotte Doyle.*
CATEGORY: E
POINT VALUE: 15

1. T	5. F	9. T	13. B
2. F	6. T	10. T	14. D
3. T	7. T	11. T	
4. F	8. F	12. B	

229

AVI. *Who Was That Masked Man, Anyway?*
CATEGORY: C
POINT VALUE: 10

1. T	5. T	9. T	13. D
2. T	6. T	10. T	14. C
3. F	7. T	11. T	
4. F	8. F	12. A	

230

Banks, Lynne Reid. *The Indian in the Cupboard.*
CATEGORY: B
POINT VALUE: 10

1. F	5. T	9. T	13. A
2. F	6. F	10. T	14. D
3. T	7. F	11. F	
4. F	8. F	12. C	

231
Banks, Lynne Reid. *The Mystery of the Cupboard.*
CATEGORY: B
POINT VALUE: 10

1. F	5. T	9. T	13. A
2. T	6. T	10. T	14. B
3. F	7. F	11. T	
4. T	8. F	12. B	

232
Banks, Lynne Reid. *One More River.*
CATEGORY: D
POINT VALUE: 15

1. F	5. T	9. F	13. A
2. T	6. F	10. T	14. B
3. T	7. T	11. T	
4. F	8. F	12. C	

233
Banks, Lynne Reid. *The Return of the Indian.*
CATEGORY: B
POINT VALUE: 10

1. T	5. F	9. F	13. A
2. T	6. F	10. T	14. A
3. F	7. F	11. T	
4. F	8. T	12. C	

234
Banks, Lynne Reid. *The Secret of the Indian.*
CATEGORY: B
POINT VALUE: 10

1. F	5. F	9. F	13. B
2. T	6. T	10. F	14. A
3. F	7. T	11. T	
4. T	8. F	12. B	

235
Bauer, Marion Dane. *Face to Face.*
CATEGORY: C
POINT VALUE: 15

1. T	5. F	9. T	13. A
2. T	6. T	10. F	14. C
3. F	7. F	11. F	
4. T	8. T	12. C	

236
Bauer, Marion Dane. *On My Honor.*
CATEGORY: C
POINT VALUE: 5

1. T	5. T	9. T	13. A
2. T	6. T	10. F	14. D
3. T	7. T	11. F	
4. F	8. F	12. C	

237
Bellairs, John. *The House with a Clock in Its Walls.*
CATEGORY: D
POINT VALUE: 10

1. T	5. F	9. F	13. D
2. T	6. T	10. F	14. B
3. T	7. T	11. F	
4. F	8. F	12. A	

238
Bellairs, John. *The Letter, the Witch, and the Ring.*
CATEGORY: C
POINT VALUE: 10

1. T	5. T	9. T	13. C
2. F	6. T	10. T	14. D
3. F	7. T	11. T	
4. T	8. F	12. A	

239
Bellairs, John. *The Mansion in the Mist.*
CATEGORY: C
POINT VALUE: 10

1. T	5. T	9. T	13. B
2. F	6. F	10. F	14. A
3. T	7. F	11. C	
4. T	8. F	12. A	

240
Blume, Judy. *Are You There God? It's Me, Margaret.*
CATEGORY: C
POINT VALUE: 10

1. F	5. F	9. T	13. A
2. F	6. F	10. F	14. A
3. T	7. T	11. F	
4. F	8. T	12. B	

241
Blume, Judy. *Fudge-A-Mania.*
CATEGORY: A
POINT VALUE: 10

1. T	5. F	9. T	13. D
2. T	6. T	10. T	14. C
3. T	7. T	11. B	
4. T	8. T	12. A	

242
Blume, Judy. *Here's to You, Rachel Robinson.*
CATEGORY: D
POINT VALUE: 10

1. F	5. F	9. F	13. A
2. F	6. T	10. T	14. A
3. F	7. T	11. T	
4. F	8. F	12. B	

243
Blume, Judy. *Then Again, Maybe I Won't.*
CATEGORY: D
POINT VALUE: 10

1. T	5. T	9. F	13. A
2. T	6. F	10. T	14. D
3. F	7. T	11. F	
4. F	8. F	12. C	

244
Byars, Betsy. *A Blossom Promise.*
CATEGORY: B
POINT VALUE: 10

1. T	5. T	9. F	13. D
2. F	6. F	10. F	14. A
3. F	7. F	11. F	
4. T	8. T	12. A	

245
Byars, Betsy. *The Blossoms and the Green Phantom.*
CATEGORY: B
POINT VALUE: 10

1. T	5. T	9. F	13. A
2. F	6. T	10. F	14. B
3. F	7. T	11. T	
4. F	8. T	12. B	

246
Byars, Betsy. *The Blossoms Meet the Vulture Lady.*
CATEGORY: B
POINT VALUE: 10

1. T	5. T	9. F	13. D
2. F	6. T	10. T	14. A
3. T	7. T	11. F	
4. F	8. T	12. A	

247
Byars, Betsy. *The Not-Just-Anybody Family.*
CATEGORY: B
POINT VALUE: 10

1. T	5. F	9. T	13. A
2. T	6. T	10. F	14. A
3. F	7. F	11. T	
4. T	8. T	12. A	

248
Byars, Betsy. *Wanted . . . Mud Blossom.*
CATEGORY: B
POINT VALUE: 10

1. F	5. F	9. T	13. B
2. F	6. F	10. T	14. C
3. T	7. F	11. T	
4. F	8. T	12. A	

249
Cassedy, Sylvia. *Behind the Attic Wall.*
CATEGORY: C
POINT VALUE: 20

1. F	5. T	9. F	13. D
2. T	6. F	10. T	14. A
3. T	7. F	11. T	
4. T	8. T	12. A	

250
Cassedy, Sylvia. *Lucie Babbidge's House.*
CATEGORY: C
POINT VALUE: 15

1. F	5. T	9. T	13. B
2. F	6. T	10. T	14. A
3. T	7. T	11. T	
4. T	8. F	12. A	

251
Christopher, Matt. *Front Court Hex.*
CATEGORY: A
POINT VALUE: 10

1.	T	5.	T	9.	T	13.	B
2.	F	6.	T	10.	T	14.	A
3.	T	7.	T	11.	T		
4.	F	8.	F	12.	B		

252
Christopher, Matt. *Johnny Long Legs.*
CATEGORY: A
POINT VALUE: 10

1.	T	5.	T	9.	T	13.	B
2.	F	6.	T	10.	F	14.	A
3.	T	7.	T	11.	F		
4.	T	8.	T	12.	D		

253
Christopher, Matt. *No Arm in Left Field.*
CATEGORY: A
POINT VALUE: 10

1.	T	5.	F	9.	T	13.	B
2.	T	6.	F	10.	T	14.	A
3.	F	7.	F	11.	T		
4.	T	8.	T	12.	B		

254
Christopher, Matt. *Red-Hot Hightops.*
CATEGORY: A
POINT VALUE: 10

1.	T	5.	F	9.	T	13.	C
2.	T	6.	F	10.	F	14.	D
3.	T	7.	T	11.	T		
4.	T	8.	F	12.	A		

255
Cleary, Beverly. *Muggie Maggie.*
CATEGORY: A
POINT VALUE: 5

1.	T	5.	T	9.	T	13.	B
2.	T	6.	T	10.	T	14.	A
3.	T	7.	T	11.	T		
4.	T	8.	F	12.	D		

256
Cleary, Beverly. *Strider.*
CATEGORY: D
POINT VALUE: 10

1.	F	5.	T	9.	F	13.	B
2.	T	6.	F	10.	T	14.	C
3.	T	7.	T	11.	T		
4.	F	8.	F	12.	C		

257
Coville, Bruce. *The Ghost in the Big Brass Bed.*
CATEGORY: C
POINT VALUE: 10

1.	T	5.	F	9.	T	13.	B
2.	F	6.	F	10.	F	14.	B
3.	T	7.	T	11.	F		
4.	T	8.	T	12.	D		

258
Coville, Bruce. *The Ghost Wore Gray.*
CATEGORY: C
POINT VALUE: 10

1.	F	5.	F	9.	F	13.	D
2.	T	6.	F	10.	F	14.	D
3.	T	7.	T	11.	T		
4.	T	8.	F	12.	A		

259
Coville, Bruce. *My Teacher Flunked the Planet.*
CATEGORY: C
POINT VALUE: 10

1.	T	5.	T	9.	T	13.	B
2.	T	6.	F	10.	T	14.	A
3.	T	7.	T	11.	F		
4.	T	8.	F	12.	C		

260
Coville, Bruce. *My Teacher Is an Alien.*
CATEGORY: C
POINT VALUE: 10

1.	F	5.	F	9.	T	13.	D
2.	T	6.	F	10.	F	14.	C
3.	F	7.	F	11.	T		
4.	T	8.	T	12.	A		

261
Dahl, Roald. *Charlie and the Chocolate Factory.*
CATEGORY: B
POINT VALUE: 10

1. T	5. F	9. T	13. C
2. T	6. T	10. T	14. D
3. T	7. T	11. F	
4. F	8. F	12. A	

262
Dahl, Roald. *Charlie and the Great Glass Elevator.*
CATEGORY: B
POINT VALUE: 10

1. F	5. T	9. T	13. A
2. F	6. T	10. T	14. B
3. F	7. F	11. T	
4. T	8. F	12. B	

263
Dahl, Roald. *James and the Giant Peach.*
CATEGORY: B
POINT VALUE: 10

1. F	5. F	9. F	13. B
2. T	6. F	10. F	14. C
3. T	7. F	11. D	
4. T	8. T	12. A	

264
Dahl, Roald. *The Witches.*
CATEGORY: B
POINT VALUE: 15

1. T	5. T	9. F	13. C
2. T	6. F	10. T	14. D
3. F	7. F	11. T	
4. F	8. T	12. A	

265
Dorris, Michael. *Morning Girl.*
CATEGORY: B
POINT VALUE: 5

1. F	5. F	9. T	13. A
2. T	6. T	10. F	14. B
3. F	7. F	11. T	
4. F	8. T	12. C	

266
Fleischman, Sid. *Jim Ugly.*
CATEGORY: B
POINT VALUE: 10

1. F	5. T	9. T	13. D
2. T	6. T	10. F	14. A
3. T	7. F	11. T	
4. T	8. T	12. C	

267
Fleischman, Sid. *The Midnight Horse.*
CATEGORY: D
POINT VALUE: 5

1. T	5. F	9. T	13. A
2. T	6. T	10. T	14. D
3. F	7. T	11. T	
4. T	8. F	12. B	

268
Fleischman, Sid. *The Whipping Boy.*
CATEGORY: C
POINT VALUE: 5

1. T	5. F	9. T	13. C
2. F	6. T	10. T	14. A
3. T	7. F	11. T	
4. T	8. F	12. A	

269
Fox, Paula. *Monkey Island.*
CATEGORY: C
POINT VALUE: 10

1. F	5. F	9. T	13. A
2. T	6. T	10. F	14. D
3. T	7. F	11. F	
4. F	8. T	12. B	

270
Freedman, Russell. *Franklin Delano Roosevelt.*
CATEGORY: E
POINT VALUE: 15

1. F	5. F	9. F	13. A
2. T	6. F	10. F	14. B
3. T	7. T	11. T	
4. T	8. T	12. D	

271
Freedman, Russell. *Lincoln: A Photobiography.*
CATEGORY: E
POINT VALUE: 15

1. T	5. F	9. T	13. D
2. F	6. F	10. F	14. A
3. F	7. T	11. F	
4. F	8. T	12. D	

272
Freedman, Russell. *The Wright Brothers.*
CATEGORY: E
POINT VALUE: 15

1. F	5. T	9. T	13. A
2. T	6. F	10. F	14. A
3. T	7. T	11. F	
4. F	8. T	12. D	

273
George, Jean Craighead. *The Missing 'Gator of Gumbo Limbo.*
CATEGORY: C
POINT VALUE: 10

1. F	5. T	9. F	13. A
2. T	6. F	10. T	14. B
3. F	7. T	11. F	
4. T	8. F	12. B	

274
George, Jean Craighead. *Shark Beneath the Reef.*
CATEGORY: C
POINT VALUE: 10

1. T	5. T	9. F	13. A
2. T	6. T	10. F	14. A
3. T	7. F	11. B	
4. F	8. F	12. C	

275
Graeber, Charlotte Towner. *Fudge.*
CATEGORY: A
POINT VALUE: 5

1. F	5. T	9. F	13. D
2. T	6. T	10. F	14. D
3. T	7. T	11. T	
4. F	8. T	12. B	

276
Hahn, Mary Downing. *Wait Till Helen Comes: A Ghost Story.*
CATEGORY: D
POINT VALUE: 10

1. T	5. T	9. T	13. A
2. T	6. T	10. F	14. C
3. F	7. F	11. T	
4. T	8. T	12. B	

277
Hamilton, Virginia. *Cousins.*
CATEGORY: D
POINT VALUE: 10

1. T	5. F	9. T	13. A
2. T	6. F	10. T	14. B
3. T	7. F	11. F	
4. T	8. T	12. D	

278
Hamilton, Virginia. *Zeely.*
CATEGORY: C
POINT VALUE: 10

1. T	5. T	9. T	13. A
2. T	6. F	10. F	14. B
3. T	7. F	11. T	
4. F	8. F	12. C	

279
Hinton, S. E. *The Outsiders.*
CATEGORY: D
POINT VALUE: 15

1. T	5. T	9. T	13. A
2. T	6. F	10. F	14. C
3. T	7. T	11. T	
4. T	8. F	12. A	

280
Hinton, S. E. *Tex.*
CATEGORY: D
POINT VALUE: 15

1. F	5. T	9. T	13. C
2. T	6. T	10. T	14. A
3. T	7. T	11. T	
4. F	8. F	12. A	

281
Hinton, S. E. *That Was Then, This Is Now.*
CATEGORY: D
POINT VALUE: 15

1. F	5. T	9. T	13. B
2. T	6. F	10. F	14. B
3. T	7. T	11. T	
4. T	8. T	12. D	

282
Howe, Deborah, and James Howe. *Bunnicula: A Rabbit Tale of Mystery.*
CATEGORY: B
POINT VALUE: 5

1. T	5. T	9. T	13. C
2. T	6. T	10. T	14. A
3. T	7. T	11. T	
4. F	8. T	12. D	

283
Howe, James. *The Celery Stalks at Midnight.*
CATEGORY: B
POINT VALUE: 5

1. T	5. F	9. F	13. C
2. F	6. F	10. T	14. A
3. T	7. T	11. F	
4. T	8. T	12. A	

284
Howe, James. *Howliday Inn.*
CATEGORY: B
POINT VALUE: 10

1. T	5. F	9. F	13. A
2. T	6. F	10. T	14. B
3. F	7. F	11. D	
4. T	8. T	12. A	

285
Howe, James. *Return to Howliday Inn.*
CATEGORY: B
POINT VALUE: 10

1. F	5. F	9. F	13. B
2. T	6. F	10. T	14. A
3. F	7. T	11. F	
4. F	8. F	12. A	

286
King-Smith, Dick. *Harry's Mad.*
CATEGORY: B
POINT VALUE: 5

1. F	5. T	9. T	13. B
2. F	6. F	10. F	14. A
3. T	7. F	11. T	
4. T	8. T	12. D	

287
Konigsburg, E. L. *T-Backs, T-Shirts, COAT and Suit.*
CATEGORY: D
POINT VALUE: 10

1. T	5. F	9. F	13. B
2. F	6. F	10. T	14. B
3. T	7. T	11. F	
4. T	8. F	12. C	

288
Lasky, Kathryn. *The Night Journey.*
CATEGORY: C
POINT VALUE: 10

1. T	5. T	9. T	13. B
2. T	6. F	10. T	14. B
3. T	7. T	11. F	
4. T	8. T	12. D	

289
Lasky, Kathryn. *Shadows in the Water.*
CATEGORY: E
POINT VALUE: 15

1. F	5. F	9. T	13. A
2. T	6. F	10. F	14. B
3. T	7. T	11. F	
4. T	8. T	12. B	

290
Lindgren, Astrid. *Pippi Goes on Board.*
CATEGORY: A
POINT VALUE: 10

1. T	5. T	9. T	13. D
2. T	6. F	10. F	14. C
3. F	7. T	11. F	
4. F	8. T	12. B	

291
Lindgren, Astrid. *Pippi in the South Seas.*
CATEGORY: A
POINT VALUE: 10

1. F	5. T	9. F	13. C
2. F	6. F	10. F	14. A
3. F	7. T	11. F	
4. T	8. T	12. B	

292
Lindgren, Astrid. *Pippi Longstocking.*
CATEGORY: A
POINT VALUE: 10

1. T	5. F	9. T	13. A
2. T	6. F	10. F	14. C
3. T	7. F	11. T	
4. T	8. F	12. A	

293
Lowry, Lois. *All About Sam.*
CATEGORY: B
POINT VALUE: 10

1. T	5. T	9. F	13. C
2. T	6. F	10. T	14. D
3. F	7. F	11. F	
4. T	8. T	12. B	

294
Lowry, Lois. *Attaboy, Sam!*
CATEGORY: B
POINT VALUE: 10

1. T	5. T	9. T	13. D
2. F	6. F	10. F	14. B
3. F	7. T	11. D	
4. T	8. F	12. C	

295
Lowry, Lois. *The Giver.*
CATEGORY: D
POINT VALUE: 10

1. T	5. T	9. T	13. B
2. F	6. T	10. T	14. B
3. F	7. F	11. T	
4. T	8. T	12. C	

296
Lowry, Lois. *Number the Stars.*
CATEGORY: D
POINT VALUE: 10

1. T	5. T	9. F	13. A
2. F	6. T	10. T	14. D
3. F	7. T	11. F	
4. F	8. T	12. C	

297
MacBride, Roger Lea. *Little House on Rocky Ridge.*
CATEGORY: C
POINT VALUE: 25

1. F	5. F	9. F	13. A
2. F	6. F	10. T	14. C
3. T	7. T	11. T	
4. F	8. F	12. B	

298
MacDonald, Betty. *Mrs. Piggle-Wiggle.*
CATEGORY: A
POINT VALUE: 10

1. T	5. T	9. F	13. B
2. F	6. T	10. T	14. B
3. T	7. F	11. T	
4. T	8. T	12. A	

299
MacDonald, Betty. *Mrs. Piggle-Wiggle's Farm.*
CATEGORY: A
POINT VALUE: 10

1. T	5. F	9. F	13. C
2. T	6. F	10. T	14. A
3. T	7. F	11. T	
4. T	8. T	12. A	

300
MacLachlan, Patricia. *Baby.*
CATEGORY: C
POINT VALUE: 10

1. T	5. F	9. T	13. A
2. T	6. T	10. F	14. B
3. F	7. F	11. F	
4. T	8. F	12. C	

301

MacLachlan, Patricia. *Journey.*
CATEGORY: C
POINT VALUE: 10

1. F	5. T	9. T	13. A
2. T	6. T	10. F	14. C
3. T	7. F	11. F	
4. F	8. F	12. B	

302

Magorian, Michelle. *Good Night, Mr. Tom.*
CATEGORY: E
POINT VALUE: 25

1. T	5. F	9. T	13. D
2. T	6. F	10. F	14. A
3. F	7. F	11. T	
4. T	8. T	12. B	

303

Martin, Ann M. *Ten Kids, No Pets.*
CATEGORY: B
POINT VALUE: 15

1. T	5. F	9. F	13. D
2. F	6. T	10. T	14. B
3. T	7. T	11. F	
4. T	8. T	12. B	

304

McKissack, Patricia C. *The Dark-Thirty: Southern Tales of the Supernatural.*
CATEGORY: D
POINT VALUE: 15

1. F	5. T	9. F	13. D
2. T	6. F	10. T	14. C
3. F	7. T	11. T	
4. T	8. T	12. B	

305

McKissack, Patricia C., and Fredrick McKissack. *A Long Hard Journey: The Story of Pullman Porter.*
CATEGORY: E
POINT VALUE: 15

1. F	5. F	9. T	13. B
2. T	6. T	10. F	14. A
3. T	7. F	11. F	
4. T	8. T	12. A	

306

Montgomery, L. M. *Anne of Avonlea.*
CATEGORY: E
POINT VALUE: 25

1. F	5. F	9. F	13. A
2. F	6. T	10. F	14. C
3. T	7. T	11. T	
4. F	8. F	12. B	

307

Montgomery, L. M. *Anne of Green Gables.*
CATEGORY: E
POINT VALUE: 25

1. F	5. T	9. F	13. B
2. F	6. F	10. F	14. A
3. T	7. T	11. F	
4. F	8. F	12. B	

308

Naylor, Phyllis Reynolds. *The Agony of Alice.*
CATEGORY: C
POINT VALUE: 10

1. T	5. F	9. T	13. B
2. F	6. T	10. F	14. A
3. T	7. F	11. F	
4. T	8. T	12. B	

309

Naylor, Phyllis Reynolds. *Beetles, Lightly Toasted.*
CATEGORY: C
POINT VALUE: 10

1. F	5. T	9. T	13. A
2. F	6. T	10. F	14. D
3. F	7. F	11. D	
4. F	8. F	12. B	

310

Naylor, Phyllis Reynolds. *The Boys Start the War.*
CATEGORY: B
POINT VALUE: 10

1. T	5. F	9. T	13. A
2. T	6. T	10. T	14. B
3. F	7. F	11. T	
4. T	8. F	12. C	

311

Naylor, Phyllis Reynolds. *The Grand Escape.*
CATEGORY: B
POINT VALUE: 10

1. T	5. F	9. T	13. C
2. F	6. F	10. T	14. C
3. F	7. T	11. F	
4. T	8. F	12. B	

312

Naylor, Phyllis Reynolds. *Shiloh.*
CATEGORY: C
POINT VALUE: 10

1. T	5. F	9. F	13. C
2. T	6. F	10. F	14. B
3. T	7. F	11. T	
4. T	8. T	12. C	

313

Nixon, Joan Lowery. *The Kidnapping of Christina Lattimore.*
CATEGORY: E
POINT VALUE: 15

1. T	5. T	9. F	13. A
2. T	6. F	10. T	14. B
3. T	7. T	11. F	
4. T	8. F	12. A	

314

Nixon, Joan Lowery. *The Other Side of Dark.*
CATEGORY: E
POINT VALUE: 15

1. T	5. T	9. T	13. D
2. F	6. T	10. F	14. B
3. F	7. F	11. T	
4. F	8. T	12. A	

315

O'Dell, Scott. *My Name Is Not Angelica.*
CATEGORY: D
POINT VALUE: 15

1. T	5. T	9. T	13. C
2. F	6. T	10. T	14. A
3. T	7. F	11. F	
4. T	8. T	12. B	

316

Paterson, Katherine. *Lyddie.*
CATEGORY: D
POINT VALUE: 15

1. F	5. F	9. T	13. D
2. T	6. F	10. T	14. A
3. T	7. T	11. T	
4. F	8. F	12. T	

317

Paterson, Katherine. *Of Nightingales That Weep.*
CATEGORY: E
POINT VALUE: 15

1. T	5. T	9. T	13. B
2. F	6. T	10. F	14. C
3. T	7. T	11. T	
4. T	8. T	12. C	

318

Paterson, Katherine. *Park's Quest.*
CATEGORY: C
POINT VALUE: 10

1. T	5. T	9. T	13. C
2. T	6. F	10. T	14. C
3. F	7. F	11. F	
4. F	8. F	12. A	

319

Paulsen, Gary. *Hatchet.*
CATEGORY: D
POINT VALUE: 10

1. T	5. F	9. T	13. A
2. F	6. T	10. F	14. A
3. F	7. T	11. T	
4. T	8. F	12. D	

320

Paulsen, Gary. *Nightjohn.*
CATEGORY: D
POINT VALUE: 5

1. F	5. T	9. F	13. C
2. T	6. T	10. F	14. A
3. T	7. F	11. D	
4. T	8. F	12. B	

321
Paulsen, Gary. *The Voyage of the* Frog.
CATEGORY: C
POINT VALUE: 10

1. F	5. F	9. F	13. B
2. F	6. T	10. F	14. A
3. F	7. T	11. A	
4. T	8. F	12. C	

322
Paulsen, Gary. *The Winter Room.*
CATEGORY: D
POINT VALUE: 10

1. F	5. F	9. F	13. B
2. T	6. F	10. T	14. B
3. T	7. F	11. T	
4. T	8. T	12. A	

323
Peck, Richard. *Are You in the House Alone?*
CATEGORY: E
POINT VALUE: 15

1. T	5. F	9. T	13. D
2. T	6. T	10. F	14. B
3. T	7. T	11. T	
4. F	8. T	12. D	

324
Peck, Richard. *Don't Look and It Won't Hurt.*
CATEGORY: E
POINT VALUE: 15

1. T	5. T	9. T	13. A
2. T	6. T	10. F	14. D
3. F	7. F	11. T	
4. T	8. F	12. B	

325
Peck, Richard. *The Ghost Belonged to Me.*
CATEGORY: D
POINT VALUE: 15

1. T	5. T	9. F	13. A
2. T	6. F	10. T	14. A
3. T	7. T	11. T	
4. F	8. T	12. B	

326
Reeder, Carolyn. *Shades of Gray.*
CATEGORY: C
POINT VALUE: 10

1. T	5. T	9. T	13. B
2. T	6. F	10. T	14. D
3. T	7. T	11. F	
4. T	8. T	12. A	

327
Rylant, Cynthia. *Missing May.*
CATEGORY: C
POINT VALUE: 10

1. T	5. F	9. F	13. A
2. T	6. T	10. T	14. B
3. T	7. T	11. T	
4. T	8. F	12. B	

328
Sachar, Louis. *There's a Boy in the Girls' Bathroom.*
CATEGORY: B
POINT VALUE: 10

1. T	5. T	9. T	13. A
2. T	6. T	10. T	14. D
3. T	7. F	11. T	
4. T	8. T	12. C	

329
Smith, Robert Kimmel. *The War with Grandpa.*
CATEGORY: B
POINT VALUE: 10

1. T	5. F	9. F	13. A
2. F	6. F	10. F	14. C
3. T	7. F	11. F	
4. T	8. F	12. B	

330
Spinelli, Jerry. *Maniac Magee.*
CATEGORY: D
POINT VALUE: 15

1. F	5. F	9. T	13. A
2. T	6. T	10. T	14. C
3. F	7. T	11. F	
4. T	8. T	12. B	

331

Spinelli, Jerry. *Space Station Seventh Grade.*
CATEGORY: D
POINT VALUE: 15

1. T	5. T	9. F	13. D
2. F	6. T	10. F	14. A
3. F	7. T	11. T	
4. F	8. F	12. A	

332

Stolz, Mary. *Stealing Home.*
CATEGORY: B
POINT VALUE: 10

1. T	5. T	9. T	13. B
2. T	6. T	10. F	14. D
3. F	7. T	11. D	
4. F	8. T	12. A	

333

Taylor, Mildred D. *Let the Circle Be Unbroken.*
CATEGORY: E
POINT VALUE: 25

1. T	5. T	9. F	13. B
2. T	6. F	10. T	14. C
3. F	7. T	11. T	
4. T	8. T	12. D	

334

Taylor, Mildred D. *The Road to Memphis.*
CATEGORY: E
POINT VALUE: 25

1. F	5. T	9. T	13. A
2. T	6. T	10. T	14. A
3. F	7. F	11. F	
4. T	8. T	12. B	

335

Warner, Gertrude Chandler. *The Boxcar Children.* (Boxcar Mystery #1)
CATEGORY: A
POINT VALUE: 10

1. T	5. T	9. T	13. C
2. T	6. T	10. T	14. A
3. F	7. T	11. F	
4. F	8. T	12. D	

336

Warner, Gertrude Chandler. *Surprise Island.* (Boxcar Mystery #2)
CATEGORY: A
POINT VALUE: 10

1. F	5. F	9. T	13. A
2. F	6. T	10. T	14. B
3. T	7. T	11. T	
4. T	8. F	12. D	

337

Warner, Gertrude Chandler. *The Yellow House Mystery.* (Boxcar Mystery #3)
CATEGORY: A
POINT VALUE: 10

1. T	5. F	9. T	13. A
2. F	6. F	10. F	14. B
3. T	7. T	11. F	
4. T	8. F	12. D	

338

Wright, Betty Ren. *Christina's Ghost.*
CATEGORY: C
POINT VALUE: 10

1. F	5. F	9. T	13. D
2. T	6. T	10. T	14. D
3. T	7. F	11. F	
4. F	8. T	12. C	

339

Wright, Betty Ren. *The Dollhouse Murders.*
CATEGORY: C
POINT VALUE: 10

1. F	5. T	9. F	13. A
2. T	6. T	10. F	14. D
3. T	7. T	11. T	
4. F	8. T	12. D	

340

Wright, Betty Ren. *Ghosts Beneath Our Feet.*
CATEGORY: C
POINT VALUE: 10

1. F	5. T	9. F	13. A
2. T	6. F	10. T	14. D
3. T	7. T	11. F	
4. F	8. T	12. B	

PART
IV

Children's
Catalog

 # Introduction

Welcome to the *Children's Catalog*. Before you select a book, ask your teacher to recommend a category of books (from A—E) for you to read. Within each category, books are given point values depending on the length of the book. Your teacher should give you a goal for the total number of points you should acquire.

When you have read a book, the teacher will give you a short test about the book to see if you understood the story.

In choosing the books you will read during this program, it would be a good idea to choose books from all kinds of topical headings. By doing this, you will find out if there are types of books that you enjoy that you might not otherwise have read. It's kind of like going to an ice cream shop that sells 33 different flavors of ice cream. You may know that you love dill pickle with pistachio nuts ice cream, but if you always order that flavor, you may never find out that you like fishy fruit better!

So if you like to read mysteries, go ahead and read a few, but also try a book or two about friendship, or horses, or ships. You might be surprised at the types of books you find yourself really enjoying!

The first half of the *Children's Catalog* presents a Subject Index of all the books included in the program. The books for each subject are listed by category (from A—E). The second half of the catalog gives short annotations describing what each book is about. Within each category, the books in the second half of the catalog are listed alphabetically by author.

Using the *Children's Catalog* is easy. Browse through the Subject Index and jot down the titles of several books that interest you. Next to each title, take note of the book's author and category. When your list is complete, turn to the second half of the catalog to read the annotations. If, for example, one of the books you have listed is *The Midnight Horse* by Sid Fleischman, turn to Category D in the second half of the catalog. Then, scanning the list of authors in Category D, look under "F" for Fleischman, and here you will find the annotation. After reading the annotations for the books on your list, decide which of the books you would like to learn even more about. Next, you might ask your teacher if you may visit the school library to locate the books on your list and to review the books there before deciding which book you would like to read next.

The *Children's Catalog* will be a useful tool for you to use in selecting books you are sure to enjoy. On the next page, you will find a complete listing of all the topics included in this program. So start browsing . . . and happy reading!

 **List of Subjects**

Abandonment
Adventure
African Americans
Aliens/Extraterrestrials
Animals
Animals as Talking Characters
Babies
Biography
Boy-Girl Relationships
Boys Growing Up
Brothers
Brothers and Sisters
Cats
Child Abuse
Child Labor
Children Living Alone
Courage
Crime
Crime—Being the Victim of a Violent Crime
Death/Dying
Divorce
Dogs
Family Life
Family Problems
Fantasy
Farms—Living on a Farm
Fathers
Friendship
Frontier Life and Pioneer Life
Gangs/Street Life
Ghosts
Girls Growing Up
Grandparents
Handicaps
Historical Fiction
Homelessness
Horses

Humor
Islands—Living on an Island
Jewish People
Kidnapping
Make Believe/Magic
Mental Illness
Mothers
Murder
Mystery
Native Americans
Nature/Ecology
Neglect
Newbery Medal Books
Orphans/Orphanages
Pets
Poverty/Financial Hardship
Prejudice
Rabbits
Relatives—Living With Relatives
Rivers
Romance
Runaways
School
Sea
Ships
Single Parents
Sisters
Slavery
Social Issues
Sports
Stepparents
Summer Vacation
Survival
Teen Pregnancy
Toddlers/Preschoolers
War—Civilian Life During Wartime
Witches/Witchcraft/Sorcery

 # Subject Index

ABANDONMENT—BEING ABANDONED BY ONE OR BY BOTH PARENTS

(*See also*: Child Abuse, Children Living Alone, Family Problems, Neglect—Being Neglected by One or by Both Parents, Orphans/Orphanages.)

Category: C
　　Fox, Paula. *Monkey Island.*
　　MacLachlan, Patricia. *Baby.*
　　MacLachlan, Patricia. *Journey.*
Category: D
　　Hinton, S. E. *Tex.*
　　Paterson, Katherine. *Lyddie.*
Category: E
　　Peck, Richard. *Don't Look and It Won't Hurt.*

ADVENTURE

(*See also*: Fantasy, Frontier Life and Pioneer Life, Islands—Living on an Island, Rivers, Sea, Ships, Survival.)

Category: A
　　Lindgren, Astrid. *Pippi Goes on Board.*
　　Lindgren, Astrid. *Pippi in the South Seas.*
　　Lindgren, Astrid. *Pippi Longstocking.*
Category: B
　　Dahl, Roald. *Charlie and the Chocolate Factory.*
　　Dahl, Roald. *Charlie and the Great Glass Elevator.*
　　Dahl, Roald. *James and the Giant Peach.*
　　Fleischman, Sid. *Jim Ugly.*
　　Naylor, Phyllis Reynolds. *The Grand Escape.*
Category: C
　　Bauer, Marion Dane. *Face to Face.*
　　Fleischman, Sid. *The Whipping Boy.*
　　Lasky, Kathryn. *The Night Journey.*
　　Paulsen, Gary. *The Voyage of the* Frog.
Category: D
　　Fleischman, Sid. *The Midnight Horse.*
　　Paulsen, Gary. *Hatchet.*
Category: E
　　AVI. *The True Confessions of Charlotte Doyle.*

AFRICAN AMERICANS

(*See also*: Prejudice, Slavery.)

Category: A
　　Porter, Connie. (American Girls Collection). *Meet Addy.*
　　Christopher, Matt. *No Arm in Left Field.*
Category: B
　　Stolz, Mary. *Stealing Home.*
Category: C
　　Hamilton, Virginia. *Zeely.*
Category: D
　　Hamilton, Virginia. *Cousins.*
　　McKissack, Patricia C. *The Dark-Thirty: Southern Tales of the Supernatural.*
　　Paulsen, Gary. *Nightjohn.*
　　Spinelli, Jerry. *Maniac Magee.*
Category: E
　　McKissack, Patricia C., and Fredrick McKissack. *A Long Hard Journey: The Story of Pullman Porter.*
　　Taylor, Mildred D. *Let the Circle Be Unbroken.*
　　Taylor, Mildred D. *The Road to Memphis.*

ALIENS/EXTRATERRESTRIALS

(*See also*: Fantasy.)

Category: B
　　Dahl, Roald. *Charlie and the Great Glass Elevator.*
Category: C
　　Coville, Bruce. *My Teacher Flunked the Planet.*
　　Coville, Bruce. *My Teacher Is an Alien.*

ANIMALS

(*See also*: Animals As Talking Characters, Cats, Dogs, Farms—Living on a Farm, Horses, Nature, Pets, Rabbits.)

Category: A
　　MacDonald, Betty. *Mrs. Piggle-Wiggle's Farm.*
Category: B
　　Martin, Ann M. *Ten Kids, No Pets.*

Category: C
> AVI. *Blue Heron.*
> George, Jean Craighead. *The Missing 'Gator of Gumbo Limbo.*
> George, Jean Craighead. *Shark Beneath the Reef.*

Category: D
> Paulsen, Gary. *Hatchet.*

Category: E
> Lasky, Kathryn. *Shadows in the Water.*

ANIMALS AS TALKING CHARACTERS

(*See also*: Animals, Cats, Dogs, Fantasy, Farms—Living on a Farm, Horses, Make Believe/Magic, Pets, Rabbits.)

Category: B
> Dahl, Roald. *James and the Giant Peach.*
> Howe, Deborah, and James Howe. *Bunnicula: A Rabbit Tale of Mystery.*
> Howe, James. *The Celery Stalks at Midnight.*
> Howe, James. *Howliday Inn.*
> Howe, James. *Return to Howliday Inn.*
> King-Smith, Dick. *Harry's Mad.*
> Naylor, Phyllis Reynolds. *The Grand Escape.*

BABIES

(*See also*: Toddlers/Preschoolers.)

Category: B
> Lowry, Lois. *All About Sam.*

Category: C
> MacLachlan, Patricia. *Baby.*

BIOGRAPHY

(*See also*: Historical Fiction.)

Category: E
> Freedman, Russell. *Franklin Delano Roosevelt.*
> Freedman, Russell. *Lincoln: A Photobiography.*
> Freedman, Russell. *The Wright Brothers.*

BOY-GIRL RELATIONSHIPS

(*See also*: Boys Growing Up, Friendship, Girls Growing Up, Romance.)

Category: A
> Blume, Judy. *Fudge-A-Mania.*

Category: B
> Byars, Betsy. *A Blossom Promise.*
> Byars, Betsy. *The Blossoms and the Green Phantom.*
> Byars, Betsy. *The Blossoms Meet the Vulture Lady.*
> Byars, Betsy. *The Not-Just-Anybody Family.*

> Byars, Betsy. *Wanted . . . Mud Blossom.*
> Naylor, Phyllis Reynolds. *The Boys Start the War.*
> Sachar, Louis. *There's a Boy in the Girls' Bathroom.*

Category: C
> Blume, Judy. *Are You There God? It's Me, Margaret.*
> MacLachlan, Patricia. *Baby*
> Naylor, Phyllis Reynolds. *The Agony of Alice.*
> Rylant, Cynthia. *Missing May.*

Category: D
> AVI. *Punch with Judy.*
> Banks, Lynne Reid. *One More River.*
> Blume, Judy. *Here's to You, Rachel Robinson.*
> Cleary, Beverly. *Strider.*
> Hinton, S. E. *The Outsiders.*
> Hinton, S. E. *Tex.*
> Hinton, S. E. *That Was Then, This Is Now.*
> Peck, Richard. *The Ghost Belonged to Me.*
> Spinelli, Jerry. *Maniac Magee.*

Category: E
> Magorian, Michelle. *Good Night, Mr. Tom.*
> Montgomery, L. M. *Anne of Avonlea.*
> Montgomery, L. M. *Anne of Green Gables.*
> Nixon, Joan Lowery. *The Other Side of Dark.*
> Taylor, Mildred D. *Let the Circle Be Unbroken.*
> Taylor, Mildred D. *The Road to Memphis.*

BOYS GROWING UP

(*See also*: Boy-Girl Relationships, Brothers, Brothers and Sisters, Family Life, Family Problems, Friendship, School.)

Category: A
> Christopher, Matt. *Front Court Hex.*
> Christopher, Matt. *Johnny Long Legs.*
> Christopher, Matt. *No Arm in Left Field.*
> Graeber, Charlotte Towner. *Fudge.*

Category: B
> Banks, Lynne Reid. *The Indian in the Cupboard.*
> Banks, Lynne Reid. *The Mystery of the Cupboard.*
> Banks, Lynne Reid. *The Return of the Indian.*
> Banks, Lynne Reid. *The Secret of the Indian.*
> Fleischman, Sid. *Jim Ugly.*
> Naylor, Phyllis Reynolds. *The Boys Start the War.*
> Sachar, Louis. *There's a Boy in the Girls' Bathroom.*
> Smith, Robert Kimmel. *The War with Grandpa.*
> Stolz, Mary. *Stealing Home.*

Category: C
> AVI. *Who Was That Masked Man, Anyway?*
> Bauer, Marion Dane. *Face to Face.*
> Bauer, Marion Dane. *On My Honor.*
> Fleischman, Sid. *The Whipping Boy.*
> Fox, Paula. *Monkey Island.*
> George, Jean Craighead. *Shark Beneath the Reef.*
> MacLachlan, Patricia. *Journey.*
> Naylor, Phyllis Reynolds. *Beetles, Lightly Toasted.*
> Naylor, Phyllis Reynolds. *Shiloh.*
> Paterson, Katherine. *Park's Quest.*
> Paulsen, Gary. *The Voyage of the* Frog.
> Reeder, Carolyn. *Shades of Gray.*

Category: D
> AVI. *Punch with Judy.*
> Blume, Judy. *Then Again, Maybe I Won't.*
> Cleary, Beverly. *Strider.*
> Hinton, S. E. *The Outsiders.*
> Hinton, S. E. *Tex.*
> Hinton, S. E. *That Was Then, This Is Now.*
> Lowry, Lois. *The Giver.*
> Paulsen, Gary. *Hatchet.*
> Paulsen, Gary. *The Winter Room.*
> Spinelli, Jerry. *Maniac Magee.*
> Spinelli, Jerry. *Space Station Seventh Grade.*

Category: E
> Magorian, Michelle. *Good Night, Mr. Tom.*

BROTHERS

(*See also*: Boys Growing Up, Brothers and Sisters, Family Life, Sisters.)

Category: B
> Naylor, Phyllis Reynolds. *The Boys Start the War.*

Category: D
> Hinton, S. E. *The Outsiders.*
> Hinton, S. E. *Tex.*
> Paulsen, Gary. *The Winter Room.*

Category: E
> Freedman, Russell. *The Wright Brothers.*

BROTHERS AND SISTERS

(*See also*: Boys Growing Up, Brothers, Family Life, Girls Growing Up, Sisters.)

Category: A
> Tripp, Valerie. (American Girls Collection). *Meet Molly.*
> Warner, Gertrude Chandler. *The Boxcar Children* (Boxcar Mystery #1).
> Warner, Gertrude Chandler. *Surprise Island* (Boxcar Mystery #2).
> Warner, Gertrude Chandler. *The Yellow House Mystery* (Boxcar Mystery #3).

Category: B
> Byars, Betsy. *A Blossom Promise.*
> Byars, Betsy. *The Blossoms and the Green Phantom.*
> Byars, Betsy. *The Blossoms Meet the Vulture Lady.*
> Byars, Betsy. *The Not-Just-Anybody Family.*
> Byars, Betsy. *Wanted . . . Mud Blossom.*
> Dorris, Michael. *Morning Girl.*
> Lowry, Lois. *All About Sam.*
> Lowry, Lois. *Attaboy, Sam!*
> Martin, Ann M. *Ten Kids, No Pets.*

Category: C
> Hamilton, Virginia. *Zeely.*
> MacLachlan, Patricia. *Journey.*
> Naylor, Phyllis Reynolds. *The Agony of Alice.*
> Paterson, Katherine. *Park's Quest.*
> Wright, Betty Ren. *Ghosts Beneath Our Feet.*

Category: D
> Blume, Judy. *Here's to You, Rachel Robinson.*

Category: E
> Taylor, Mildred D. *Let the Circle Be Unbroken.*
> Taylor, Mildred D. *The Road to Memphis.*

CATS

(*See also*: Animals, Animals as Talking Characters, Dogs, Farms—Living on a Farm, Horses, Pets, Rabbits.)

Category: B
> Howe, Deborah, and James Howe. *Bunnicula: A Rabbit Tale of Mystery.*
> Howe, James. *The Celery Stalks at Midnight.*
> Howe, James. *Howliday Inn.*
> Howe, James. *Return to Howliday Inn.*
> Naylor, Phyllis Reynolds. *The Grand Escape.*

CHILD ABUSE

(*See also*: Abandonment—Being Abandoned by One or by Both Parents, Child Labor, Crime—Being the Victim of a Violent Crime, Neglect—Being Neglected by One or by Both Parents.)

Category: C
> AVI. *Blue Heron.*

Category: E
> AVI. *The True Confessions of Charlotte Doyle.*
> Magorian, Michelle. *Good Night, Mr. Tom.*

CHILD LABOR

(*See also*: Abandonment—Being Abandoned by One or by Both Parents, Child Abuse, Children Living Alone, Historical Fiction, Poverty/Financial Hardship, Runaways.)

Category: A

Adler, Susan S. (American Girls Collection). *Meet Samantha.*

Category: D

Paterson, Katherine. *Lyddie.*

CHILDREN LIVING ALONE

(*See also*: Abandonment—Being Abandoned by One or by Both Parents, Gangs/Street Life, Neglect—Being Neglected by One or by Both Parents, Orphans/Orphanages, Runaways.)

Category: A

Lindgren, Astrid. *Pippi Goes on Board.*
Lindgren, Astrid. *Pippi in the South Seas.*
Lindgren, Astrid. *Pippi Longstocking.*
Warner, Gertrude Chandler. *The Boxcar Children* (Boxcar Mystery #1).

Category: C

Fox, Paula. *Monkey Island.*
Paulsen, Gary. *The Voyage of the* Frog.

Category: D

Hinton, S. E. *The Outsiders.*
Hinton, S. E. *Tex.*
Paterson, Katherine. *Lyddie.*
Paulsen, Gary. *Hatchet.*
Spinelli, Jerry. *Maniac Magee.*

COURAGE

(*See also*: Adventure, Survival.)

Category: A

Porter, Connie. (American Girls Collection). *Meet Addy.*

Category: C

Bauer, Marion Dane. *Face to Face.*
Lasky, Kathryn. *The Night Journey.*
Paulsen, Gary. *The Voyage of the* Frog.

Category: D

Lowry, Lois. *The Giver.*
Lowry, Lois. *Number the Stars.*
O'Dell, Scott. *My Name Is Not Angelica.*
Paterson, Katherine. *Lyddie.*
Paulsen, Gary. *Hatchet.*
Paulsen, Gary. *Nightjohn.*

Category: E

AVI. *The True Confessions of Charlotte Doyle.*
Taylor, Mildred D. *Let the Circle Be Unbroken.*
Taylor, Mildred D. *The Road to Memphis.*

CRIME

(*See also*: Crime—Being the Victim of a Violent Crime, Gangs/Street Life, Kidnapping, Murder.)

Category: C

Coville, Bruce. *The Ghost in the Big Brass Bed.*
Coville, Bruce. *The Ghost Wore Gray.*

Category: D

Hinton, S. E. *The Outsiders.*
Hinton, S. E. *Tex.*
Hinton, S. E. *That Was Then, This Is Now.*

Category: E

Lasky, Kathryn. *Shadows in the Water.*

CRIME—BEING THE VICTIM OF A VIOLENT CRIME

(*See also*: Child Abuse, Gangs/Street Life, Kidnapping, Murder.)

Category: D

Hinton, S. E. *Tex.*

Category: E

Nixon, Joan Lowery. *The Kidnapping of Christina Lattimore.*
Nixon, Joan Lowery. *The Other Side of Dark.*
Peck, Richard. *Are You in the House Alone?*

DEATH/DYING

Category: C

Bauer, Marion Dane. *On My Honor.*
MacLachlan, Patricia. *Baby.*
Paterson, Katherine. *Park's Quest.*
Rylant, Cynthia. *Missing May.*

Category: D

Hamilton, Virginia. *Cousins.*
Hinton, S. E. *The Outsiders.*
Hinton, S. E. *That Was Then, This Is Now.*
Lowry, Lois. *The Giver.*
Paterson, Katherine. *Lyddie.*
Spinelli, Jerry. *Space Station Seventh Grade.*

Category: E

Freedman, Russell. *Lincoln: A Photobiography.*
Magorian, Michelle. *Good Night, Mr. Tom.*
Nixon, Joan Lowery. *The Other Side of Dark.*
Paterson, Katherine. *Of Nightingales That Weep.*

DIVORCE

(See also: Abandonment—Being Abandoned by One or by Both Parents, Family Problems, Fathers, Mothers, Single Parents—Living in a Single Parent Home, Stepparents.)

Category: C
AVI. *Blue Heron.*
Bauer, Marion Dane. *Face to Face.*
Paterson, Katherine. *Park's Quest.*

Category: D
Cleary, Beverly. *Strider.*
Hamilton, Virginia. *Cousins.*
Paulsen, Gary. *Hatchet.*

Category: E
Peck, Richard. *Don't Look and It Won't Hurt.*

DOGS

(See also: Animals, Animals as Talking Characters, Cats, Farms—Living on a Farm, Horses, Pets, Rabbits.)

Category: A
Blume, Judy. *Fudge-A-Mania.*
Graeber, Charlotte Towner. *Fudge.*

Category: B
Byars, Betsy. *A Blossom Promise.*
Byars, Betsy. *The Blossoms and the Green Phantom.*
Byars, Betsy. *The Blossoms Meet the Vulture Lady.*
Byars, Betsy. *The Not-Just-Anybody Family.*
Byars, Betsy. *Wanted . . . Mud Blossom.*
Fleischman, Sid. *Jim Ugly.*
Howe, Deborah, and James Howe. *Bunnicula: A Rabbit Tale of Mystery.*
Howe, James. *The Celery Stalks at Midnight.*
Howe, James. *Howliday Inn.*
Howe, James. *Return to Howliday Inn.*

Category: C
Naylor, Phyllis Reynolds. *Shiloh.*

Category: D
Cleary, Beverly. *Strider.*
Konigsburg, E. L. *T-Backs, T-Shirts, COAT and Suit.*

FAMILY LIFE

(See also: Boys Growing Up, Brothers, Brothers and Sisters, Family Problems, Fathers, Girls Growing Up, Grandparents, Mothers, Sisters.)

Category: A
Blume, Judy. *Fudge-A-Mania.*

Category: B
Byars, Betsy. *A Blossom Promise.*
Byars, Betsy. *The Blossoms and the Green Phantom.*

Byars, Betsy. *The Blossoms Meet the Vulture Lady.*
Byars, Betsy. *The Not-Just-Anybody Family.*
Byars, Betsy. *Wanted . . . Mud Blossom.*
Dorris, Michael. *Morning Girl.*
Lowry, Lois. *All About Sam.*
Lowry, Lois. *Attaboy, Sam!*
Martin, Ann M. *Ten Kids, No Pets.*
Stolz, Mary. *Stealing Home.*

Category: C
AVI. *Who Was That Masked Man, Anyway?*
George, Jean Craighead. *Shark Beneath the Reef.*
Lasky, Kathryn. *The Night Journey.*
MacBride, Roger Lea. *Little House on Rocky Ridge.*
MacLachlan, Patricia. *Baby.*
MacLachlan, Patricia. *Journey.*

Category: D
Paulsen, Gary. *The Winter Room.*
Spinelli, Jerry. *Space Station Seventh Grade.*

Category: E
Montgomery, L. M. *Anne of Avonlea.*
Montgomery, L. M. *Anne of Green Gables.*

FAMILY PROBLEMS

(See also: Divorce, Family Life, Neglect—Being Neglected by One or by Both Parents, Poverty/Financial Hardship, Single Parents—Living in a Single Parent Home, Stepparents.)

Category: B
Smith, Robert Kimmel. *The War with Grandpa.*

Category: C
Bauer, Marion Dane. *Face to Face.*
Naylor, Phyllis Reynolds. *The Agony of Alice.*
Paterson, Katherine. *Park's Quest.*
Reeder, Carolyn. *Shades of Gray.*
Rylant, Cynthia. *Missing May.*
Wright, Betty Ren. *The Dollhouse Murders.*
Wright, Betty Ren. *Ghosts Beneath Our Feet.*

Category: D
Banks, Lynne Reid. *One More River.*
Blume, Judy. *Here's to You, Rachel Robinson.*
Blume, Judy. *Then Again, Maybe I Won't.*
Hamilton, Virginia. *Cousins.*
Paterson, Katherine. *Lyddie.*

Category: E
Magorian, Michelle. *Good Night, Mr. Tom.*
Nixon, Joan Lowery. *The Other Side of Dark.*
Peck, Richard. *Don't Look and It Won't Hurt.*

Taylor, Mildred D. *Let the Circle Be Unbroken*.
Taylor, Mildred D. *The Road to Memphis*.

FANTASY

(*See also*: Adventure, Aliens/ Extraterrestrials, Animals as Talking Characters, Make Believe/Magic.)

Category: B

Banks, Lynne Reid. *The Indian in the Cupboard*.
Banks, Lynne Reid. *The Mystery of the Cupboard*.
Banks, Lynne Reid. *The Return of the Indian*.
Banks, Lynne Reid. *The Secret of the Indian*.
Dahl, Roald. *Charlie and the Chocolate Factory*.
Dahl, Roald. *Charlie and the Great Glass Elevator*.
Dahl, Roald. *James and the Giant Peach*.

Category: C

Cassedy, Sylvia. *Behind the Attic Wall*.
Cassedy, Sylvia. *Lucie Babbidge's House*.
Coville, Bruce. *My Teacher Flunked the Planet*.
Coville, Bruce. *My Teacher Is an Alien*.

FARMS—LIVING ON A FARM

(*See also*: Animals, Cats, Dogs, Horses, Nature, Pets, Rabbits.)

Category: A

MacDonald, Betty. *Mrs. Piggle-Wiggle's Farm*.

Category: C

Bauer, Marion Dane. *Face to Face*.
Reeder, Carolyn. *Shades of Gray*.
MacBride, Roger Lea. *Little House on Rocky Ridge*.

Category: D

Banks, Lynne Reid. *One More River*.
Paulsen, Gary. *The Winter Room*.

Category: E

Montgomery, L. M. *Anne of Avonlea*.
Montgomery, L. M. *Anne of Green Gables*.
Taylor, Mildred D. *Let the Circle Be Unbroken*.
Taylor, Mildred D. *The Road to Memphis*.

FATHERS

(*See also*: Family Life, Family Problems, Mothers, Stepparents.)

Category: B

Fleischman, Sid. *Jim Ugly*.

Category: C

AVI. *Blue Heron*.
Bauer, Marion Dane. *Face to Face*.
Bauer, Marion Dane. *On My Honor*.
Naylor, Phyllis Reynolds. *The Agony of Alice*.

Category: D

Banks, Lynne Reid. *One More River*.
Cleary, Beverly. *Strider*.

FRIENDSHIP

(*See also*: Boy-Girl Relationships, Boys Growing Up, Girls Growing Up, School.)

Category: A

Adler, Susan S. (American Girls Collection). *Meet Samantha*.
Tripp, Valerie. (American Girls Collection). *Meet Molly*.

Category: B

Banks, Lynne Reid. *The Indian in the Cupboard*.
Banks, Lynne Reid. *The Mystery of the Cupboard*.
Banks, Lynne Reid. *The Return of the Indian*.
Banks, Lynne Reid. *The Secret of the Indian*.
Byars, Betsy. *A Blossom Promise*.
Byars, Betsy. *The Blossoms and the Green Phantom*.
Byars, Betsy. *The Blossoms Meet the Vulture Lady*.
Byars, Betsy. *The Not-Just-Anybody Family*.
Byars, Betsy. *Wanted . . . Mud Blossom*.
Sachar, Louis. *There's a Boy in the Girls' Bathroom*.

Category: C

AVI. *Blue Heron*.
AVI. *Who Was That Masked Man, Anyway?*
Blume, Judy. *Are You There God? It's Me, Margaret*.
Fleischman, Sid. *The Whipping Boy*.
MacLachlan, Patricia. *Baby*.

Category: D

AVI. *Punch with Judy*.
Banks, Lynne Reid. *One More River*.
Blume, Judy. *Then Again, Maybe I Won't*.
Cleary, Beverly. *Strider*.
Hamilton, Virginia. *Cousins*.
Hinton, S. E. *The Outsiders*.
Hinton, S. E. *Tex*.
Hinton, S. E. *That Was Then, This Is Now*.
Lowry, Lois. *Number the Stars*.
Spinelli, Jerry. *Maniac Magee*.
Spinelli, Jerry. *Space Station Seventh Grade*.

Category: E

Magorian, Michelle. *Good Night, Mr. Tom*.
Montgomery, L. M. *Anne of Avonlea*.
Montgomery, L. M. *Anne of Green Gables*.

Taylor, Mildred D. *Let the Circle Be Unbroken.*
Taylor, Mildred D. *The Road to Memphis.*

FRONTIER LIFE AND PIONEER LIFE

(*See also*: Adventure, Family Life, Historical Fiction.)
Category: B
Fleischman, Sid. *Jim Ugly.*
Category: C
MacBride, Roger Lea. *Little House on Rocky Ridge.*

GANGS/STREET LIFE

(*See also*: Children Living Alone, Crime, Homelessness, Runaways.)
Category: C
Fox, Paula. *Monkey Island.*
Category: D
Hinton, S. E. *The Outsiders.*
Hinton, S. E. *Tex.*
Hinton, S. E. *That Was Then, This Is Now.*
Spinelli, Jerry. *Maniac Magee.*

GHOSTS

(*See also*: Mystery, Witches/Witchcraft/Sorcery.)
Category: C
Coville, Bruce. *The Ghost in the Big Brass Bed.*
Coville, Bruce. *The Ghost Wore Gray.*
Wright, Betty Ren. *Christina's Ghost.*
Wright, Betty Ren. *The Dollhouse Murders.*
Wright, Betty Ren. *Ghosts Beneath Our Feet.*
Category: D
Fleischman, Sid. *The Midnight Horse.*
Hahn, Mary Downing. *Wait Till Helen Comes: A Ghost Story.*
McKissack, Patricia C. *The Dark-Thirty: Southern Tales of the Supernatural.*
Peck, Richard. *The Ghost Belonged to Me.*

GIRLS GROWING UP

(*See also*: Boy-Girl Relationships, Brothers and Sisters, Family Life, Family Problems, Friendship, School, Sisters.)
Category: A
Adler, Susan S. (American Girls Collection). *Meet Samantha.*
Porter, Connie. (American Girls Collection). *Meet Addy.*
Shaw, Janet. (American Girls Collection). *Meet Kirsten.*

Tripp, Valerie. (American Girls Collection). *Meet Felicity.*
Tripp, Valerie. (American Girls Collection). *Meet Molly.*
Christopher, Matt. *Red-Hot Hightops.*
Cleary, Beverly. *Muggie Maggie.*
Category: B
Dorris, Michael. *Morning Girl.*
Category: C
AVI. *Blue Heron.*
Blume, Judy. *Are You There God? It's Me, Margaret.*
Cassedy, Sylvia. *Behind the Attic Wall.*
Cassedy, Sylvia. *Lucie Babbidge's House.*
Coville, Bruce. *The Ghost in the Big Brass Bed.*
Coville, Bruce. *The Ghost Wore Gray.*
Hamilton, Virginia. *Zeely.*
Lasky, Kathryn. *The Night Journey.*
MacBride, Roger Lea. *Little House on Rocky Ridge.*
MacLachlan, Patricia. *Baby.*
Naylor, Phyllis Reynolds. *The Agony of Alice.*
Rylant, Cynthia. *Missing May.*
Wright, Betty Ren. *Christina's Ghost.*
Wright, Betty Ren. *The Dollhouse Murders.*
Wright, Betty Ren. *Ghosts Beneath Our Feet.*
Category: D
Banks, Lynne Reid. *One More River.*
Blume, Judy. *Here's to You, Rachel Robinson.*
Hahn, Mary Downing. *Wait Till Helen Comes: A Ghost Story.*
Hamilton, Virginia. *Cousins.*
Konigsburg, E. L. *T-Backs, T-Shirts, COAT and Suit.*
Lowry, Lois. *Number the Stars.*
O'Dell, Scott. *My Name Is Not Angelica.*
Paterson, Katherine. *Lyddie.*
Paulsen, Gary. *Nightjohn.*
Category: E
AVI. *The True Confessions of Charlotte Doyle.*
Montgomery, L. M. *Anne of Avonlea.*
Montgomery, L. M. *Anne of Green Gables.*
Nixon, Joan Lowery. *The Kidnapping of Christina Lattimore.*
Nixon, Joan Lowery. *The Other Side of Dark.*
Paterson, Katherine. *Of Nightingales That Weep.*
Peck, Richard. *Are You in the House Alone?*
Peck, Richard. *Don't Look and It Won't Hurt.*
Taylor, Mildred D. *Let the Circle Be Unbroken.*
Taylor, Mildred D. *The Road to Memphis.*

GRANDPARENTS

(*See also*: Family Life, Relatives—Living with Relatives.)

Category: A
  Adler, Susan S. (American Girls Collection). *Meet Samantha.*
Category: B
  Smith, Robert Kimmel. *The War with Grandpa.*
  Stolz, Mary. *Stealing Home.*
Category: C
  Blume, Judy. *Are You There God? It's Me, Margaret.*
  Lasky, Kathryn. *The Night Journey.*
  MacLachlan, Patricia. *Journey.*
  Paterson, Katherine. *Park's Quest.*

HANDICAPS

Category: C
  Wright, Betty Ren. *The Dollhouse Murders.*
Category: E
  Freedman, Russell. *Franklin Delano Roosevelt.*

HISTORICAL FICTION

(*See also*: Biography, Child Labor, Frontier Life and Pioneer Life, War—Civilian Life During Wartime.)

Category: A
  Adler, Susan S. (American Girls Collection). *Meet Samantha.*
  Porter, Connie. (American Girls Collection). *Meet Addy.*
  Shaw, Janet. (American Girls Collection). *Meet Kirsten.*
  Tripp, Valerie. (American Girls Collection). *Meet Felicity.*
  Tripp, Valerie. (American Girls Collection). *Meet Molly.*
Category: C
  Reeder, Carolyn. *Shades of Gray.*
Category: D
  Lowry, Lois. *Number the Stars.*
  O'Dell, Scott. *My Name Is Not Angelica.*
  Paterson, Katherine. *Lyddie.*
  Paulsen, Gary. *Nightjohn.*
Category: E
  AVI. *The True Confessions of Charlotte Doyle.*
  Magorian, Michelle. *Good Night, Mr. Tom.*
  Paterson, Katherine. *Of Nightingales That Weep.*
  Taylor, Mildred D. *Let the Circle Be Unbroken.*
  Taylor, Mildred D. *The Road to Memphis.*

HOMELESSNESS

(*See also*: Children Living Alone, Gangs/Street Life, Poverty/Financial Hardship, Social Issues, Survival.)

Category: A
  Warner, Gertrude Chandler. *The Boxcar Children* (Boxcar Mystery #1).
Category: C
  Fox, Paula. *Monkey Island.*
  George, Jean Craighead. *The Missing 'Gator of Gumbo Limbo.*
Category: D
  Paterson, Katherine. *Lyddie.*
  Spinelli, Jerry. *Maniac Magee.*

HORSES

(*See also*: Animals, Animals as Talking Characters, Cats, Dogs, Farms—Living on a Farm, Pets, Rabbits.)

Category: A
  Tripp, Valerie. (American Girls Collection). *Meet Felicity.*
Category: D.
  Fleischman, Sid. *The Midnight Horse.*

HUMOR

(*See also*: Animals as Talking Characters, Babies, Make Believe/Magic, Toddlers/Preschoolers.)

Category: A
  Blume, Judy. *Fudge-A-Mania.*
  Cleary, Beverly. *Muggie Maggie.*
  Lindgren, Astrid. *Pippi Goes on Board.*
  Lindgren, Astrid. *Pippi in the South Seas.*
  Lindgren, Astrid. *Pippi Longstocking.*
  MacDonald, Betty. *Mrs. Piggle-Wiggle.*
  MacDonald, Betty. *Mrs. Piggle-Wiggle's Farm.*
Category: B
  Byars, Betsy. *A Blossom Promise.*
  Byars, Betsy. *The Blossoms and the Green Phantom.*
  Byars, Betsy. *The Blossoms Meet the Vulture Lady.*
  Byars, Betsy. *The Not-Just-Anybody Family.*
  Byars, Betsy. *Wanted . . . Mud Blossom.*
  Dahl, Roald. *Charlie and the Chocolate Factory.*
  Dahl, Roald. *Charlie and the Great Glass Elevator.*
  Dahl, Roald. *James and the Giant Peach.*
  Dahl, Roald. *The Witches.*
  Howe, Deborah, and James Howe. *Bunnicula: A Rabbit Tale of Mystery.*
  Howe, James. *The Celery Stalks at Midnight.*

Howe, James. *Howliday Inn.*
Howe, James. *Return to Howliday Inn.*
King-Smith, Dick. *Harry's Mad.*
Lowry, Lois. *All About Sam.*
Lowry, Lois. *Attaboy, Sam!*
Naylor, Phyllis Reynolds. *The Boys Start the War.*
Naylor, Phyllis Reynolds. *The Grand Escape.*
Smith, Robert Kimmel. *The War with Grandpa.*
Category: C
AVI. *Who Was That Masked Man, Anyway?*
Blume, Judy. *Are You There God? It's Me, Margaret.*
Naylor, Phyllis Reynolds. *The Agony of Alice.*
Naylor, Phyllis Reynolds. *Beetles, Lightly Toasted.*
Category: D
Cleary, Beverly. *Strider.*

ISLANDS—LIVING ON AN ISLAND

(*See also*: Adventure, Nature, Rivers, Sea, Ships, Survival.)

Category: A
Lindgren, Astrid. *Pippi in the South Seas.*
Warner, Gertrude Chandler. *Surprise Island* (Boxcar Mystery #2).
Category: B
Dorris, Michael. *Morning Girl.*
Category: C
MacLachlan, Patricia. *Baby.*
Category: D
O'Dell, Scott. *My Name Is Not Angelica.*
Category: E
Lasky, Kathryn. *Shadows in the Water.*
Montgomery, L. M. *Anne of Avonlea.*
Montgomery, L. M. *Anne of Green Gables.*

JEWISH PEOPLE

(*See also*: Prejudice.)

Category: C
Blume, Judy. *Are You There God? It's Me, Margaret.*
Lasky, Kathryn. *The Night Journey.*
Category: D
Banks, Lynne Reid. *One More River.*
Lowry, Lois. *Number the Stars.*

KIDNAPPING

(*See also*: Crime—Being the Victim of a Violent Crime.)

Category: C
Fleischman, Sid. *The Whipping Boy.*

Category: E
Nixon, Joan Lowery. *The Kidnapping of Christina Lattimore.*

MAKE BELIEVE/MAGIC

(*See also*: Animals as Talking Characters, Fantasy, Humor.)

Category: A
Christopher, Matt. *Red-Hot Hightops.*
Lindgren, Astrid. *Pippi Goes on Board.*
Lindgren, Astrid. *Pippi in the South Seas.*
Lindgren, Astrid. *Pippi Longstocking.*
MacDonald, Betty. *Mrs. Piggle-Wiggle.*
MacDonald, Betty. *Mrs. Piggle-Wiggle's Farm.*
Category: B
Howe, Deborah, and James Howe. *Bunnicula: A Rabbit Tale of Mystery.*
Howe, James. *The Celery Stalks at Midnight.*
Howe, James. *Howliday Inn.*
Howe, James. *Return to Howliday Inn.*
King-Smith, Dick. *Harry's Mad.*
Naylor, Phyllis Reynolds. *The Grand Escape.*
Category: C
AVI. *Who Was That Masked Man, Anyway?*
Cassedy, Sylvia. *Behind the Attic Wall.*
Cassedy, Sylvia. *Lucie Babbidge's House.*
Category: D
Fleischman, Sid. *The Midnight Horse.*

MENTAL ILLNESS

(*See also*: Family Problems.)

Category: C
Fox, Paula. *Monkey Island.*
Category: E
Magorian, Michelle. *Good Night, Mr. Tom.*

MOTHERS

(*See also*: Family Life, Family Problems, Fathers, Stepparents.)

Category: A
Porter, Connie. (American Girls Collection). *Meet Addy.*
Tripp, Valerie. (American Girls Collection). *Meet Molly.*

MURDER

(*See also*: Crime, Ghosts, Mystery.)

Category: C
Wright, Betty Ren. *Christina's Ghost.*
Wright, Betty Ren. *The Dollhouse Murders*

Category: D
> Hinton, S. E. *The Outsiders.*
> Lowry, Lois. *The Giver.*

Category: E
> Nixon, Joan Lowery. *The Other Side of Dark.*

MYSTERY

(*See also*: Ghosts, Murder.)

Category: A
> Warner, Gertrude Chandler. *The Boxcar Children* (Boxcar Mystery #1).
> Warner, Gertrude Chandler. *Surprise Island* (Boxcar Mystery #2).
> Warner, Gertrude Chandler. *The Yellow House Mystery* (Boxcar Mystery #3).

Category: B
> Howe, Deborah, and James Howe. *Bunnicula: A Rabbit Tale of Mystery.*
> Howe, James. *The Celery Stalks at Midnight.*
> Howe, James. *Howliday Inn.*
> Howe, James. *Return to Howliday Inn.*

Category: C
> Bellairs, John. *The Letter, the Witch, and the Ring.*
> Bellairs, John. *The Mansion in the Mist.*
> Coville, Bruce. *The Ghost in the Big Brass Bed.*
> Coville, Bruce. *The Ghost Wore Gray.*
> George, Jean Craighead. *The Missing 'Gator of Gumbo Limbo.*
> Wright, Betty Ren. *Christina's Ghost.*
> Wright, Betty Ren. *The Dollhouse Murders.*
> Wright, Betty Ren. *Ghosts Beneath Our Feet.*

Category: D
> Bellairs, John. *The House with a Clock in Its Walls.*
> Hahn, Mary Downing. *Wait Till Helen Comes: A Ghost Story.*
> Peck, Richard. *The Ghost Belonged to Me.*

Category: E
> Nixon, Joan Lowery. *The Kidnapping of Christina Lattimore.*
> Nixon, Joan Lowery. *The Other Side of Dark.*

NATIVE AMERICANS

(*See also*: Historical Fiction, Prejudice, Slavery.)

Category: B
> Banks, Lynne Reid. *The Indian in the Cupboard* .
> Banks, Lynne Reid. *The Mystery of the Cupboard.*

Banks, Lynne Reid. *The Return of the Indian..*
Banks, Lynne Reid. *The Secret of the Indian.*
Dorris, Michael. *Morning Girl.*

NATURE/ECOLOGY

(*See also*: Animals, Farms—Living on a Farm, Islands—Living on an Island, Rivers, Sea.)

Category: C
> George, Jean Craighead. *The Missing 'Gator of Gumbo Limbo.*

Category: D
> Paulsen, Gary. *Hatchet.*

Category: E
> Lasky, Kathryn. *Shadows in the Water.*

NEGLECT—BEING NEGLECTED BY ONE OR BY BOTH PARENTS

(*See also*: Abandonment—Being Abandoned by One or by Both Parents, Child Abuse, Children Living Alone, Family Problems, Orphans/Orphanages.)

Category: D
> Hinton, S. E. *Tex.*

Category: E
> Magorian, Michelle. *Good Night, Mr. Tom.*

NEWBERY MEDAL BOOKS

(Listed with the year, in parentheses, in which the award was given.)

Category: C
> Rylant, Cynthia. *Missing May.* (1993)
> Naylor, Phyllis Reynolds. *Shiloh.* (1992)
> Fleischman, Sid. *The Whipping Boy.* (1987)

Category: D
> Lowry, Lois. *The Giver.* (1994)
> Lowry, Lois. *Number the Stars.* (1990)
> Spinelli, Jerry. *Maniac Magee.* (1991)

Category: E
> Freedman, Russell. *Lincoln: A Photobiography.* (1988)

ORPHANS/ORPHANAGES

(*See also*: Abandonment—Being Abandoned by One or by Both Parents, Children Living Alone, Neglect—Being Neglected by One or by Both Parents.)

Category: A
> Warner, Gertrude Chandler. *The Boxcar Children* (Boxcar Mystery #1).

Category: C
> Cassedy, Sylvia. *Behind the Attic Wall.*
> Cassedy, Sylvia. *Lucie Babbidge's House.*

Category: D
>   AVI. *Punch with Judy.*
>   Hinton, S. E. *The Outsiders.*
>   Spinelli, Jerry. *Maniac Magee.*

Category: E
>   Montgomery, L. M. *Anne of Green Gables.*

PETS

(*See also*: Animals, Animals as Talking Characters, Cats, Dogs, Farms—Living on a Farm, Horses, Mice/Rats, Rabbits.)

Category: A
>   Graeber, Charlotte Towner. *Fudge.*

Category: B
>   Martin, Ann M. *Ten Kids, No Pets.*

Category: C
>   Naylor, Phyllis Reynolds. *Shiloh.*

Category: D
>   Cleary, Beverly. *Strider.*

POVERTY/FINANCIAL HARDSHIP

(*See also*: Family Problems, Homelessness, Survival.)

Category: C
>   Fox, Paula. *Monkey Island.*
>   Naylor, Phyllis Reynolds. *Shiloh.*

Category: D
>   Hinton, S. E. *Tex.*

PREJUDICE

(*See also*: African Americans, Handicaps, Jewish People, Native Americans, Slavery.)

Category: A
>   Porter, Connie. (American Girls Collection). *Meet Addy.*
>   Christopher, Matt. *No Arm in Left Field.*

Category: D
>   Banks, Lynne Reid. *One More River.*
>   McKissack, Patricia C. *The Dark-Thirty: Southern Tales of the Supernatural.*
>   O'Dell, Scott. *My Name Is Not Angelica.*
>   Paulsen, Gary. *Nightjohn.*
>   Spinelli, Jerry. *Maniac Magee.*

Category: E
>   McKissack, Patricia C., and Fredrick McKissack. *A Long Hard Journey: The Story of Pullman Porter.*
>   Taylor, Mildred D. *Let the Circle Be Unbroken.*
>   Taylor, Mildred D. *The Road to Memphis.*

RABBITS

(*See also*: Animals, Animals as Talking Characters, Cats, Dogs, Farms—Living on a Farm, Horses, Pets.)

Category: B
>   Howe, Deborah, and James Howe. *Bunnicula: A Rabbit Tale of Mystery.*
>   Howe, James. *The Celery Stalks at Midnight.*

RELATIVES—LIVING WITH RELATIVES

(*See also*: Family Life, Grandparents.)

Category: A
>   Adler, Susan S. (American Girls Collection). *Meet Samantha.*

Category: B
>   Smith, Robert Kimmel. *The War with Grandpa.*
>   Stolz, Mary. *Stealing Home.*

Category: C
>   MacLachlan, Patricia. *Journey.*
>   Paterson, Katherine. *Park's Quest.*
>   Reeder, Carolyn. *Shades of Gray.*
>   Rylant, Cynthia. *Missing May.*
>   Wright, Betty Ren. *Christina's Ghost.*
>   Wright, Betty Ren. *Ghosts Beneath Our Feet.*

Category: D
>   Konigsburg, E. L. *T-Backs, T-Shirts, COAT and Suit.*

RIVERS

(*See also*: Adventure, Islands—Living on an Island, Nature, Sea, Ships.)

Category: C
>   Bauer, Marion Dane. *Face to Face.*
>   Bauer, Marion Dane. *On My Honor.*

Category: D
>   Banks, Lynne Reid. *One More River.*

ROMANCE

(*See also*: Boy-Girl Relationships, Friendship.)

Category: D
>   Blume, Judy. *Here's to You, Rachel Robinson.*
>   Hinton, S. E. *That Was Then, This Is Now.*

Category: E
>   Montgomery, L. M. *Anne of Avonlea.*
>   Nixon, Joan Lowery. *The Other Side of Dark.*
>   Paterson, Katherine. *Of Nightingales That Weep.*

RUNAWAYS

(*See also*: Children Living Alone, Gangs/Street Life, Homelessness.)

Category: C

Fleischman, Sid. *The Whipping Boy.*

Category: D

Spinelli, Jerry. *Maniac Magee.*

SEA

(*See also*: Adventure, Islands—Living on an Island, Nature, Rivers, Ships.)

Category: A

Lindgren, Astrid. *Pippi Goes on Board.*

Lindgren, Astrid. *Pippi in the South Seas.*

Category: C

Paulsen, Gary. *The Voyage of the* Frog.

Category: E

AVI. *The True Confessions of Charlotte Doyle.*

Lasky, Kathryn. *Shadows in the Water.*

SCHOOL

(*See also*: Boys Growing Up, Friendship, Girls Growing Up.)

Category: A

Cleary, Beverly. *Muggie Maggie.*

Category: B

Sachar, Louis. *There's a Boy in the Girls' Bathroom.*

Category: C

Naylor, Phyllis Reynolds. *The Agony of Alice.*

Naylor, Phyllis Reynolds. *Beetles, Lightly Toasted.*

Category: D

Spinelli, Jerry. *Space Station Seventh Grade.*

SHIPS

(*See also*: Adventure, Islands—Living on an Island, Rivers, Sea.)

Category: A

Lindgren, Astrid. *Pippi Goes on Board.*

Lindgren, Astrid. *Pippi in the South Seas.*

Category: C

Paulsen, Gary. *The Voyage of the* Frog.

Category: E

AVI. *The True Confessions of Charlotte Doyle.*

SINGLE PARENTS—LIVING IN A SINGLE PARENT HOME

(*See also*: Divorce, Family Problems, Stepparents.)

Category: B

Byars, Betsy. *A Blossom Promise.*

Byars, Betsy. *The Blossoms and the Green Phantom.*

Byars, Betsy. *The Blossoms Meet the Vulture Lady.*

Byars, Betsy. *The Not-Just-Anybody Family.*

Byars, Betsy. *Wanted . . . Mud Blossom.*

Category: C

Naylor, Phyllis Reynolds. *The Agony of Alice.*

Category: D

Cleary, Beverly. *Strider.*

Hamilton, Virginia. *Cousins.*

Hinton, S. E. *Tex.*

Hinton, S. E. *That Was Then, This Is Now.*

Category: E

Peck, Richard. *Don't Look and It Won't Hurt.*

SISTERS

(*See also*: Brothers, Brothers and Sisters, Family Life, Girls Growing Up.)

Category: C

Paterson, Katherine. *Park's Quest.*

Wright, Betty Ren. *The Dollhouse Murders.*

Category: D

Hahn, Mary Downing. *Wait Till Helen Comes: A Ghost Story.*

Category: E

Peck, Richard. *Don't Look and It Won't Hurt.*

SLAVERY

(*See also*: African Americans, Native Americans, Prejudice.)

Category: A

Porter, Connie. (American Girls Collection). *Meet Addy.*

Category: D

O'Dell, Scott. *My Name Is Not Angelica.*

Paulsen, Gary. *Nightjohn.*

Category: E

Freedman, Russell. *Lincoln: A Photobiography.*

SOCIAL ISSUES

(*See also*: Child Abuse, Child Labor, Homelessness, Poverty/Financial Hardship, Prejudice.)

Category: A

Adler, Susan S. (American Girls Collection). *Meet Samantha.*

Category: C

Coville, Bruce. *My Teacher Flunked the Planet.*

Reeder, Carolyn. *Shades of Gray.*

Category: D
>   Konigsburg, E. L. *T-Backs, T-Shirts, COAT and Suit.*
>   Lowry, Lois. *The Giver.*

Category: E
>   Freedman, Russell. *Franklin Delano Roosevelt.*
>   Freedman, Russell. *Lincoln: A Photobiography.*

SPORTS

Category: A
>   Christopher, Matt. *Front Court Hex.*
>   Christopher, Matt. *Johnny Long Legs.*
>   Christopher, Matt. *No Arm in Left Field.*
>   Christopher, Matt. *Red-Hot Hightops.*

STEPPARENTS

(*See also*: Divorce, Family Problems, Single Parents—Living in a Single Parent Home.)

Category: C
>   AVI. *Blue Heron.*
>   Bauer, Marion Dane. *Face to Face.*

SUMMER VACATION

(*See also*: Boys Growing Up, Family Life, Friendship, Girls Growing Up.)

Category: C
>   Hamilton, Virginia. *Zeely.*

Category: D
>   Konigsburg, E. L. *T-Backs, T-Shirts, COAT and Suit.*

SURVIVAL

(*See also*: Adventure, Animals, Frontier Life and Pioneer Life, Gangs/Street Life, Islands—Living on an Island.)

Category: C
>   Paulsen, Gary. *The Voyage of the* Frog.

Category: D
>   Paulsen, Gary. *Hatchet.*

TEEN PREGNANCY

Category: E
>   Peck, Richard. *Don't Look and It Won't Hurt.*

TODDLERS/PRESCHOOLERS

(*See also*: Babies, Humor.)

Category: B
>   Lowry, Lois. *All About Sam.*
>   Lowry, Lois. *Attaboy, Sam!*

WAR—CIVILIAN LIFE DURING WARTIME

(*See also*: Historical Fiction.)

Category: A
>   Tripp, Valerie. (American Girls Collection). *Meet Molly.*

Category: D
>   Lowry, Lois. *Number the Stars.*

Category: E
>   Magorian, Michelle. *Good Night, Mr. Tom.*
>   Paterson, Katherine. *Of Nightingales That Weep.*

WITCHES/WITCHCRAFT/SORCERY

(*See also*: Ghosts, Make Believe/Magic.)

Category: A
>   Christopher, Matt. *Front Court Hex.*

Category: B
>   Dahl, Roald. *The Witches.*

Category: C
>   Bellairs, John. *The Letter, the Witch, and the Ring.*
>   Bellairs, John. *The Mansion in the Mist.*

Category: D
>   Bellairs, John. *The House with a Clock in Its Walls.*

Annotations—Category A

Adler, Susan S. (American Girls Collection). 1986. *Meet Samantha*. Middleton, Wis.: Pleasant Company Publications. Category: A. Point Value: 5. Book #221.

It is 1904 and Samantha is an orphan being raised by her rich grandmother. When Samantha becomes friends with Nellie, the girl next door, and with Jessie, the African American seamstress, Samantha learns that life is very difficult for the poor families living nearby.

Blume, Judy. 1990. *Fudge-A-Mania*. New York: Dutton Children's Books. Category: A. Point Value: 10. Book #241.

Get ready for some wild and wacky reading! In Fudge-A-Mania, Fudge and his family are going on vacation, and they're taking the family dog and Fudge's parrot with them!

Christopher, Matt. 1974. *Front Court Hex*. Boston: Little, Brown. Category: A. Point Value: 10. Book #251.

Last year Jerry was the best on the team. This year, he's the worst. Is it just bad luck, or has someone put a spell on him?

Christopher, Matt. 1970. *Johnny Long Legs*. Boston: Little, Brown. Category: A. Point Value: 10. Book #252.

Johnny wants his team to win, but how can Johnny help when everyone who is shorter than him can outjump him?

Christopher, Matt. 1974. *No Arm in Left Field*. Boston: Little, Brown. Category: A. Point Value: 10. Book #253.

Terry is the only black player on his team. Tony dislikes Terry because Terry is black and also because Terry can't throw well. Can Tony and Terry work out their problems and lead their team to victory?

Christopher, Matt. 1987. *Red-Hot Hightops*. Boston: Little, Brown. Category: A. Point Value: 10. Book #254.

Kelly is shy and quiet until a pair of red shoes turns her into a basketball star.

Cleary, Beverly. 1990. *Muggie Maggie*. New York: William Morrow. Category: A. Point Value: 5. Book #255.

Maggie likes to print but now that she is in the third grade, it's time to learn to write in cursive. What will happen when Maggie refuses to learn?!

Graeber, Charlotte Towner. 1987. *Fudge*. New York: Lothrop, Lee & Shepard Books. Category: A. Point Value: 5. Book #275.

Chad has seven days to prove to his parents that he is responsible enough to care for a dog. Will he be able to do it?

Lindgren, Astrid. 1957. *Pippi Goes on Board*. New York: The Viking Press. Category: A. Point Value: 10. Book #290.

Pippi, the world's most unusual girl, finally sees her father, the cannibal king. Will Pippi stay in Villa Villekulla or will she go to be a cannibal princess?

Lindgren, Astrid. 1959. *Pippi in the South Seas*. New York: The Viking Press. Category: A. Point Value: 10. Book #291.

From fighting off filthy thieves to rescuing each other from sharks, Pippi, Tommy, and Annika have many fun-filled days when they vacation on a tropical island.

Lindgren, Astrid. 1950. *Pippi Longstocking*. New York: The Viking Press. Category: A. Point Value: 10. Book #292.

Amazing! Unbelievable! Shocking! What else can you say about a girl as strong as 10 men, who lives with a horse and a monkey, who doesn't go to school, and who has a chest full of gold coins? Who is this girl? Pippi Longstocking, of course!

MacDonald, Betty. 1947. *Mrs. Piggle-Wiggle*. New York: HarperCollins Children's Books. Category: A. Point Value: 10. Book #298.

Mrs. Piggle-Wiggle loves and understands children, and for every problem, she has a cure. Some of Mrs. Piggle-Wiggle's cures are a little unusual, like planting radish seeds in the filthy head of the little girl who refused to take a bath, but what can you expect from a little woman who lives in an upside-down house?!

MacDonald, Betty. 1954. *Mrs. Piggle-Wiggle's Farm*. New York: HarperCollins Children's Books. Category: A. Point Value: 10. Book #299.
Mrs. Piggle-Wiggle has moved to a farm, but she still loves children. And with the help of her unusual animals, Mrs. Piggle-Wiggle helps children solve difficult problems.

Porter, Connie. (American Girls Collection). 1993. *Meet Addy*. Middleton, Wis.: Pleasant Company Publications. Category: A. Point Value: 5. Book #222.
Freedom! Freedom from slavery is what Addy and her family want the most, and they've come up with a plan to escape the tobacco plantation where they live. However, when the plantation owner, Master Stevens, unexpectedly sells Addy's father and brother, the plan is ruined, and Addy and her mother must decide what to do. Will Addy and her mother be able to escape on their own?

Shaw, Janet. (American Girls Collection). 1986. *Meet Kirsten*. Middleton, Wis.: Pleasant Company Publications. Category: A. Point Value: 5. Book #223.
Nine-year-old Kirsten and her family are traveling from Sweden to a new life in America. Kirsten tries to be brave as she and her family face storms, disease, and even death on their way to Minnesota.

Tripp, Valerie. (American Girls Collection). 1991. *Meet Felicity*. Middleton, Wis.: Pleasant Company Publications. Category: A. Point Value: 5. Book #224.
Felicity loves horses, but the horse she loves the most is owned by a cruel man who mistreats his animals. Felicity wants to rescue the horse, but first she will have to come up with a plan!

Tripp, Valerie. (American Girls Collection). 1986. *Meet Molly*. Middleton, Wis.: Pleasant Company Publications. Category: A. Point Value: 5. Book #225.
When America is at war, everyone, including Molly, must make sacrifices to help the cause. Molly tries to be helpful and pleasant most of the time—even when she has to eat vegetables for dinner—but when Molly's brother ruins Halloween for Molly and her friends, Molly makes plans to get even!

Warner, Gertrude Chandler. 1942. *The Boxcar Children*. (Boxcar Mystery #1). Niles, Ill.: Albert Whitman. Category: A. Point Value: 10. Book #335.
Jessie, Bennie, Violet, and Henry are brothers and sisters whose parents are dead and who have no place to live. When the four children find an empty boxcar, they turn it into a home. The children are doing fine living by themselves, but then their grandfather comes looking for them. Should the Boxcar Children run away and hide?

Warner, Gertrude Chandler. 1949. *Surprise Island*. (Boxcar Mystery #2). Niles, Ill.: Albert Whitman. Category: A. Point Value: 10. Book #336.
The Boxcar Children spend a summer alone on an island with only Captain Daniel and a mysterious stranger.

Warner, Gertrude Chandler. 1953. *The Yellow House Mystery*. (Boxcar Mystery #3). Niles, Ill.: Albert Whitman. Category: A. Point Value: 10. Book #337.
Long ago, a man from the island disappeared with $10,000. Where did the man go and why did he leave? Can the Boxcar Children follow the old clues and solve the mystery?

Annotations—Category B

Banks, Lynne Reid. 1980. *The Indian in the Cupboard*. New York: Delacorte Press. Category: B. Point Value: 10. Book #230.
Omri's mother gives him a cupboard for his birthday, but when Omri puts a toy Indian in the cupboard, something very strange happens: the toy Indian becomes a real live miniature Indian! What will Omri do with this little person? And what will the small but powerful Indian do with Omri?

Banks, Lynne Reid. 1993. *The Mystery of the Cupboard*. New York: William Morrow. Category: B. Point Value: 10. Book #231.
Omri finally solves the mystery of why the magic cupboard works, but in solving the mystery, Omri runs the risk of changing the course of history forever.

Banks, Lynne Reid. 1986. *The Return of the Indian*. New York: Doubleday. Category: B. Point Value: 10. Book #233.
Omri brings Little Bear back and finds that he is in terrible danger.

Banks, Lynne Reid. 1989. *The Secret of the Indian*. New York: Doubleday. Category: B. Point Value: 10. Book #234.
Omri and Patrick find that keeping the cupboard a secret is almost impossible, but this problem seems small when Omri and Patrick learn that their lives, as well as the lives of their tiny friends, are all in danger.

Byars, Betsy. 1987. *A Blossom Promise*. New York: Dell Publishing. Category: B. Point Value: 10. Book #244.
When a flood brings tragedy to the Blossom family, the Blossoms deal with it in true Blossom style.

Byars, Betsy. 1987. *The Blossoms and the Green Phantom*. New York: Dell Publishing. Category: B. Point Value: 10. Book #245.
Trouble seems to follow the Blossom family like flies follow a garbage truck! In this Blossom adventure, Pap spends the night in a garbage dumpster, and one of Junior's inventions has Junior hiding from an angry neighbor with a loaded shotgun!

Byars, Betsy. 1986. *The Blossoms Meet the Vulture Lady*. New York: Dell Publishing. Category: B. Point Value: 10. Book #246.
Junior loves to invent things, but when Junior invents a coyote trap, the only thing he traps is himself!

Byars, Betsy. 1986. *The Not-Just-Anybody Family*. New York: Dell Publishing. Category: B. Point Value: 10. Book #247.
In the Blossom family, you never know what's going to happen next. Whether they're breaking into jail or jumping off barns, the Blossoms are always entertaining!

Byars, Betsy. 1991. *Wanted . . . Mud Blossom*. New York: Dell Publishing. Category: B. Point Value: 10. Book #248.
Guilty! There are pine needles in his fur and there is dirt on his nose. Mud, the family dog, has eaten Scooty, the school hamster. Or has he?

Dahl, Roald. 1964. *Charlie and the Chocolate Factory*. New York: Puffin Books. Category: B. Point Value: 10. Book #261.
Never in his wildest dreams did little Charlie Bucket ever think that he would be able to see the inside of Willy Wonka's mysterious chocolate factory. But when Charlie finds a golden ticket inside of a chocolate candy bar, he wins a tour of the magical factory — a tour that will prove to be as dangerous as it is amazing!

Dahl, Roald. 1972. *Charlie and the Great Glass Elevator*. New York: Puffin Books. Category: B. Point Value: 10. Book #262.
Charlie, Willy Wonka, and the Bucket family zip from one adventure to another as they travel in Wonka's Great Glass Elevator.

Dahl, Roald. 1961. *James and the Giant Peach*. New York: Puffin Books. Category: B. Point Value: 10. Book #263.
After James accidentally drops some magic crystals, he ends up in a giant peach with a group of large, talking bugs.

Dahl, Roald. 1983. *The Witches*. New York: Farrar, Straus & Giroux. Category: B. Point Value: 15. Book #264.
Beware! There are hundreds of evil witches lurking around, and this book will help you spot them!

Dorris, Michael. 1992. *Morning Girl*. New York: Hyperion Books for Children. Category: B. Point Value: 5. Book #265.
Morning Girl lives in the Bahamas where it is always warm, where there is plenty of food, and where everyone in her tribe works peacefully together. In other words, Morning Girl thinks that her life in the Bahamas is paradise. At least it *would* be paradise if her brother would quit bothering her so much.

Fleischman, Sid. 1992. *Jim Ugly*. New York: Dell Publishing. Category: B. Point Value: 10. Book #266.
Is Jake's father really dead? Jake isn't sure, so with the aid of the wolf-like dog, Jim Ugly, Jake tries to follow his father's trail.

Howe, Deborah, and James Howe. 1979. *Bunnicula: A Rabbit Tale of Mystery*. New York: Atheneum. Category: B. Point Value: 5. Book #282.
Chester, the cat, is convinced that the cute little bunny that the Monroes have found is really a vampire.

Howe, James. 1983. *The Celery Stalks at Midnight*. New York: Atheneum. Category: B. Point Value: 5. Book #283.
Convinced that Bunnicula, the vampire bunny, is on the loose and is stalking the entire town, Harold, Howie, and Chester set out to stop Bunnicula and Bunnicula's evil minions.

Howe, James. 1982. *Howliday Inn*. New York: Atheneum. Category: B. Point Value: 10. Book #284.
The Monroe family has gone on vacation and left Chester and Harold at the Chateau Bow-Wow. However, instead of being a place to relax, Chester and Harold find that the Chateau Bow-Wow is a place of mystery and danger.

Howe, James. 1992. *Return to Howliday Inn*. New York: Atheneum. Category: B. Point Value: 10. Book #285.

Once again, Harold and his friends are sent to the Chateau Bow-Wow where ghostly voices convince Chester that danger is again all around.

King-Smith, Dick. 1987. *Harry's Mad*. New York: Crown Publishers. Category: B. Point Value: 5. Book #286.
When Harry's great-uncle from America dies, he sends Harry a talking parrot named Madison that changes Harry's life. Squawk!

Lowry, Lois. 1988. *All About Sam*. Boston: Houghton Mifflin. Category: B. Point Value: 10. Book #293.
When a baby as smart as Sam is born, he can't believe his eyes or his ears! Why, for example, do people talk so foolishly to him? "Goo goo, ga, ga?" Puh–lease!

Lowry, Lois. 1992. *Attaboy, Sam!* Boston: Houghton Mifflin. Category: B. Point Value: 10. Book #294.
Sam's mother is having a birthday, and Sam is going to give her the best present in the world! At least he *was* going to give her the best present in the world until it exploded. Now what is Sam going to do?

Martin, Ann M. 1988. *Ten Kids, No Pets*. New York: Holiday House. Category: B. Point Value: 15. Book #303.
All the Rosso kids want is a pet, but even 10 kids seem to be no match for Mom's no-pet rule. How can they get Mom to change her mind?

Naylor, Phyllis Reynolds. 1993. *The Boys Start the War*. New York: Delacorte Press. Category: B. Point Value: 10. Book #310.
When a family of girls moves in across the river, the Halford boys try to make them leave by starting a practical joke war.

Naylor, Phyllis Reynolds. 1993. *The Grand Escape*. New York: Atheneum. Category: B. Point Value: 10. Book #311.
Marco and Polo are two house cats who escape to the exciting outside world where they meet a tomcat named Texas Jake. Texas Jake says that he will give Marco and Polo a place to stay but only if they can solve three mysteries. What Marco and Polo don't know, however, is that Texas Jake's mysteries are designed to kill them. Are two house cats able to outwit Texas Jake, or will they die trying?

Sachar, Louis. 1987. *There's a Boy in the Girls' Bathroom.* New York: Random House. Category: B. Point Value: 10. Book #328.
Bradley Chalkers is disliked by everybody except the new school counselor, who believes that Bradley can be a good student and not the terror of the school. But is it possible to change when everyone thinks you're a monster?

Smith, Robert Kimmel. 1984. *The War with Grandpa.* New York: Delacorte Press. Category: B. Point Value: 10. Book #329.
When Peter hears that Grandpa is coming to live with Peter and his family, Peter is very happy. But then Peter hears the rest of the news: Grandpa will be taking over his room. What?! Give up his room? Never! Peter has just one message for Grandpa: This means war! But Grandpa proves to be a worthy foe. Who will be the winner?

Stolz, Mary. 1992. *Stealing Home.* New York: HarperCollins Children's Books. Category: B. Point Value: 10. Book #332.
Thomas and his grandfather are like two peas in a pod, but then bossy Great-Aunt Linzy, who hates everything that Thomas and his grandfather love, comes to live with them. Can Thomas, Grandpa, and Aunt Linzy survive in the same small house without driving each other crazy?

Annotations—Category C

AVI. 1992. *Blue Heron.* New York: Macmillan. Category: C. Point Value: 15. Book #226.
Maggie's visit with her father turns sour when Maggie's father acts strangely and someone tries to kill the heron that Maggie loves.

AVI. 1992. *Who Was That Masked Man, Anyway?* New York: Orchard Books. Category: C. Point Value: 10. Book #229.
Hi ho, Silver! Away! Frankie spends so much of his time listening to radio adventures that he is about to flunk the sixth grade. Not to worry, though . . . when the going gets rough, Frankie becomes Chet Barker, ace detective, the wonder boy who can solve every problem.

Bauer, Marion Dane. 1991. *Face to Face.* Boston: Houghton Mifflin. Category: C. Point Value: 15. Book #235.
For years, Michael has dreamed of seeing his real father. Now, finally, an unexpected call leads Michael to his father and into a trip down a river that could cost him his life.

Bauer, Marion Dane. 1986. *On My Honor.* Boston: Houghton Mifflin. Category: C. Point Value: 5. Book #236.
Joel and Tony went swimming in a river they knew was dangerous and Tony drowned. Now Joel must face both sets of parents and deal with his own feelings of horror and guilt.

Bellairs, John. 1976. *The Letter, the Witch, and the Ring.* New York: The Dial Press. Category: C. Point Value: 10. Book #238.
Rita Rose goes on a trip with Mrs. Zimmerman and ends up in a deadly struggle with an evil witch over a magic ring.

Bellairs, John. 1992. *The Mansion in the Mist.* New York: Penguin Books USA. Category: C. Point Value: 10. Book #239.
Some evil beings from a different dimension are trying to take over Earth. Anthony and his friends must unravel some mysterious clues in order to stop them.

Blume, Judy. 1970. *Are You There God? It's Me, Margaret*. New York: Macmillan Books for Young Readers. Category: C. Point Value: 10. Book #240.
Problems, problems, problems! Besides having to make a very important decision about religion, Margaret also has to worry about buying a bra, starting her period, and learning how to kiss boys. All this, and she's only in the sixth grade! Will Margaret survive the year?

Cassedy, Sylvia. 1993. *Behind the Attic Wall*. New York: Thomas Y. Crowell Junior Books. Category: C. Point Value: 20. Book #249.
Maggie has no parents, no friends, and no place to live. Reluctantly, Maggie's elderly great-aunts accept Maggie into their home. Life with the aunts is not a pleasant one for Maggie, but when Maggie makes a startling discovery in the attic of the great-aunts' old house, everything begins to change.

Cassedy, Sylvia. 1989. *Lucie Babbidge's House*. New York: Thomas Y. Crowell Junior Books. Category: C. Point Value: 15. Book #250.
Lucie creates a secret life with a dollhouse that has unknown magical powers.

Coville, Bruce. 1991. *The Ghost in the Big Brass Bed*. New York: Bantam Books. Category: C. Point Value: 10. Book #257.
A short trip to pick up an antique leads Chris and Nina into an adventure with two ghosts in a haunted house.

Coville, Bruce. 1988. *The Ghost Wore Gray*. New York: Bantam Books. Category: C. Point Value: 10. Book #258.
Chris and Nina find a handsome ghost who almost gets them killed.

Coville, Bruce. 1992. *My Teacher Flunked the Planet*. New York: Pocket Books. Category: C. Point Value: 10. Book #259.
Aliens want to destroy the earth, and it is up to Peter, Susan, and Duncan to convince the aliens to let humanity survive.

Coville, Bruce. 1989. *My Teacher Is an Alien*. New York: Pocket Books. Category: C. Point Value: 10. Book #260.
When Susan sneaks into her teacher's house, she sees him pull off a mask to reveal a lime green alien face. Ahhhh!!!!

Fleischman, Sid. 1986. *The Whipping Boy*. New York: Greenwillow Books. Category: C. Point Value: 5. Book #268.
Jemmy and the prince have been captured by two outlaws. Will Jemmy be able to outwit the outlaws? Perhaps. But only if Prince Brat doesn't live up to his name.

Fox, Paula. 1991. *Monkey Island*. New York: Dell Publishing. Category: C. Point Value: 10. Book #269.
Clay's father left after he lost his job. After that, Clay's mother left the welfare hotel room where they were staying. Now Clay, who is only 11, is living on the streets of New York City, struggling to eat and keep warm.

George, Jean Craighead. 1992. *The Missing 'Gator of Gumbo Limbo*. New York: HarperCollins Children's Books. Category: C. Point Value: 10. Book #273.
Dajun is a huge alligator that lives in Gumbo Limbo Hammock, which is one of the last unspoiled places in Florida. But when Dajun gets too large, the government wants him killed. Dajun's only hope for survival rests with a group of homeless woods people who live in Gumbo Limbo Hammock. Will the people of the Hammock be able to save Dajun? Will they want to?

George, Jean Craighead. 1989. *Shark Beneath the Reef*. New York: HarperCollins Children's Books. Category: C. Point Value: 10. Book #274.
For three generations, all of the men in the Torres family have been shark fishermen. Now their way of life is being threatened. Fourteen-year-old Tomás must decide soon if he should drop out of school to help or if he should continue his education.

Hamilton, Virginia. 1967. *Zeely*. New York: Macmillan. Category: C. Point Value: 10. Book #278.
Geeder is visiting her uncle for the summer. When she sees her uncle's neighbor, the tall, silent, and mysterious, Zeely Tayber, Geeder wonders if Zeely is a descendant of African royalty. Later, when Geeder finds a picture of a Watutsi queen who looks like Zeely, Geeder is convinced that her suspicions about Zeely are true, and Geeder's imagination runs wild.

Lasky, Kathryn. 1986. *The Night Journey*. New York: Puffin Books. Category: C. Point Value: 10. Book #288.
When Nana Sashie was a little girl, she and her family made a dramatic and dangerous escape from Russia to avoid being killed because they were Jews. Rachel's parents don't want Rachel to hear Nana Sashie's stories, but Rachel is determined that she will. Late each night, after everyone else in the house is asleep, Rachel sneaks into her great-grandmother's room to hear the stories and to forge a bond that is precious to them both.

MacBride, Roger Lea. 1993. *Little House on Rocky Ridge*. New York: HarperCollins Children's Books. Category: C. Point Value: 25. Book #297.
Rose and her family face storms, rats, chiggers, and many other dangers as they travel to a new home in Missouri.

MacLachlan, Patricia. 1993. *Baby*. New York: Delacorte Press. Category: C. Point Value: 10. Book #300.
Larkin finds a baby in a basket in front of her house. But can Larkin's family, which has already lost a child, love another baby that might be taken away again?

MacLachlan, Patricia. 1991. *Journey*. New York: Delacorte Press. Category: C. Point Value: 10. Book #301.
Cameras don't lie, says Journey's grandfather, and Journey knows that his grandfather is right. Still, sometimes the truth can be too painful to face. Journey must decide if he will accept the truth about his mother or reject his grandfather's words.

Naylor, Phyllis Reynolds. 1985. *The Agony of Alice*. New York: Atheneum. Category: C. Point Value: 10. Book #308.
Alice's mother died long ago, and when Alice's brother takes Alice shopping for clothes, Alice accidentally walks into the wrong dressing room and sees a boy she knows from school in his underwear! How embarrassing! How humiliating! How TYPICAL! All Alice wants is to be a beautiful and mature woman who behaves in an elegant manner, but Alice is convinced that the only way she can do this is to find the right role model.

Naylor, Phyllis Reynolds. 1987. *Beetles, Lightly Toasted*. New York: Macmillan. Category: C. Point Value: 10. Book #309.
Is it possible to save food supplies by eating bugs? Andy thinks so, and he tests out his unusual recipes on his family and friends. Gross!

Naylor, Phyllis Reynolds. 1991. *Shiloh*. New York: Atheneum. Category: C. Point Value: 10. Book #312.
Marty has found a dog that has been mistreated. Marty knows he should return the dog, but he hides it instead. Will the dog's owner come looking for Marty?

Paterson, Katherine. 1988. *Park's Quest*. New York: Puffin Books. Category: C. Point Value: 10. Book #318.
Eleven-year-old Park goes to his grandfather's farm to learn about his father, who died in the Vietnam War.

Paulsen, Gary. 1989. *The Voyage of the* Frog. New York: Orchard Books. Category: C. Point Value: 10. Book #321.
David enjoys sailing and has sailed many times out on the ocean with his uncle in his uncle's small sailboat. When David's uncle dies, he has one last request: that his ashes be scattered at sea. In an attempt to honor his uncle's wishes, David sets out alone in the sailboat. When a freak storm sweeps David's boat out into the empty wastes of the ocean, David is stranded at sea with just enough food and water to last a few days.

Reeder, Carolyn. 1989. *Shades of Gray*. New York: Macmillan. Category: C. Point Value: 10. Book #326.
Will's whole family died during the Civil War, and now Will must go live with an uncle who wouldn't fight for the cause Will passionately believes in.

Rylant, Cynthia. 1992. *Missing May*. New York: Orchard Books. Category: C. Point Value: 10. Book #327.
Summer is an orphan who is taken in by her poor aunt and uncle who live in the mountains of West Virginia. She is very happy living with her aunt and uncle, but Summer's happiness ends several years later when Aunt May dies and Uncle Ob goes into a deep depression.

Wright, Betty Ren. 1985. *Christina's Ghost*. New York: Holiday House. Category: C. Point Value: 10. Book #338.
Christina quickly learns that the house she and her crabby uncle are living in is haunted.

Wright, Betty Ren. 1983. *The Dollhouse Murders*. New York: Holiday House. Category: C. Point Value: 10. Book #339.
The dolls in the haunted dollhouse are trying to give Amy and her sister a message. But what do the mysterious, moving dolls want?

Wright, Betty Ren. 1984. *Ghosts Beneath Our Feet*. New York: Holiday House. Category: C. Point Value: 10. Book #340.
The ghost girl that Katie sees seems to be trying to tell her something urgently important, but what can that message be?

 # Annotations—Category D

AVI. 1993. *Punch with Judy*. New York: Bradbury Press. Category: D. Point Value: 10. Book #227.
Punch is an orphan boy traveling with a show that is changing its act to comedy. But how can you be funny when the law is after you, when you're hungry, and when your only friend seems to hate you?

Banks, Lynne Reid. 1973. *One More River*. New York: William Morrow. Category: D. Point Value: 15. Book #232.
Lesley has everything: money, clothes, looks, and popularity. But when Lesley's father announces that the family is giving everything up and moving to Israel, all of that is about to change.

Bellairs, John. 1973. *The House with a Clock in Its Walls*. New York: Penguin Books. Category: D. Point Value: 10. Book #237.
Lewis has experimented with Uncle Jonathan's magic and unleashed a force evil enough to destroy the world.

Blume, Judy. 1993. *Here's to You, Rachel Robinson*. New York: Bantam Doubleday Dell Books for Young Readers. Category: D. Point Value: 10. Book #242.
Rachel's life is going along just fine until her rude and difficult brother, Charles, comes back home.

Blume, Judy. 1971. *Then Again, Maybe I Won't*. New York: Dell Publishing. Category: D. Point Value: 10. Book #243.
Tony's family is suddenly rich, so why isn't everybody happy?

Cleary, Beverly. 1991. *Strider*. New York: William Morrow. Category: D. Point Value: 10. Book #256.
When Leigh and Barry find a dog sitting on a beach, they decide that the dog will belong to both of them. But joint custody of a dog has its problems. Will Leigh and Barry's friendship survive?

Fleischman, Sid. 1990. *The Midnight Horse*. New York: Dell Publishing. Category: D. Point Value: 5. Book #267.
Touch's only relative is the evil Judge Wigglesworth who is planning to cheat Touch and take over an inn down in the village. It is up to Touch, with the help of a magician's ghost, to stop the judge.

Hahn, Mary Downing. 1986. *Wait Till Helen Comes: A Ghost Story*. Boston: Houghton Mifflin. Category: D. Point Value: 10. Book #276.
Molly must try to keep a ghost from killing her new, bratty stepsister!

Hamilton, Virginia. 1990. *Cousins*. New York: Philomel Books. Category: D. Point Value: 10. Book #277.

Cammy is a tough girl who seems to be able to handle anything, but when Cammy's cousin dies, she almost has a nervous breakdown.

Hinton, S. E. 1967. *The Outsiders*. New York: The Viking Press. Category: D. Point Value: 15. Book #279.

Ponyboy is only 14, but he has lost both parents and his life is filled with violence as he and his friends battle their rivals in dangerous rumbles.

Hinton, S. E. 1979. *Tex*. New York: Delacorte Press. Category: D. Point Value: 15. Book #280.

Tex and his older brother, Mason, have been alone for five months. But now the money has run out, and Tex and his brother must decide what to do.

Hinton, S. E. 1971. *That Was Then, This Is Now*. New York: The Viking Press. Category: D. Point Value: 15. Book #281.

Byron and Mark have lived a life of hustling and violence since childhood. Now Byron is beginning to ask questions while Mark accepts things as they are. What will happen when these best friends grow apart?

Konigsburg, E. L. 1993. *T-Backs, T-Shirts, COAT and Suit*. New York: Hyperion Books for Children. Category: D. Point Value: 10. Book #287.

When 12-year-old Chlöe goes to spend a summer in Florida with her aunt, she becomes the center of a noisy battle over T-back swimming suits.

Lowry, Lois. 1993. *The Giver*. Boston: Houghton Mifflin. Category: D. Point Value: 10. Book #295.

Jonas lives in an ideal community. There are no problems. Everyone is polite and friendly all the time, and everyone works at a job that is exactly suited to his personality. It sounds like a perfect life, but when Jonas discovers the horrifying secret which makes the community work, he must make a desperate decision.

Lowry, Lois. 1993. *Number the Stars*. Boston: Houghton Mifflin. Category: D. Point Value: 10. Book #296.

Ten-year-old Annemarie learns what real courage is when she helps her young Jewish friend flee from the Nazis.

McKissack, Patricia C. 1992. *The Dark-Thirty: Southern Tales of the Supernatural*. New York: Alfred A. Knopf. Category: D. Point Value: 15. Book #304.

This collection of African American ghost stories is only for readers who enjoy being scared. It is not recommended for the faint-hearted or for anyone who still sleeps with a teddy bear and a night light! Proceed at your own risk!

O'Dell, Scott. 1989. *My Name Is Not Angelica*. Boston: Houghton Mifflin. Category: D. Point Value: 15. Book #315.

Raisha is a young African girl who is captured and sold into slavery in the West Indies. Horrified by the conditions which she and the other slaves must endure, Raisha risks her life by joining in the plans for a revolt.

Paterson, Katherine. 1991. *Lyddie*. New York: Puffin Books. Category: D. Point Value: 15. Book #316.

Lyddie Worthen is a young girl with lots of spirit and determination. In Lowell, Massachusetts, Lyddie finds a place to live and an all-day job in a factory. But where is Lyddie's family?

Paulsen, Gary. 1987. *Hatchet*. New York: Puffin Books. Category: D. Point Value: 10. Book #319.

Brian is alone in the Canadian wilderness after a plane wreck with only his wits and a hatchet to help him survive.

Paulsen, Gary. 1993. *Nightjohn*. New York: Delacorte Press. Category: D. Point Value: 5. Book #320.

The punishment for teaching slaves to read is severe, but Nightjohn is an escaped slave who is willing to risk anything as he attempts to teach slaves to read and write.

Paulsen, Gary. 1989. *The Winter Room*. New York: Orchard Books. Category: D. Point Value: 10. Book #322.

Life on a farm in Minnesota is difficult, but Eldon's family has survived and enjoyed life by working together. When Wayne gets angry at Uncle David, life seems as bleak as the cold forests that surround the farm.

Peck, Richard. 1975. *The Ghost Belonged to Me.* New York: Dell Publishing. Category: D. Point Value: 15. Book #325.
Blossom claims there is a ghost in Alexander's barn. Alexander thinks Blossom is lying until he sees a strange green light shining out the loft window. Is someone trying to play a joke on him? Alexander hopes so!

Spinelli, Jerry. 1990. *Maniac Magee.* Boston: Little, Brown. Category: D. Point Value: 15. Book #330.

Maniac is a legend in Two Mills; he can outhit, outrun, and outkick any kid in town. The only thing Maniac can't do is go home.

Spinelli, Jerry. 1982. *Space Station Seventh Grade.* Boston: Little, Brown. Category: D. Point Value: 15. Book #331.
Jason has always been well-behaved and a model student, but when he enters the seventh grade, all of that begins to change.

Annotations—Category E

AVI. 1990. *The True Confessions of Charlotte Doyle.* New York: Orchard Books. Category: E. Point Value: 15. Book #228.
In 1832, Charlotte finds that she is the only passenger (and the only girl!) on a ship with a cruel captain and a crew planning a mutiny. Once at sea, Charlotte is forced to choose between the captain and the crew, and the choice she makes could prove to be a deadly one.

Freedman, Russell. 1990. *Franklin Delano Roosevelt.* Boston: Clarion Books. Category: E. Point Value: 15. Book #270.
Franklin Delano Roosevelt was born to a life of ease and riches. His life was a smooth path to power until the dreaded polio virus left Roosevelt confined to a wheelchair.

Freedman, Russell. 1987. *Lincoln: A Photobiography.* New York: Clarion Books. Category: E. Point Value: 15. Book #271.
Was Abraham Lincoln really Honest Abe the rail splitter, or was he Abe Lincoln, the gorilla in the White House? You'll find the answers to these questions in this biography of the *real* Abraham Lincoln!

Freedman, Russell. 1991. *The Wright Brothers.* New York: Holiday House. Category: E. Point Value: 15. Book #272.
It didn't work the first time. And it didn't work the second, third, fourth, or fifth time.

But after dozens and dozens of failed attempts, the Wright brothers achieved their dream at last. This book tells the true story of how two brothers did what almost everyone said was impossible: they designed, built, and flew the first airplane in the world.

Lasky, Kathryn. 1992. *Shadows in the Water.* Orlando, Florida: Harcourt Brace Jovanovich, Category: E. Point Value: 15. Book #289.
In the Starbuck household, there are two sets of twins who can communicate to one another without speaking. All they have to do is to "teleflash," as they call it, and they can mentally send messages back and forth. When the Starbuck twins are in the Florida Keys, they hear clicking sounds in their minds. What is going on? Are dolphins trying to communicate with the twins? If they are, what could the dolphins want to tell them?

Magorian, Michelle. 1981. *Good Night, Mr. Tom.* New York: HarperCollins Children's Books. Category: E. Point Value: 25. Book #302.
During World War II, Willie is sent to the country so that he will be safe from German bombers. There, for the first time, Willie has friends and security. This newfound security is torn from Willie, however, when his abusive mother demands that he return home to London. Will anyone be able to help Willie escape his mother and find happiness again?

McKissack, Patricia C., and Fredrick McKissack. 1989. *A Long Hard Journey: The Story of Pullman Porter.* New York: Walker and Company. Category: E. Point Value: 15. Book #305.

Everyone knew that it was a hopeless cause. The poor, black sleeping car porters didn't have a chance of forcing the mighty Pullman Company to treat them fairly. This is the incredible but true story of how the impossible did happen.

Montgomery, L. M. 1909. *Anne of Avonlea.* New York: Farrar, Straus & Giroux. Category: E. Point Value: 25. Book #306.

The second book in the Anne of Green Gables series. In this volume, Anne returns to Avonlea to teach in her old school. Most of Anne's old friends are nearby, but Anne also meets some mysterious new neighbors with hidden and tragic pasts.

Montgomery, L. M. 1908. *Anne of Green Gables.* New York: Farrar, Straus & Giroux. Category: E. Point Value: 25. Book #307.

Matthew and Marilla hoped to adopt a quiet and hard-working boy to help out on their farm, but what they found instead was a whirlwind of activity and chatter named Anne. This book is the story of an impetuous young girl who won the hearts of all who came to know her.

Nixon, Joan Lowery. 1979. *The Kidnapping of Christina Lattimore.* Orlando, Fla.: Harcourt Brace Jovanovich. Category: E. Point Value: 15. Book #313.

Christina is kidnapped and locked up in a basement. When she is finally rescued, she is accused of having been involved in her own kidnapping. How can Christina convince everyone of the truth?

Nixon, Joan Lowery. 1986. *The Other Side of Dark.* New York: Delacorte Press. Category: E. Point Value: 15. Book #314.

An intruder walks into Stacy's home, kills Stacy's mother, and shoots Stacy. Stacy goes into a coma and doesn't wake up for four years. When Stacy comes out of the coma, will she remember what happened to her and to her mother?

Paterson, Katherine. 1974. *Of Nightingales That Weep.* New York: HarperCollins Children's Books. Category: E. Point Value: 15. Book #317.

Takiko, who is caught up in the middle of a terrible war in which her father has already died, finds out that the man she loves is an enemy spy.

Peck, Richard. 1976. *Are You in the House Alone?* New York: Viking Penguin. Category: E. Point Value: 15. Book #323.

First, it's the phone calls that follow Gail everywhere she goes. Next, Gail finds obscene, threatening notes hidden in her locker at school. Terrified and certain that she is being stalked, Gail tells the school counselor and the principal what is happening to her, but she is told not to worry. Bad advice. Days later, Gail's worst fears come true, and she is attacked and raped.

Peck, Richard. 1972. *Don't Look and It Won't Hurt.* New York: Henry Holt. Category: E. Point Value: 15. Book #324.

Sixteen-year-old Carol Patterson's life is no bed of roses. Her father abandoned the family years ago, her older sister barely talks to her, and her mother is often cross and tired from working hard to support the family. But when Carol's older sister, Ellen, becomes pregnant, things at home go from bad to worse.

Taylor, Mildred D. 1981. *Let the Circle Be Unbroken.* New York: Puffin Books. Category: E. Point Value: 25. Book #333.

In this sequel to *Roll of Thunder, Hear My Cry*, the Logan family's troubles build as T. J. goes on trial, Stacey runs away, and a half-white cousin arouses too much attention.

Taylor, Mildred D. 1990. *The Road to Memphis.* New York: Puffin Books. Category: E. Point Value: 25. Book #334.

In this third book in *The Roll of Thunder* series, Moe does the unthinkable by badly beating three white men. Moe's only hope is to flee the state, and only Cassie, Stacey, and their friends can help him.